MONEY AND CREDIT

Their Influence on
Jobs, Prices, and Growth

MONEY AND CREDIT

Their Influence on
Jobs, Prices, and Growth

The Report of the Commission on Money and Credit

PRENTICE-HALL, INC.
Englewood Cliffs, N.J.
1961

PRINTED IN THE UNITED STATES OF AMERICA
60041-C

The Commission on Money and Credit was established by the unanimous vote of the Board of Trustees of the Committee for Economic Development. The by-laws governing the Commission on Money and Credit state that "it shall be the responsibility of the Commission to initiate studies into the United States monetary and financial system. All research is to be thoroughly objective in character and the approach in each instance is to be from the standpoint of the general welfare and not from that of any special political or economic group." The Commission, however, "shall fix its own rules and determine the scope of its studies." Publication of this report does *not* necessarily constitute endorsement of the recommendations presented in the Report by the Commission's advisory board, its research staff, or any member of any board or committee (other than the Commission) or any officer, of the Committee for Economic Development or any other organization participating in the work of the Commission.

MEMBERSHIP OF COMMISSION

J. IRWIN MILLER
Chairman of the Board, Cummins Engine Company

ROBERT R. NATHAN
Robert R. Nathan Associates, Inc.

EMIL RIEVE
President Emeritus,
Textile Workers of America, AFL-CIO
(Appointed May 19, 1960.)

DAVID ROCKEFELLER
President, The Chase Manhattan Bank

BEARDSLEY RUML
New York, New York
(Died April 18, 1960.)

STANLEY H. RUTTENBERG
Director, Department of Research, AFL-CIO

CHARLES SAWYER
Taft, Stettinius & Hollister

WILLIAM F. SCHNITZLER
Secretary-Treasurer, AFL-CIO
(Resigned April 28, 1960.)

EARL B. SCHWULST
President and Chairman of the Board,
The Bowery Savings Bank

CHARLES B. SHUMAN
President,
American Farm Bureau Federation

JESSE W. TAPP
Chairman of the Board,
Bank of America, N.T. and S.A.

J. CAMERON THOMSON
Retired Chairman of the Board,
Northwest Bancorporation

WILLARD L. THORP
Director, Merrill Center for Economics,
Amherst College

THEODORE O. YNTEMA
Chairman, Finance Committee,
Ford Motor Company

This report represents the deliberations of a diverse group of American citizens. They were assisted by an able staff of scholars and by a group of advisers of great competence. The members of the Commission were deliberately selected with the advice of a distinguished Selection Committee to provide a group of men with different backgrounds: banking, business, government, labor, and the professions. All members had broad, practical economic experience. It could fairly be said that their conclusions represent a consensus of American philosophy and economic judgment today.

No member of the Commission, whether or not he has written or joined in specific footnotes, endorses personally every specific proposal in its entirety or concurs fully with every statement in the supporting analysis, but all approve the major substance of the report and urge careful consideration of its interrelated recommendations.

The funds for this effort were provided by the Ford Foundation, the Merrill Foundation, and the Committee for Economic Development. None of these organizations exerted the slightest pressure. There were no restrictions as to the scope and method of the work, and certainly no restrictions as to the judgments reached.

This report is deliberately short, perhaps too short in view of the vital importance of the areas covered. The purpose was to gain more readers. We have not attempted to set forth in the report itself the mass of evidence on which our recommendations and conclusions are based. Much of the material used in reaching conclusions will be published separately as supporting papers. These will appear under the names of their authors with no indication of concurrence or disagreement by members of the Commission, its advisers, or its staff. They will be published for the benefit of those dealing with the same problems and to stimulate scholars to probe further into areas where firm knowledge is patently inadequate.

The Commission hopes that many Americans will be interested to read the entire report, because any summary in matters of such complexity as those discussed suffers by oversimplification.

The reader will no doubt gain the impression that this report stresses particularly the significance of government in our affairs, using the term government in its broadest sense. This is natural since the subject of the Commission's work is the responsibility of governmental institutions in promoting the success of our economy.

The Commission recognizes that our society is based upon the dynamics of the market place. Individual decisions largely determine the direction and growth of our product and its distribution. The greater part of American activity by far is based upon the private sector. What is emphasized is the important and vital complementary role of government in helping a relatively free society to do a better job—and a better job does not envisage economic Utopia.

Although the Commission is concerned with the attainment of our national goals, it recommends no precise and specific formula for this purpose. To do so would be inconsistent with our traditions and practices and probably totally unrealistic.

If we are to be free, some fluctuation in our economic growth pattern is unavoidable. If the Commission's recommendations were to be adopted, one could hope and expect that the degree of fluctuations might be further reduced. They have been reduced in the last decade.

A fundamental and basic element in this report is the recommendation that the help of government in its various phases requires more liaison between the different institutions involved and more coordination. The significant role of the President in this regard is pointed out but that is not to say that the Chief of State is solely responsible for the success of a free country which must grow and prosper by the individual initiative, industry, and judgment of free citizens.

FRAZAR B. WILDE
Chairman, Commission on Money and Credit

ACKNOWLEDGMENTS

The Commission on Money and Credit has had a great deal of cooperation and assistance in the preparation of this Report. We wish to acknowledge our indebtedness to those who have made this Report possible.

The United States Department of the Treasury and the Board of Governors of the Federal Reserve System, in particular, were helpful in providing data and answers to our extensive formal inquiries about their operations. Also, many other government agencies supplied information freely upon request.

Many associations of financial institutions were extremely helpful in supplying information and analyses in the form of monographs. The associations which supplied monographs as a part of the research program of the Commission were:

The American Bankers Association
American Finance Conference, Inc.
American Mutual Insurance Alliance
Association of Casualty and Surety Companies
Credit Union National Association, Inc.
Life Insurance Association of America
Mortgage Bankers Association of America
National Association of Investment Companies
National Association of Mutual Savings Banks
National Board of Fire Underwriters
National Consumer Finance Association
United States Savings and Loan League

We wish to acknowledge our debt to the many scholars who prepared memoranda and research studies on various aspects of the problems under consideration.

The Advisory Board of the Commission, a group of distinguished scholars who are listed elsewhere in this report, have given us wise counsel and many hours of time in our deliberations.

We also wish to thank the three organizations whose joint effort created the Commission and financed its work. They are the Ford Foundation, the Merrill Foundation for the Advancement of Financial Knowledge, and the Committee for Economic Development.

The staff, under the direction of Bertrand Fox and Eli Shapiro, created a great body of basic research material upon which the Commission was able to draw in its deliberations. They also prepared and revised a large number of drafts of the Commission Report with care and concern for various points of view. We wish to thank the staff who are listed elsewhere in the report for their excellent work.

The Commission on Money and Credit

TABLE OF CONTENTS

TABLES

CHARTS

MONEY AND CREDIT

Their Influence on
Jobs, Prices, and Growth

CHAPTER ONE

INTRODUCTION

Our monetary, credit, and fiscal policies and the instruments and institutions through which they operate must be so designed that they can make an essential contribution in the decades ahead to the improvement of our standards of living through simultaneously achieving low levels of unemployment, an adequate rate of economic growth, and reasonable price stability. And the more successful we are in achieving these goals, the better able we will be to achieve our most fundamental goals: to enhance the freedom and dignity of our citizens, indeed of men everywhere, and to ensure the survival of our country and its system of government.

The Commission on Money and Credit was established in 1958 in response to widespread concern as to the adequacy of the nation's monetary and financial structure and its regulation and control. It was directed to study these broad general problems as it saw fit and to make recommendations on what changes, if any, should be made.*

Since the Federal Reserve System was established in 1913 following the comprehensive study of the monetary system by the Aldrich Commission, there have been two world wars, the great depression, periods of unprecedented prosperity, a fourfold growth of the gross national product in real terms, and a more than twofold increase in real product per capita. The nation has become much more industrialized and urban. Our people enjoy much higher real incomes and hold more assets. The industrial and labor structure has changed markedly. We have witnessed the introduction of radically new products and methods of production made possible by rapid scientific and technological advances and increased investment of capital.

---

* EMIL RIEVE—I agree with the foreword that careful consideration should be given to the Commission's recommendations, without any suggestion that each member of the Commission endorses every detail. There are various recommendations with which I disagree, completely or in part. In the main, I tend to concur with the dissents and comments of Stanley Ruttenberg and Robert Nathan.

In addition, the United States has assumed during this period the responsibilities of a world power. The dollar has become the keystone of the world payments system. Our financial system now influences and must be responsive to conditions abroad. We have taken leadership in helping to accelerate the development of less advanced nations, and to provide a stronger defense for the free world.

There have been great changes in the relationship between the public and private spheres. Government—federal and state and local—has become an increasingly important factor in the economy. State and local government expenditures and debt have increased sharply in dollar amounts and in relation to the national income. The actions of the federal government have become increasingly significant for finance, because of:

1. The enlarged scope of public expenditures and taxes
2. The development of federal lending and guaranteeing institutions
3. The enormous growth of the federal debt and federal trust funds

A new and important concept of the federal government's role in the economy is reflected in the Employment Act of 1946, which makes it a continuing government responsibility to promote high and stable levels of production, employment, and purchasing power.

In the private financial structure we have witnessed a very rapid growth in financial institutions. The assets of all private financial institutions have increased at a growth rate well above the rate of growth of population, real output, or national wealth; and the share of financial institutions in all assets, financial and nonfinancial, has increased. Many financial institutions, such as life insurance companies and savings and loan institutions, have grown at a rate far greater than that of commercial banks. New types of institutions, such as pension funds and investment companies, have found an important place in our financial structure. There have been important changes in our corporate financial practices and in the lending procedures of credit organizations. Consumer installment credit has become an important part of the debt structure of the American economy.

The postwar period has reflected economic developments of World War II, to a marked degree in the earlier part of the period and to a decreasing degree in the later years. Because the United States borrowed heavily to finance the war, and because the Federal Reserve permitted a large increase in the money supply to support the many debt issues of the Treasury, we emerged from the war with a large national debt and a money supply high in relation to national income. Individuals and businesses held abnormally large money balances and stocks of liquid assets. These holdings facilitated the financing of expenditures to meet the pent-up demands of consumers for goods of all kinds and the demands of businesses for new plants and equipment to convert from the production of munitions to civilian products. Under the pressure of these demands, output rose rapidly and prices and wages rose sharply.

From certain points of view the record of the U.S. economy in the postwar period has been a good one. Reconversion from war production to civilian production was rapid. A major depression such as followed other great wars has been avoided. The Korean mobilization was handled with minimal disruptive effects in the economy. Output, incomes, and employment have grown substantially. While there have been four recessions, the period has been on the whole one of the more prosperous of our history.

From other points of view the postwar performance of the economy has not been satisfactory. The rising trend of unemployment and the large number of pockets of sustained unemployment, the lagging growth rate of the economy, the inflations of the immediate postwar and Korean war periods and the continued upward drift of the price level since 1952, the series of four recessions and the fact that the last two recoveries have failed to bring low-level unemployment, the large balance of payments deficits and the losses of gold, all are cause for concern and raise questions related to our money and credit system.

Has the nature of the economy so changed that traditional adjustment and control mechanisms are no longer adequate?

Has the growth of nonbank financial intermediaries, the decreased share of financial assets held by commercial banks, and the increased size of the federal debt diminished significantly the strength of monetary control mechanisms?

Has the legacy of excess liquidity in the economy now been wrung out and is a change in Federal Reserve policy in regard to the growth of the money supply now required?

Is the structure of the Federal Reserve System and are the control measures available to it adequate to the tasks ahead?

Has too much reliance been placed on monetary policy and not enough on debt management, fiscal, and other credit policies to achieve national objectives?

Are federal credit agency operations responsive to general monetary policy and can they reinforce the general stabilization and growth policies of the federal government?

Can the regulation of the private financial structure contribute more effectively to stability and growth?

Can the balance of payments situation and the international position of the dollar be managed without disturbing the internal stability of the economy and the domestic monetary system?

How might the control measures available to the government be combined more effectively to meet specific situations?

How can government procedures be developed to ensure the necessary interchange of views on economic policy matters among the affected agencies and to coordinate policy measures to meet national objectives?

These are some of the questions that gave rise to the Commission and which it has considered. The Commission has endeavored to ascertain the more critical problems relating to our monetary and credit system and its control and regulation: those that have appeared in the past, are currently with us, and seem likely to be important in the future. The Commission's major concern, however, is with the future, and it has tried to be alert to the emerging problems of at least the decade ahead.*

---

* H. CHRISTIAN SONNE—My criticism is directed mainly at the Commission's failure to deal adequately with the past and especially with the future.

As regards the past. I fail to see how a Commission on Money and Credit can ignore the basic question of what money and other circulating media in the U.S.A. should be based on. This question seems the more important during the present period when the public is worried about "inflation" or the shrinking value of the dollar.

When discussing "The Causes of Inflation" in Chapter Two (page 15, ff.) a distinction is made between price increases resulting from demand-pull and those resulting from demand-shift and cost-push. But all we are told is that if the latter are dominant, certain difficulties arise, and so forth. No answer is given to this natural question: Is perhaps something wrong with the methods by which our circulating media of approximately $140 billion have been created? Have these media the proper underlying values in goods and services?

The public is entitled to be told whether the Commission concludes—based on its concept of the meaning of money—that recent price rises have or have not been influenced by the quality or quantity of our circulating media. The report should also deal fully with the fundamental rules and regulations governing the commercial banks and with the operations of the Federal Reserve System influencing our money supply.

A clear analysis of the events affecting monetary policy from 1914 to 1940, coupled with the Commission's admirable analysis of such events in the recent past and the present, should provide an excellent basis for considering—

The monetary problems that seem likely to be important in the future.

To the ten queries raised in Chapter One (page 3, ff.), I would add an all important question.

We find in many fields of activity, such as those of foreign relations, military organization, communication, such profound underlying transformations that old methods have to be discarded to make room for new procedures.

Does the same apply to economic policies when we take a new look at the problems of the sixties?

Considering the changes described in Chapter One (third through sixth paragraphs) it would seem strange if the answer were not in the affirmative. Yet, I see nothing in the report that suggests any really important new approach.

In my opinion the report fails to deal adequately with the main economic changes and problems that we are likely to face during the crucial decade that lies ahead. The major issues include: The risk of heavy reliance on the traditional counter-cyclical measures; the need for growth as a national necessity; and our rising price and cost structure with its increasing effect on our balance of payments.

If the past had been adequately treated in the report we would have seen how:

—The Federal Reserve Act was conceived at a time when government budgets were relatively small and a laissez-faire ideology prevailed.

—The countercyclical policy of the thirties was conceived at a time when *temporary* increases in public works were believed necessary for priming the pump of our free enterprise system.

—After tax rates became high in the post-World War II period *temporary* (automatic or formula-determined) tax reductions were regarded as the panacea.

The basic question now is whether this traditional "shot in the arm" treatment is still an adequate policy for the next foreseeable phase of domestic and international developments.

The answer is "No" for the following reasons:

1. So many things—both at home and abroad—need to be done to strengthen this nation, its international position, its trade balance and its domestic well being.

2. We must achieve increased production of goods and services to provide for over 3 million new jobs a year.

3. To accomplish these goals requires a higher and more sustained rate of growth than can be assured through the traditional policies of fiscal and monetary pump priming.

Hence, adequate growth is needed in support of the strength of the nation, its well-being, high employment.

In these circumstances, I must disassociate myself from the following astounding conclusions of the paragraph in Chapter Two which says: *"Although not satisfied with recent rates of growth, the Commission does not recommend the establishment of any specific rate of growth as a target"* (page 31).

As we have seen at recent peaks of recovery, countercyclical measures in the form of temporary pump priming are not enough to find employment for the ever increasing number of chronically unemployed. The solution no longer lies in using "shot in the arm" methods but in applying deliberate, continuing, constructive measures.

We can no longer treat cyclical stabilization and growth as unrelated aims to be achieved by unrelated policies; nor can we effectively separate short-term and long-term measures.

During the decade ahead, growth should be the predominant aim—cyclical stabilization a subordinate, yet important aspect.

To support continuing economic growth during the coming decade, large scale programs are needed which require cooperation between the public and the private sectors of the economy.

Once these programs have been initiated countercyclical policy can make its most effective contribution by purchase or sale of the securities used to finance them (see my comment on page 37).

In the coming decade we are likely to see emerge a large scale pattern of semi-private, semi-public new national programs to achieve national growth in those fields where it is lagging. Such programs could be conducted in an economically sound manner without interfering with our traditional free enterprise system.

In the light of the future probabilities, some of which I have sketched, I consider the coverage of the CMC report inadequate.

It is my strong belief that the public—particularly under the precarious circumstances now prevailing—is entitled to expect recommendations from the CMC which will deal also with the economic and monetary consequences of problems that are most likely to become important in the near future.

I have therefore prepared some suggestions for monetary policy that, in my view, would facilitate the changes most likely to occur. In preparing some of these suggestions, I have attempted to break new ground.

This requires adequate explanation and more space than is available to me here. I am, therefore, arranging to have my complete statement printed separately.

The great complexity of our monetary and credit structure and its myriad ramifications throughout the economy have imposed limitations on what the Commission has been able to do in its less than three years of existence. It has examined the nature of the monetary and credit system, the role of the central bank and the effectiveness of its control measures, the debt management and monetary activities of the Treasury, the broad aspects of fiscal policy, the lending and loan guarantee activities of federal credit agencies, the regulatory policies of the federal and state governments and their effect on the dominant parts of our private financial system, and the problems of government organization, administration, and coordination of monetary, credit, and fiscal policies. Certain problems of international liquidity, international credit, and the balance of payments adjustment mechanism have also been considered.

Nature of the Recommendations

The Commission has been mindful that monetary and credit policies and measures are not ends in themselves. Like the money and credit they are designed to regulate, they are important for their effectiveness in helping us to attain basic national economic objectives. Such policies have been analyzed within the context of the operation of the economic system as a whole and especially in relation to the major economic objectives of adequate economic growth, high levels of production and employment, and reasonable stability of the price level. The investigation has led necessarily beyond the narrow area of money and credit because many policies and measures in addition to monetary and credit measures bear on these objectives. The Commission has commented on other measures and has shown their relationship to monetary and credit measures, but in general recommendations have been confined to the areas of money and credit.

For the most part the recommendations propose either structural and institutional changes designed to contribute to the more effective functioning of the economy or propose broad guides for specific policy decisions. The Commission has tried to avoid offering specific policy prescriptions for particular current problems. It has tried to confine its recommendations and suggestions for change only to situations where the present structure has not worked well. The recommendations do not call for the wholesale overhaul of our financial structure. They consist of many small changes, which frequently reflect evolving trends. It has avoided recommendations for change merely for the sake of change or merely to achieve a more logically consistent structure. The Commission has also been mindful of the distinction between defects in structure and defects due to weak policy or to the poor judgment of human beings. There is no assurance that errors in judgment will be avoided by structural changes, but an effective structure will enable competent men to perform more effectively. There is no substitute, however, for competent, responsive, and responsible officials in both public agencies and private organizations.

The recommendations are based on the fundamental assumption that the economy will continue to be largely a private enterprise economy. This form of economic organization with its stimulus to individual initiative has been a key element in explaining our outstanding record of economic growth and national well-being and is well suited to perform effectively in the years ahead. The Commission believes, however, that both private enterprise and government have major and complementary roles to play in achieving national objectives, and that neither one nor the other can do the whole job. Consequently, the recommendations deal with both government and private enterprise, and they try to strengthen the effectiveness of both.

In the private sector, the recommendations aim largely at changes designed to stimulate the forces of enterprise and competition by relaxing the constraints imposed by too restrictive government regulation by eliminating specific controls that distort the workings of the market mechanism, and by creating an environment conducive to growth. In the government sector, they emphasize the interrelationship of monetary, debt management, fiscal, and credit agency control measures in their influence on the levels and composition of demand in the economy. A coherent combination of these measures is essential to an effective national economic policy. It is also emphasized that monetary, credit, and fiscal measures are only part of a broad national economic policy, and that they must be supplemented with other measures in a systematic way if we are to improve our performance toward attaining our national economic objectives. The Commission believes that national economic policy is an integrated whole, and recommendations are made as to how the relationship among monetary, credit, and fiscal measures might be planned, reviewed, and related to other measures at the presidential level.

The Commission recognizes clearly the limitations of what a study such as this can accomplish. We do not live in a perfect world, and neither the Commission nor anyone else can prescribe mechanisms, structures, and policy guides which will guarantee the ideal attainment of national objectives. We can and should strive for a significant improvement in performance, and the Commission believes that the changes suggested will contribute toward that improvement.

Outline of the Report

The report is in three main sections. The first is introductory and consists of Chapters One and Two. Chapter Two discusses the major national economic objectives and analyzes in some detail the three objectives of economic growth, low levels of unemployment, and stable prices; the potential conflicts and the extent of compatibility among them; and the relationships of monetary, credit, and fiscal policy measures to them.

The second section, Chapters Three to Nine, consists of discussions of the strengths and limitations of the various kinds of policy measures in affecting our broad economic objectives, conclusions and recommendations relating to individual measures, and a discussion of how they might be combined for specific purposes. First the Commission takes up the Federal Reserve System and monetary policy (Chapter Three), Treasury debt management policy and the Treasury securities market (Chapter Four), and then the broad aspects of fiscal policy (Chapter Five). In Chapter Six the regulation of the major types of private financial institutions and in Chapter Seven the nature, structure, and operations of government credit agencies are covered. Chapter Eight discusses selected problems of our international balance of payments, international liquidity, foreign credits, and international adjustment mechanisms. Finally, in Chapter Nine the problems of combining the various measures under varying circumstances to achieve national objectives are outlined.

The final section, Chapter Ten, consists of a discussion of the problems of organizational structure and government administration to develop and to carry out effectively an integrated approach to national economic policy. It proposes a mechanism for review at the presidential level of the impacts of and the interrelationships among policy measures employed throughout the federal government and for formulation of a balanced coherent approach to the achievement of national economic objectives.

CHAPTER TWO

NATIONAL ECONOMIC GOALS

An adequate rate of economic growth, sustained high levels of production and employment, and reasonable stability of prices are clearly the three objectives of central concern for monetary, credit, and fiscal policies. These three goals, however, must be sought in the context of other important national objectives which necessarily impose constraints on their pursuit. Among such other objectives the provision of adequate national security is of high priority. The maintenance of harmonious international economic relations and contributions to economic development abroad are also important. The Commission holds that a desirable degree of economic freedom and reliance on the market mechanism for the allocation of products and resources is a continuing national objective.* At the same time it recognizes the role of government in providing proper degree of useful goods and services and of appropriate coordinating and regulatory functions. It is imperative also to preserve and strengthen workable competition in the private enterprise system to assure the proper functioning of the economy and the efficient use of resources in

---

* J. CAMERON THOMSON—The two sentences "The Commission holds that a desirable degree of economic freedom and reliance on the market mechanism for the allocation of products and resources is a continuing national objective" and "The Commission believes that a mixed private and public system best meets our national needs" are inconsistent with the reference in the Employment Act of 1946 to our "free competitive enterprise" and create uncertainty as to the extent of the Commission's giving priority to free competitive enterprise. Specifically I would eliminate the second sentence referred to in this note and change the first sentence to read as follows: "The Commission holds that primary reliance on economic freedom and reliance on the market mechanism for the allocation of products and resources is a continuing national objective."

Mr. SHUMAN wishes to be associated with Mr. THOMSON'S comment.

response to market forces. And assurance of an equitable distribution of opportunity and income is important.*

As we shall see, no single economic goal can be wholly unqualified, because each may have to be sought subject to constraints imposed by other goals or at costs representing sacrifices, to some degree, of other goals.

Even though our economy is usually described as a free enterprise economy, it has always involved government participation. In large part the decisions of what and how much to produce, how the proceeds of production are shared among participants, and what and how much is purchased by consumers and users of goods and services are made freely by individuals in response to market forces. But the federal, state, and local governments provide many goods and services which could be provided less satisfactorily, if at all, by the private sector, such as national defense, economic aid to other countries, highways, and public schools. And in the private sector many decisions as to what is to be produced are influenced in important ways by government activities, such as credit aids, subsidies and tax concessions, tariffs, price supports, and direct regulations. The Commission believes that a mixed private and public system best meets our national needs.** Commission members differ, however, as to what constitutes the proper balance between private and governmental activities and also within the governmental sphere on the division of responsibility among federal, state, and local governments.

A primary duty of government is to provide an appropriate climate and set of conditions to enable private enterprise to meet our economic needs through a competitive market system to the maximum extent practicable. The pressure of competition should ensure that resources are used efficiently. It is the function of government to ensure among other things that competition is effective, operates fairly, and functions with adequate protection to the consumer.

The Commission is concerned, however, that government regulation should not thwart the competition it is trying to stimulate, that it should not chill the forces making for innovation and growth, and that regulatory bodies should not become vehicles for protecting an industry or group at the expense of the public interest. There is equal concern that government regulation should restrain those forces which would destroy competition.

There exists today a widespread network of government regulation of our private economic system. The members of the Commission differ on

---

* CHARLES B. SHUMAN—I do not accept the theory that it is the responsibility of government to assure an equitable distribution of income. Equality of opportunity is all that any citizen should ask. If he has opportunity and does his part, income will be equitable.

** See Mr. THOMSON'S comment on page 9.

whether some regulation goes too far or not far enough and on whether additional regulation is needed.

Agreement exists also that there are many services which we want as a people, which we cannot provide for ourselves effectively, and which we want the government to provide for us. Again Commission members differ on the urgency and the magnitude of various needs. Some members urge increased federal activity in such fields as education, health, urban renewal, low-cost housing, natural resources, and aid to under-developed nations; others urge a possible decrease in some federal activities and great caution in moving into fields ordinarily the province of state and local governments. These are political decisions and should be made by elected representatives in response to the expressed wishes of voters.

One responsibility of government, however, is of special interest to the Commission. The consensus reached and expressed in the Employment Act of 1946 is that:

> It is the continuing policy and responsibility of the Federal Government to use all practicable means consistent with its needs and obligations and other essential considerations of national policy, with the assistance and cooperation of industry, agriculture, labor, and State and local governments, to coordinate and utilize all its plans, functions, and resources for the purpose of creating and maintaining, in a manner calculated to foster and promote free competitive enterprise and the general welfare, conditions under which there will be afforded useful employment opportunities, including self-employment, for those able, willing, and seeking to work, and to promote maximum employment, production, and purchasing power.

This stated responsibility parallels that expressed by most advanced governments of the Western world. It is not an exclusive responsibility of the federal government but one that is shared with the private economy. The more fully this joint responsibility is met, the greater will be the health and vigor of the private enterprise system.*

---

* J. IRWIN MILLER—In the achievement of national economic goals the quality and the behavior of the citizens of our society may in the long run prove to have been more influential than any of the systems and plans and programs here studied. Since it is our unquestioned national desire to achieve our material goals within an atmosphere of personal opportunity and individual freedom, it cannot be said often enough that the price of freedom is self-discipline. Unless individuals and groups of individuals in a free society voluntarily claim less than the law allows and voluntarily do more than the law requires, then the protection of all society will continuously demand more law, more government, and less freedom. The alternative to voluntary self-restraint is the imposition of restraint from mobilized public opinion leading to the intervention of government.

Messrs. BLACK, LAZARUS, SONNE, and THOMSON wish to be associated with Mr. MILLER'S comment.

J. CAMERON THOMSON—After the word "responsibility" I would add "to-

The Central Goals

It is the Commission's view that effective cooperation of government and individuals participating in the private economy can achieve to a satisfactory degree the objectives of adequate economic growth, low levels of unemployment, and reasonable price stability. Indeed, to a large degree, the attainment of one is likely to be helpful if not essential to the attainment of others. This basic compatibility of the three objectives is one of the most important facts about the relationships among them.

Despite this fundamental compatibility, however, the possibility of conflict among these goals is a very real one. Three problems must be recognized in their relationships. Adequate economic growth, reasonable price stability, and low-level unemployment are equally important as long-term objectives.* If one objective such as price stability were sought with utmost rigor, the sacrifice of other objectives such as low unemployment and growth might be so great that there would be general agreement that it had been pushed too far. From time to time, however, circumstances may force one objective to move ahead of the others. For example, rapid inflation might involve such costs that stabilizing the price level would be given top priority, and the possible costs in terms of unemployment and growth would be borne with little question. These black and white situations seldom occur, and in the more usual situation the task is to seek them all simultaneously and in reasonable degree.

Second, the extent of compatibility among these goals will be greatly influenced by the measures used to achieve them. Some policies to advance a goal may serve their purpose at virtually no cost in terms of other ends. Other policies may clearly sacrifice one objective for the attainment of another. For example, a program to expand growth by improving efficiency may involve no sacrifice in current consumption.

Third, monetary, credit, and fiscal measures *alone* will not be able to achieve a satisfactory performance in terms of all three goals simultaneously if resources move too slowly from one use to another in response to shifts in demand and if some groups enjoy and exercise substantial market power to push up or to maintain prices or wages at unduly high levels. Under some conditions in the past, both here and abroad, reducing

gether with price stability which was not a specific objective of the Employment Act of 1946."

Mr. MILLER wishes to be associated with Mr. THOMSON'S comment.

* WILLARD L. THORP—If one grants that all three objectives are important, the idea of equality is unnecessary and confusing. On the basis of most criteria which I can think of, I would put low-level unemployment first, if there were any point in ranking them.

Mr. RUTTENBERG wishes to be associated with Mr. THORP'S comment.

unemployment beyond some level has been achieved only at the cost
of a rising price level. Correspondingly, restrictions on price increases
beyond some point by tight monetary, credit, and fiscal policies have led
to increased levels of unemployment and to restrictions on the growth of
output.

In stressing the need for other measures, it is not suggested that they
are more important than the monetary, credit, and fiscal measures that
are the Commission's primary concern. On the contrary, the Commission
believes that the latter are the major governmental means available to
deal with both employment and price stability and that their proper
use is an absolute prerequisite for adequate economic growth. However,
if the other required measures are not in effect, then monetary, credit,
and fiscal measures will not be able to attain all three goals simultaneously.

Reasonable Price Stability

The Commission's concern with reasonable price stability is directed
primarily to the avoidance of sustained, moderate increases in the general
price level and of rapid increases even of limited duration.

The fear of inflation and the desire for a dollar of stable purchasing
power are widespread in this country and arise largely from the undesirable effects which are believed to result from inflation. The adverse
consequences cited are many, and among the most frequently heard are
the arbitrary and regressive changes in the distribution of wealth and
income, a slowing down of growth resulting from the discouragement of
savings, distortion and waste in the allocation of resources, reduced
productive efficiency, a flight from the dollar, and the tendency of inflation to feed on itself and thus to become ever greater, leading eventually
to complete collapse.

Most of the arguments on the harmful consequences of inflation have
been derived from studies of the great wartime inflations and the hyper-
inflations of the past. There is no denial from any quarter that the consequences of such price-level increases are so disastrous and costly compared to measures to contain them that they must be avoided. Few
believe that such an inflation is a real threat in this country. No explosive
inflationary situations have occurred without the reckless behavior of
governments through the extremely rapid creation of money. There is
every reason to presume that the federal government will avoid the kind
of excesses that lead to galloping inflation.

The arbitrary redistribution of real incomes and real wealth are
matters of major concern in mild as well as severe inflations. These effects,
however, are far less drastic in mild than in rapid inflations. Our national

policy clearly should be to avoid even mild sustained increases in the price level so long as the cost in terms of other equally vital objectives is not excessive.

The prevention of inflation has nearly always been an important objective of domestic monetary policy if only because of its effects internally. The level of prices is of critical international importance as well. It is clear that if price levels rise in the United States relative to those abroad, our ability to sell goods in foreign markets will decrease. Our international competitive position will improve under conditions of reasonable price-level stability in the United States whenever prices abroad rise more than here. Of course, it is the relationships among the prices of individual products that move internationally that are important in such comparisons, and although they are influenced by the same factors leading to changes in the general price level, each is also affected separately by technological and other factors influencing its costs. If rapid gains in productivity in the manufacture of such commodities in the United States are to be of benefit in international competition, they must bring relatively lower prices.

MEANING AND MEASUREMENT

To devise policies for reasonable price stability which will simultaneously permit the achievement of other goals, the first need is for an understanding of the causes of inflation in general and of the American postwar inflation in particular.

The term inflation is used in this Report to refer to continued increases in the general level of prices, but this meaning is not precise. There would be no general agreement as to how rapidly or how continuously the general price level would have to rise to justify the term inflation.

Both inflation and price stability refer to some general level of prices, but the terms are incompletely defined until an appropriate basket of goods for their measure is specified. Because a major purpose of economic activity is to provide for consumers' needs, a good case can be made for including in the basket only consumers' goods and services. The Consumer Price Index of the Bureau of Labor Statistics attempts to measure the prices of such a basket, and this index is widely used to measure inflation.

This index, however, omits prices of other important elements in the economy, for example, the price of government output and prices of newly produced capital goods. To measure these price changes as well, an index known as the implicit price deflator of gross national product

(hereafter GNP deflator), which includes them, would be better.[1]
Whether one or the other index should be used as a measure of price-
level change depends partly on the question being asked. In addition,
other index numbers, such as the Wholesale Price Index of the Bureau
of Labor Statistics, are used in the study of price-level behavior. In
analyzing price-level changes an examination of many indexes and their
components is essential. In the following, however, references to price-
level changes usually refer to the Consumer Price Index.

Index numbers, however, have serious limitations. To measure price
changes the same basket of goods and services should be priced each time.
But in a dynamic economy some products will change in quality or disappear from use; new products will appear. Putting a price on such changes
is difficult. If a $10,000 house built this year is less durable but more
convenient than one built ten years ago, how does one determine whether
its price is higher or lower? The miracle drugs, improvements in hospital
care, and new diagnostic tools have all increased medical costs but have
cut death rates and the duration of many illnesses; what price tag can be
put on these changes?

There are many other technical difficulties in constructing index numbers. The construction of the sample, the relationship of the reported
price data to prices actually paid, the changes in services made available
with goods and included in their price, the effects on prices of different
levels and types of taxation, all these present problems. Thus any small
change in the Consumer Price Index or GNP deflator may not reflect
a "true" change in prices but merely quality changes or other imperfections in the indexes. A modest upward drift in the indexes, perhaps
as great as 1 percent per year, may not really indicate a true price increase, especially as many experts believe that the inability of index
numbers to allow for a trend of net improvement in quality gives most
index numbers an inherent upward bias. However, the two indexes
may be relied upon with considerable confidence for recording substantial
movements of prices.

THE CAUSES OF INFLATION

General price increases may result from either or both of two major
types of causation. One is the pull of excessive demand in relation to
supply. The other is the upward push that may result from a varied group
of factors on the supply side, such as price or wage setting by economic

---

[1] The Department of Commerce prepares regular data on gross national product both
in money values and in real terms. In the latter, correction is made for price changes.
The ratio of the first to the second of these series implies a price average, and this
average is called the implicit price deflator of the GNP.

groups with market power, increased price of imports, downward inflexibility of prices and wages, and the immobility of productive agents.

The time-honored theory of inflation is that it is caused by the pull
of excessive demand. In older theories this demand was often seen
as the result of an excessive expansion in the supply of money. But
demand-induced inflation is not conceived narrowly as resulting from
demand forces in abstraction from supply. The well-worn expression that
inflation results from "too many dollars chasing too few goods" neatly
includes the major elements of a wide variety of schools of thought within
the fold of those emphasizing demand forces as the cause of inflation;
there may be "too many dollars" (emphasizing the quantity of money),
those dollars may be "chasing" goods too hard (emphasizing the velocity
of money and all the determinants of spending), and there may be "too
few goods" (emphasizing the supply side).

The second type of cause of inflation—from the supply side—includes at
least two variants. The first may be called cost-push inflation. It may stem
from the exercise of market power by business or labor groups, or it may
be the result of such things as higher import prices or higher taxes.*
Business firms may have sufficient power to raise prices even when demand
is not adequate to sustain the former output at the new price, and this
product at the higher price may be a purchased material for other
producers, thereby causing cost-push for other product prices.** Unions
may also have sufficient power to demand and secure higher wages in excess of productivity increases, which increase labor costs and which in
turn may lead to higher prices. Alternatively higher costs may result
from higher import prices, from increased interest rates, from increased
excise taxes, from higher depreciation charges, increased research and
development expenses, or from the exhaustion of readily available resources like oil, gas, or coal. The increased costs may also arise from

---

* STANLEY H. RUTTENBERG—The term market power is used frequently in the
document to indicate the exercise by business and labor groups of unreasonable influence over sectors of the American economy. A clear distinction must be made between the existence, and the abusive use, of market power.

Market power exists in most markets and certainly in the key markets in the American economy. The existence of market power cannot be eliminated without tearing
down a considerable portion of the present economic structure. Attempts to curb it
should be directed at its abusive use—not at its existence.

The report, therefore, would have been much enhanced if the modifying word
"abusive" had been inserted before the term market power wherever it is used in the
text.

** JAMES B. BLACK—A statement is made that "business firms may have sufficient
power to raise prices even when demand is not adequate to sustain the former output
at the new prices." I think we should insert the word "temporary" after "prices," as
I do not believe that any business has the power to permanently raise prices under
the conditions stated.

Mr. SHUMAN wishes to be associated with Mr. BLACK'S comment.

government price-support activities in agriculture or from stock-piling activities. The individual firm may experience cost-push pressures because of rising prices of purchased services and materials which result from inflationary forces of any kind, including demand-pull, elsewhere in the economy.

The other variant stems from shifts of demand for particular products in the presence of immobile factors of production and downward price or wage rigidity. Shifts of demands may raise prices in the area of expanding demand. If in the areas where demand is falling prices are inflexible downward, then shifts of demand may raise the general price level. Such price-level increases are likely to be accompanied by unemployment. Downward rigidity of prices and wages may result from the conscious use of market power, from long-term contractual arrangements, or from inherent resistances in the economy.

Although sustained and prolonged general price rises are usually the result of interactions of forces both from the demand side and the supply side which have cumulative effects on each other, nevertheless the distinction between price increases resulting from demand-pull on the one hand and from market power, demand-shift, and cost-push on the other is important. If the second group are dominant, monetary, credit, and fiscal measures which influence the level of demand may, if operating alone, face a serious dilemma because the actions taken to achieve greater price stability may add to the number of unemployed or retard growth.*

THE POSTWAR EXPERIENCE

There has been a net upward movement in the level of prices over the last 100 years in the United States. Beginning in 1869, data are available

---

* CHARLES B. SHUMAN—The effort to distinguish between the so-called "cost-push" and "demand-pull" types of inflation tends to obscure the importance of monetary factors. A rise in the general price level is not necessarily a matter of serious concern unless it becomes a part of an upward spiral.

The phenomenon referred to as "excessive demand" almost always reflects either a disruption of production by war or other disaster, government policies that expand money and credit, or a combination of these factors. The most common cause of "excessive demand" is deficit spending.

The "cost-push" theory is based on conditions in recent postwar years—a period in which the economy was still feeling the effects of inflation generated by World War II.

Assuming that certain cost factors can lead to an increase in the general price level in the absence of inflationary government policies, it is still true that prices cannot continue to increase over a prolonged period without action by the government to increase the money supply.

WILLARD L. THORP—Even if the price rise is due to demand pull, the attempt to check it by reducing the amount of demand may have more effect on production and employment than on prices, since many prices have a greater flexibility for rising than declining from the point at which they are—the so-called "ratchet effect."

Mr. LUBIN and Mr. NATHAN wish to be associated with Mr. THORP'S comment.

for both consumer prices and the GNP deflator. Since that date, there have been periods of gradual price decline such as 1873-97, of price stability such as 1923-29, of gradual increase such as 1900-15, of sharp increases such as during the two world wars, as well as sharp cyclical declines such as following 1920 and 1929. On balance, over the years 1869-1960, the net movement has been upward, at an average rate for both indexes of greater than 1 percent per year. In the years 1899-1960 the average annual rate of increase of consumer prices was just under 2 percent and for the GNP deflator slightly over 2 percent. And in the years 1919-60 the average annual rate of increase of consumer prices was about 1.3 percent and for the GNP deflator about 1.4 percent. It is clear, therefore, that the upward drift in price indexes is not a new phenomenon in this country. (See Chart 1.)

A study of the course of prices since World War II, however, is more relevant here. It provides an opportunity to analyze the possible causes of rising prices, it gives hints regarding the seriousness of the inflationary threat for the future, and it provides background for consideration of policies that might be followed to achieve price stability. An examination of this record led the Commission to the following conclusions.

The postwar price increases (measured by the Consumer Price Index) have been substantial, averaging 3.3 percent per year over a 15-year span, ending in December 1960. Three-fourths of the entire price increase of the period, however, occurred before 1953 and was directly related to war. More meaningful implications for the future may be gained from study of the period beginning with 1953. Between the end of 1952 and the end of 1960 the Consumer Price Index rose at an average rate of 1.4 percent per year. As was true in the entire postwar period, the major contributor to this increase has been the price of services, which has risen at an average rate of nearly 3 percent per year, whereas the prices of the commodities included in the index have risen only at an average rate of less than 1 percent per year. Differences appear also among the broad commodity groups; foods have risen at an average rate of 0.8 percent per year and other nondurable goods at 1.3 percent per year, whereas durable goods actually *fell* slightly over the eight years at an average rate of 0.3 percent per year. (See Chart 2.)

The Wholesale Price Index rose at a rate of about 1 percent per year from the end of 1952 to the end of 1960. The index was relatively stable from 1952 to 1955 and from the end of 1957 to the end of 1960 but rose during the years 1956 and 1957. This behavior is explained largely by the divergence between the movements of the prices of farm and food products and the prices of other commodities. Throughout the period the prices of nonfarm, nonfood products rose. Declines in farm and food product prices from 1952 to 1955 and from early 1958 to the end of 1959 offset increases in industrial and consumer products to keep the total

Chart 1

CONSUMER PRICE INDEX AND
IMPLICIT PRICE DEFLATOR OF THE GROSS NATIONAL PRODUCT,
1889-1960

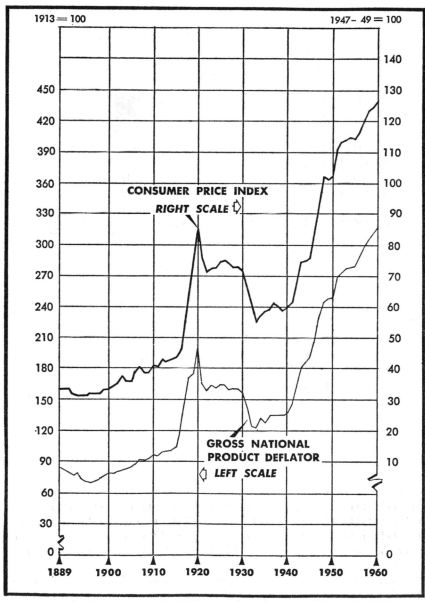

SOURCE: Federal Reserve Bank of New York and National Bureau of Economic Research.

Chart 2

CONSUMER PRICE INDEX

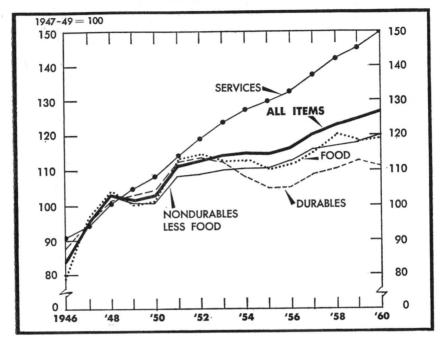

WHOLESALE PRICE INDEX

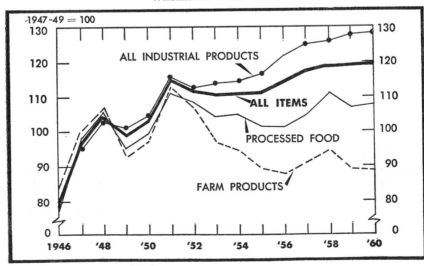

SOURCE: Department of Labor.

index stable in these periods. But when farm and food prices rose in 1956 and 1957 at the same time as other prices were rising sharply, the entire index rose. The sharpest price rises for nonfarm, nonfood products occurred in capital equipment, where the rise was very sharp from December 1954 to December 1957 and where the average rate of increase for the eight years, 1953-60, was about 3 percent per year.

The postwar experience reveals all the varieties of inflationary pressure described in the previous section. Despite the predominant influence of demand, forces on the supply side have also affected the behavior of prices in recent years. Market power and frictions of various kinds have continued to operate and may have been in some respects even more significant since the war than they were before. Various groups have continued to try to increase their income by using market power or pressure through government to raise the prices of the products or services they sell. Moreover downward rigidity in both wages and prices has persisted, especially, but not exclusively, in enterprises which are both highly concentrated and strongly unionized. This downward rigidity in wages and prices has also permitted shifting demand to cause increases in the general price level. Although forces on the supply side may have played some inflationary role throughout the entire postwar period, they were overshadowed by excess demand before 1953, and they did not operate in all industries even after that time.

A number of special conditions made the control of inflation during the postwar years particularly difficult. For example, the rapid increase in prices and wages immediately after World War II following the lifting of direct controls and the renewed outbreak of inflation at the start of the Korean War undoubtedly made both employers and employees expect that wages would continue to rise each year, and these expectations contributed to the tendency for wages and prices to rise even when there was no excess demand. The relatively slower pace of inflation and the continued efforts to control inflation in the past few years may moderate those attitudes.

FUTURE PROSPECTS

What is the prospect for future price movements? Does an examination of the past record provide any insights into the probable course of future events? Given the imperfections of our knowledge, forecasting is hazardous.

In a general way we know that the long-term trend of prices is determined by how prices behave between inflationary movements as well as by the strength of the inflations themselves. Inflationary trends have often been prevented not by the avoidance of periods when prices rose but by the compensating declines at other times. A period of noticeably falling prices has occurred only once since the war—a mild drop in the recession of 1948-49. An important question is whether we now face a new economic environment, with more inflationary bias than existed in the past, and whether it is subject to control by monetary, credit, and fiscal policies. Many persons believe that our economic setting is significantly different from the prewar past, and that some of today's inflationary forces are less subject to monetary and fiscal influence than those of earlier years.

Four major elements present difficulties for achieving price stability in the future.

1. The United States has an announced national policy of maintaining high-level production and employment. Success in achieving this objective operates to prevent severe depressions, which formerly brought price declines as an offset to the price increases in periods of strong demand.

2. Prices and wages are rigid against downward movements. While such rigidities do exist, the unresolved issue is how far this is new. The record also shows the presence of considerable price and wage rigidity in the minor recessions before World War II.

3. There is a tendency of productivity increases to be shared among employees and employers through higher incomes rather than with the consumer through lower prices. Furthermore, wage-rate increases in industries with rapidly rising productivity tend to reflect those productivity increases. Wage-rate increases in industries with limited productivity gains tend to be based on estimated changes in productivity for the economy as a whole. The combination of these practices and the maintenance of aggregate demand tend to contribute to a rising price level.

4. Payments for services are an increasingly important part of consumer spending and now account for more than one-third of the expenditures recorded in the Consumer Price Index. Since the war there has been an unbroken rising trend in the prices of services which has greatly exceeded the increase in other prices.

Four important developments are favorable for achieving price stability.

1. Our knowledge about stabilization techniques is substantially greater than it was a quarter of a century ago. We should increase our efforts to find means to curb price-level increases without compromising our objectives of high-level employment and economic growth.

2. Plant capacity is a much less limiting factor in relation to the supply of goods than it was before 1956. Plant capacity utilization was abnormally high at the end of the war, and it continued to be so for some years. With the relatively slow growth in industrial output in recent years, however, capital has grown faster than output. Levels of utilization

in early 1961 were lower than normal, but barring another episode like the Korean War we are not likely to return to such high utilization rates as we had before 1956. The result should be an increase in competitive pressure on employers to reduce costs and less readiness to give way to wage demands to keep output flowing than in the earlier postwar years. In addition, the proportion of output accounted for by efficient plants is increasing average productivity in the economy as a whole.*

3. Foreign competition has become much more effective than it was in earlier years. If we do not give way to protectionist demands, actual and potential foreign competition should have effects similar to the change in utilization rates in moderating prospective price increases.

4. The abnormally high ratios of liquid assets to incomes and the very low ratios of consumer and business debt to incomes which prevailed at the end of the war have now been restored to more usual levels. These abnormal ratios provided strong pressure for business and consumer spending in the postwar years.

Taking all these factors into account and focussing attention on the objective of price stability, the Commission believes that with appropriate monetary, credit, and fiscal policies we should be able to achieve a better record with regard to price movements in the next decade than in the years since the Korean War. If other public and private economic measures are pursued to improve the efficiency of the economy, we can have an even more satisfactory record of price stability.

Low Levels of Unemployment

By the Employment Act of 1946 the nation set high and stable levels of employment as an objective of national economic policy. The Commission uses instead "low levels of unemployment" in referring to the same objective, for the rate of unemployment is the central concern. This rate may rise at the same time as the number of workers employed is rising because the size of the labor force as a whole is increasing faster than employment. Such a situation is not a satisfactory achievement of the real purpose of the high-employment objective.

There are two main reasons for the continuous concern with unemployment. One is its direct effect upon those who are unemployed; the second is its effect upon total output and its rate of growth.

The unemployed do not enjoy the benefits of prosperity. When the

---

* STANLEY H. RUTTENBERG—Industry cannot be expected to operate at full capacity because certain small proportions of capacity may well be inefficient and costly. But this does not mean, however, that we should be satisfied with the permanently lower level of capacity utilization we have had in the period since 1956.

percentage of the civilian labor force unemployed is used as the measure of unemployment, we must not forget the actual numbers involved. With a civilian labor force of more than 70 million persons, each increase of 1 percentage point in the unemployment rate means a loss of jobs for more than 700,000 persons. For the unemployed, being without a job means not only a loss of income and hardship for the family but also a possible loss of self-respect, a sense of personal failure, and, at times, a loss of social standing in the community. In addition, unemployment represents a waste of productive resources.

Nevertheless, the goal of low-level unemployment cannot be taken to mean an absence of unemployment. Even under the pressure of wartime demands, no economy has ever succeeded in completely eliminating unemployment. In a given place, it is impossible to achieve a perfect and instantaneous match between the demand for workers of a specific skill category and work experience and the supply of such workers. All workers could conceivably be employed only if there are so many unfilled vacancies that any worker could be used in any place. And if there are more vacancies than unemployed, voluntary quit rates rise, resulting in voluntary unemployment while workers shift or are in transit between jobs.

MEANING AND MEASUREMENT

The most widely used data on national unemployment are collected in surveys conducted by the Bureau of the Census and published by the Bureau of Labor Statistics. Monthly and annual average rates of unemployment, data on the duration of unemployment, and yearly totals of the unemployed and of weeks of unemployment are among the statistics provided.

A worker is defined as unemployed if he has not received pay or profit from one hour or more of work or has not worked 15 hours or more as an unpaid family worker during the week of the survey. Among the unemployed two groups are distinguished. The "active" unemployed are those who are "looking for work"—registering with an employment service, placing or answering advertisements, writing letters of application, and so forth. The "inactive" unemployed are those who have volunteered to the interviewer that they were not seeking work because they had been laid off but expected to be called back to the job, or because they were temporarily ill, or because they thought there was no work available in their line or in the community.

The present system of reporting unemployment makes no allowance for the loss of manhours which occur when people work fewer hours than they wish. There are monthly estimates by the BLS of persons in nonagricultural industries who are not working full time for economic reasons, such as slack production, material shortages, and inability to find full-time work. The number has been quite large, ranging from an annual average of 2 million in 1956 to 3 million in the recession year of 1958. Efforts have been made to convert the working hours lost by those who worked part time involuntarily into a full-time equivalent. An estimate of this full-time equivalent for 1959 was 1 million unemployed.

THE RECORD

Chart 3 sets forth annual averages of the percentage of the civilian labor force unemployed for the years 1921-60. The huge unemployment problem of the depressed thirties and the low figures for the years of forced demand of World War II and the Korean conflict are clearly apparent as are the fluctuations of unemployment over the course of business cycles.

A disturbing feature of recent years is that the rate of unemployment, after the last two recessions, has not fallen back to the lower levels preceding the recessions. Unemployment rates for the years 1955-57 were clearly higher than for the immediate postwar years as well as for the years of the Korean conflict, and the rates for 1959 and 1960 were clearly above those for 1955-57. Part-time employment, which does not show up in the percent of the civilian labor force unemployed, was also at high levels. The 1960 year-end level of unemployment, 6.8 percent on a seasonably adjusted basis (6.4 percent unadjusted), was clearly an excessive level of unemployment.*

Another measure of unemployment relates to the duration of unemployment. The monthly survey of the BLS records the duration of unemployment at the date of the survey. The annual survey of work experience gives the cumulative total of weeks unemployed in the course of a year. Both sets of data show the same pattern of an increasing average duration of unemployment in recent years and an increasing proportion of the unemployed experiencing longer periods of unemployment. Both series also show the same pattern of incidence among different groups. For example, long-term unemployment, defined as 15 weeks or longer, which in 1960 amounted to more than 20 percent of unemployment, strikes harder at older people and at nonwhites.

---

* CHARLES B. SHUMAN—A number of factors need to be taken into account in evaluating the trend in unemployment. We have been going through a period of adjustment from conditions created by war. Rapid increases in wage rates—including the minimum wage—have tended to accelerate the adoption of labor-saving technology, and to shift demand from the unskilled to the more highly trained types of workers. Employers cannot continue to hire handicapped or unskilled workers when the value of their product is below the established wage rate. Many workers are priced out of the labor market. Finally, our method of measuring unemployment leaves much to be desired.

Chart 3

CIVILIAN LABOR FORCE AND UNEMPLOYMENT AS A PERCENTAGE OF THE CIVILIAN LABOR FORCE, 1921-1960

CIVILIAN LABOR FORCE

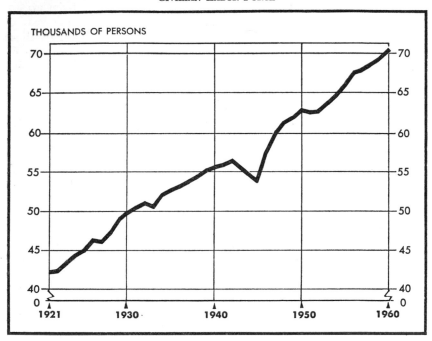

UNEMPLOYMENT RATE

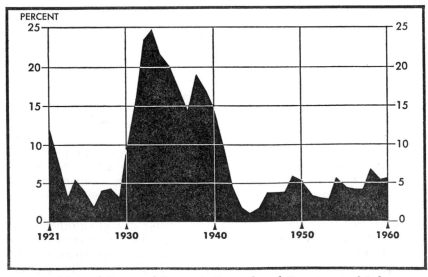

SOURCE: National Bureau of Economic Research and Department of Labor.

26

THE CAUSES OF UNEMPLOYMENT

In examining the causes of unemployment it is useful to make a rough distinction between unemployment as a result of just not enough jobs and structural, frictional, and seasonal causes, although the distinction sometimes is not clear. In a major depression, lack of demand is unambiguously the cause of most of the unemployment. In periods of slow growth, unemployment may also stem from a demand which is too weak. This type of unemployment is called *lack-of-demand unemployment*.

There are times when the number of jobs available is about equal to or greater than the number of workers in the labor force, but there is still unemployment. Here one cause of unemployment lies in the imbalances between the types and locations of the unemployed and the types and location of workers wanted by employers, as exemplified by the distressed area problem. This is designated as *structural unemployment*.

Alternatively, there may be a crude balance between the number of available jobs and the number of workers in each town or city. Some plants may be expanding production and hiring new workers while others are temporarily contracting. Substantial numbers of workers quit jobs voluntarily for a variety of personal reasons without having another job; others are released from one job but are employable in another. If workers are poorly informed as to employment possibilities, those who become unemployed may remain so for some time even though there are jobs which they could fill. In addition, when workers know that their unemployment will be temporary, they may not look for a new job. This type of unemployment is described as *frictional unemployment*.

Finally, there may be seasonal variations in the number of jobs available in a community. While some of the unemployed may find work in other industries with a different seasonal pattern, this is not always possible. This type of unemployment is called *seasonal unemployment*.

In practice, however, the distinction often is not so clear between unemployment due to inadequate demand and structural, frictional, and seasonal unemployment. If the total demand for labor increases, structural, frictional, and seasonal unemployment may be expected to decline along with lack-of-demand unemployment. Structural unemployment will fall because activity will expand and because workers will be encouraged to shift more readily when jobs are easy to get. Frictional unemployment will fall because when there are more jobs available the unemployed will more quickly find one into which they can fit. Seasonal unemployment may fall because those laid off have a better chance of finding other work.

Despite the wealth of detail available on the characteristics of the unemployed, there are no reliable ways of determining from current figures how many are unemployed as a result of which cause. The distinctions, however, are significant for policy choices. For the greater the amount of structural maladjustment, seasonal fluctuations, and labor market frictions the more unfilled vacancies there will have to be in order to reduce unemployment to a given level.

EMPLOYMENT TARGETS

The above considerations make it clear that there is no really satisfactory definition or precise measure of high-level employment or low-level unemployment. However, a working notion can be based on a decision that at some level of unemployment, which would vary from time to time with the structural and other characteristics of the labor market, to reduce unemployment by monetary or fiscal measures is not economically justified. The cost in terms of inflation of generating the aggregate demand needed to create enough job vacancies to achieve further reduction in unemployment would be excessive compared with the cost of achieving the same reduction of unemployment by other means.*

The Commission believes that an appropriate target for low level unemployment to use as a guide for monetary, credit, and fiscal measures is one somewhere near the point where the number of unfilled vacancies is about the same as the number of unemployed. In those circumstances there would still be unemployment and there would also be unfilled vacancies. But both conditions could be relieved by measures to improve the functioning of labor markets and to increase the mobility of workers geographically and among jobs of different skills so as to reduce structural, seasonal, and frictional unemployment.**

---

* J. IRWIN MILLER—Because of the methods used, the unemployed figures published by our government are at considerable variance with those used by other nations. Furthermore, they are open to wide debate in terms of their absolute significance. To regard them as absolute measures of unemployment would be a serious mistake. This is the reason I was one of the Commission who felt it imperative to avoid the use of any precise unemployment figures as our goal.

Mr. SHUMAN wishes to be associated with Mr. MILLER'S comment.

** STANLEY H. RUTTENBERG—Instead of making this its goal, the Commission has failed to quantify its goal of low levels of unemployment. The Commission, in this paragraph, defines a low level of unemployment as somewhere "near the point where the number of unfilled vacancies is about the same as the number of unemployed." The goal of low levels of unemployment, attainable through the proper mixture of monetary, credit and fiscal measures combined with appropriate measures to reduce the levels of structural non-demand unemployment, should be 3 percent or less of the labor force.

In the paragraph at the end of this section, the Commission ". . . calls for effective use of monetary, credit and fiscal policy to induce adequate levels of demand and to stimulate economic growth. It also requires new and imaginative programs to deal directly with structural unemployment. . . ." When one combines this comment with

FUTURE PROSPECTS

What is the prospect for future levels of unemployment? Unfortunately the trend of unemployment has not been improving. Not only were unployment rates higher in 1959 and early 1960 than in earlier recovery periods, but the proportion of long-duration unemployment has been higher. This long-duration unemployment continues to be serious in depressed areas, and it has become more widespread. Technological displacement of workers in manufacturing and agriculture has been heavy, and the total number of jobs in those sectors as a percentage of total employment has been decreasing.

Two factors of special importance may make more difficult the achievement of low-level unemployment in the decade ahead. First, the expected rate of growth of the labor force increases sharply in the sixties, compared to the fifties, as the population bulge reaches the employable age. Many more jobs per year will be required to keep the unemployment rate low. Second, the pace of technological change, typified by the term automation, shows no sign of abating; on the contrary it may be increasing. Whether technological change will create new job opportunities as rapidly as it displaces other workers is not predictable. In addition, there are the problems of obsolete skills of some workers and resistances to labor mobility flowing from such things as nontransferable pensions and labor union restrictions on entry into some occupations.*

Among the factors on the favorable side are the stated responsibility of government embodied in the Employment Act, greater knowledge of stabilization techniques, increased training programs in industry to develop the new skills required, increased government interest in education and training, which will develop greater skills and adaptability in workers and postpone the age of entry into the labor force, improved information programs on job availabilities, and some increased mobility of workers.

The employment problem ahead is formidable. It calls for effective use of monetary, credit, and fiscal policies to induce adequate levels of demand and to stimulate economic growth. It also requires new and imaginative programs to deal directly with structural unemployment—

---

the one to be found on page 42, "If special measures were adopted to deal with depressed areas and with social and age discrimination in employment, the level of unemployment at high levels of demand might be reduced to perhaps 3 percent," a definite and affirmative goal would be established.

Mr. NATHAN wishes to be associated with Mr. RUTTENBERG'S comment.

* STANLEY H. RUTTENBERG—The major resistances to labor mobility are not "labor union restrictions" or "nontransferable pensions," but are the absence of adequate retraining programs, an ineffective national employment service, and the absence of adequate relocation allowances.

programs for distressed areas, education and training of new and displaced workers, an improved job information service. Action is also needed to ease the burdens of the technologically unemployed lest restrictive work practices develop which will inhibit productivity gains.*

Economic Growth

Economic growth is a major American objective, not as an end in itself but because it is a means and a prerequisite for the attainment of economic and other fundamental goals. Economic growth makes it possible to improve the standards of living of our own and future generations and to help raise standards of living in other parts of the world. The dynamic adjustments required by technological advances are more easily made in an expanding economy; competing demands for higher income can be most easily reconciled if total output is expanding. Finally growth provides the challenges and the sense of achievement that distinguish a growing society from a stagnant society.

Withal, growth is but one goal among many, and at some point any further increase in the rate of economic growth may be obtainable only

---

* See Mr. RUTTENBERG'S comment on page 28.

H. CHRISTIAN SONNE—In 1953 the chronically unemployed amounted statistically to less than ½ million. They had risen to approximately 1½ million in 1956 and to about 2 million early in 1960—near peaks of recoveries. Counter-cyclical policies are not adequate for combating this increasingly serious problem of chronic unemployment.

1. The needed job opportunities can be provided only by growth, or as a by-product of growth, for these reasons:

a. With average production gains and no substantial change in the work week, present output could be produced a year from now with about 1½ to 2 million fewer workers than today. This, in turn, means that due to our improved skill an increase in production is needed to provide employment not only for those now unemployed, but also for the increase in productivity of those now employed.

b. Our balance of payment problem can only be met by maintaining or improving the competitiveness of American industry. This will make it necessary to press forward to the utmost with technological improvements. We may expect that this will aggravate technological unemployment.

c. If we add to these considerations the fact that the yearly net influx of persons into the labor market is over 1 million, it is no wonder that the number of chronically unemployed, which now exceed 2 million, may increase at a more serious rate over the years, even during the peaks of recovery periods.

2. The alternatives of slowing down technological and managerial advances, or drastically reducing hours of work, would not be possible because we can only fulfill our international commitments over and above our domestic needs by working hard and intelligently. This means that we must enlarge our export surplus of goods and services; we must maintain and improve competitiveness (in costs and/or quality) of American products and services; which in turn means that we must press for technological advances.

by an increasing sacrifice of other goals. The maintenance of a level of aggregate demand sufficient to achieve high-level employment will result in a substantial rate of growth. Whether this rate will be widely judged adequate is uncertain. Because the costs and benefits are not reducible to any common terms that permit their objective measurement and comparison, the Commission knows of no optimum cut-off point for the rate of growth. This point will depend significantly upon the means used to achieve greater growth. Although not satisfied with recent rates of growth, the Commission does not recommend the establishment of any specific rate of growth as a target.*

MEANING AND MEASUREMENT

There are many concepts and measures of economic growth, but all refer to the output, or the capacity to produce the output, of goods and services. In its most usual sense, the economic growth of a country may be measured by the increase of its *total real output*. But if output increases only at the same rate as population increases, the average individual will not be better off. For this reason, *output per capita* is also frequently used as a measure of economic growth. Not all improvements in productivity, however, are reflected in output per capita; they may instead be taken in the form of greater leisure made possible by a shorter workweek. Hence, *output per manhour* is used as a measure of the productivity per unit of employed labor. Gross national product at constant prices and related measures of GNP per capita and GNP per manhour

---

* STANLEY H. RUTTENBERG—I heartily disagree with the statement, "the Commission does not recommend the establishment of any specific rate of growth as a target."

The Commission should set a target rate of economic growth boldly and forthrightly.

Rising productivity and a growing labor force, if fully utilized should produce an average annual economic growth rate of approximately 5 percent in the present decade. The failure to state such a growth rate is, I think, an abdication of the responsibility of this Commission to define what is actually meant by its continual reference to an adequate rate of economic growth. Only by stating an anticipated level of growth, and then relating future developments to that goal, can we determine what appropriate economic policies should be pursued.

If our normal potential growth rate from full utilization of our manpower and physical resources, without reallocation of resources between the major sectors of the economy, is considerably less than our goal of 5 percent a year, then we know that we have to reallocate resources between consumption and investment to accomplish a higher rate of economic growth.

On the other hand, if our goal is 5 percent and we attain that goal without reallocation of resources between investment and consumption, then we know that present allocation of existing levels of resources is adequate.

Mr. NATHAN wishes to be associated with Mr. RUTTENBERG'S comment.
See Mr. SONNE'S comment on page 5.

are used here as the measures of output and the bases for calculating rates
of economic growth.

THE RECORD

In terms of real GNP the U.S. economy of 1960 produced nearly ten
times as much in goods and services for consumers, business, and government as it did in 1890. Output per manhour increased about five times.
Because of a shorter workweek, output per capita rose about three and a
half times. (See Chart 4.) These figures highlight the impressive long-term
record of growth. Our country has the highest standard of living in the
world by a very wide margin.

Yet this growth did not come smoothly. The saw-tooth appearance of
graphs which depict the rise of GNP, GNP per capita, and GNP per
manhour indicate the fluctuations in the rate of growth caused by business cycles and wars. Despite these, however, data on GNP per capita for
the last 70 years held within 10 percent of a trend line of its growth except during the depression of the thirties and World War II.

The increase in productivity as measured by GNP per manhour has
been the most important single factor in the growth of total real GNP and
of GNP per capita. It is also this increase in material goods per hour's
work of labor which has enabled Americans to work fewer hours per
week and to enjoy annual vacations along with increased output.

DETERMINANTS OF GROWTH

The precise combination of forces which determines a nation's growth
is unfortunately not yet known. Growth is a product of the entire social
fabric of a people; for many elements that seemingly explain differing
rates of growth among nations, or of one nation over time, derive from
their cultural, political, moral, and economic systems.

The United States has been blessed with an abundance of resources
essential for economic growth. Moreover, a dynamic, innovative, risk-
taking management of private business has enhanced the efficiency with
which these resources are employed. Private property, a responsive and
responsible labor force, a stable political and social system, a healthy
climate for scientific and technological advance—all are involved in the
explanation of the American growth record.

Our free enterprise system is also crucial in explaining our growth
record. This system has demonstrated great capacity to develop and to
adjust to new products and new means of production. When competition
is effective, production responds to meet the changing desires of the
consumer. The achievement of satisfactory growth requires that private
and public policies should continually be designed to reduce barriers to

Chart 4

INDEXES OF REAL GROSS NATIONAL PRODUCT, AGGREGATE,
PER CAPITA, AND PER MANHOUR, 1889-1960

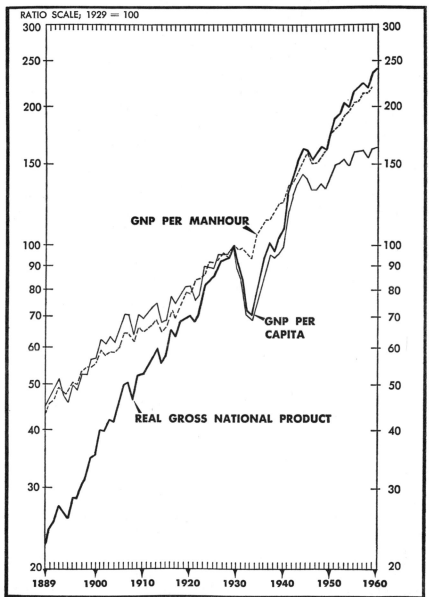

All measures based on 1929 prices. In this chart equal percentage changes in the indexes are shown as equal vertical distances.

SOURCE: National Bureau of Economic Research.

the mobility of resources and to provide a favorable environment for continued enterprise.

The rate of growth of potential output—in the sense of the output forthcoming from the economy's use of its human and physical resources at a high level—depends on the rate of growth of the quantity and quality of our productive resources—labor, capital goods, natural resources, management, and technology—and on the efficiency with which they are used. And potential output cannot be realized unless the total demand for goods and services increases at a rate equal to the growth of potential output.

The maintenance of a level of demand appropriate to high-level employment encourages the best use of resources for current output and also provides an effective incentive for promoting the abundance and quality of resources for future production. High levels of expenditure for capital goods and for research and development are generally associated with and are dependent on high levels of production and consumption.

On occasion, however, a marked increase in investment, while contributing in the short run to economic growth, may prove to be excessive and subsequently may stand in the way of high-level output and employment for a time. If innovation lags, so that producers cannot find new activities in which expansion may be confidently assumed to provide profits worth the risks involved, then the successive exploitation of existing opportunities may make further expansion less profitable. This is one of the factors involved in the problem of sustainable growth.

John Kendrick has found that in the period from 1889 to 1958, the real net national product in the private domestic economy grew at an annual rate of 3.4 percent. About half of this increase was attributed to increases in the quantity of labor and capital goods and half to increased productivity. Thus improvements in technology and its application and the increased productive ability of labor and management account for at least half of our past growth. Increases in the *quantity* of labor and capital alone will not enable us to match the past growth record, let alone surpass it. Increased *quality* of productive factors and their organization are necessary for the improved productivity that is needed for satisfactory future growth.

LABOR RESOURCES

The growth of the labor force depends primarily on the size and age distribution of the population, the length of the workweek and work year, and the proportion of the population that enters the labor force because of youth, sex, physical incapacity, or old age. Consequently the prospective labor force is already in large part determined for the next 20 years.

In this country the decision to seek work is left to the free choice of individuals, but this does not mean that the rates of labor force participation—the proportion of the population that seeks work—are not influenced by private and public policies. Educational arrangements and opportunities may delay the entry of younger persons into the labor force. Willingness to seek work is for some groups partly dependent on the probable ease of finding it. Sizable unemployment reduces the participation rates for older men and for women of all ages. Participation rates for older persons are dampened at present by the earning limitations of social security. Many older workers leave the labor force when they become unemployed. Some at least could continue to work if ready opportunities existed, and more might be retained in the labor force if suitable retraining programs were available. Participation rates for married women could be influenced by tax law changes permitting larger deductions for the expenses incurred by working.

Working hours are also determined primarily by private agreement, but they are influenced significantly by the Fair Labor Standards Act. It is apparent also that workweek reductions rise with unemployment.

The productive quality of our labor resources depends on the education and skill of the labor force, its health, and the complex of factors subsumed under morale. As technology and organization become more complex, educational levels must be raised in order to take full advantage of these developments. Admittedly crude estimates suggest that investment in education yields returns which are at least equal to returns on other types of investment.

Improved education is a major national goal in its own right because of its contribution to the development and satisfaction of individuals and to enlightened citizenship as well as for its effect on the growth of output. Similarly measures to improve the health of the population are valued for the direct benefits they provide as well as for their economic benefits.

An important addition and improvement in labor resources would be also achieved by reducing job discrimination. Not only does this keep ethnic minorities and women out of some types of work, but it imposes limits to the level of responsibility to which they can aspire. Aside from its moral implications, job discrimination robs the community of skills which are needed and are potentially available.

Measures which improve the efficiency of labor will also contribute to growth. Incentives for advancement in income and job responsibility, effective employment services, retraining programs for workers displaced by technological change, programs to help move workers from depressed areas and industries into others, policies to move marginal farm workers into more productive nonfarm employment, elimination of redundant workers—all are measures that have favorable effects upon the growth rate.

TECHNOLOGY AND CAPITAL RESOURCES

The record of continuous growth of output per manhour has been in large measure due to improvements in technical knowledge and the organization of production. It has also been due to the willingness and ability of business firms to invest in the capital equipment necessary to exploit new techniques as they are developed.

A high rate of development of new products and new techniques is necessary for the attainment of our growth objectives. This will require a high level of research and development expenditures. Current research expenditures are large in comparison with the past, but a large part is directed toward the development of military end products. Many developments useful to civilian industry arise as by-products of military research. This is an indirect and unsystematic way to seek useful civilian contributions. In many industries much more research could profitably be directed to reducing the gap between existing scientific knowledge and its application to production processes.

In spite of the large amount spent on what is called research and development, many believe that too small a fraction of this total is devoted to basic science.

To fill these gaps may require more government expenditures on non-military research, a continuance of liberal tax treatment of business expenditures on research and development, and possibly outright subsidies to stimulate basic scientific research. Measures which intensify competitive pressures to innovate can also be helpful.

To get the full benefit from improvements in technical knowledge, however, requires a level of gross investment in industry high enough to provide capital equipment for an expanding work force, to provide the amounts and types of capital per worker in line with the requirements of improving technology, and to replace obsolete plant and equipment fast enough to assure declining unit costs of production. With adequate incentives and enough saving it would be possible to increase the rate of growth by speeding up replacement so as to reduce the average age of plant and equipment.

PROSPECTIVE GROWTH

What rate of growth can be expected in the next ten or fifteen years? Many projections have been made and published in recent years of the potential rate of growth of aggregate real output for the period to 1970 or 1975. Assumptions are made about such variables as population increase, size of the labor force, length of the workweek, amount of unemployment, productivity per manhour, shifts in the composition of demand and output, growth of plant and equipment, and the average age of capital equipment. Essentially these are assumptions about the quantity and quality of resources and the efficiency with which they are used and thus about the principal determinants of growth. The resultant projections vary because they use different assumptions for the underlying factors. They also differ in their assumptions as to whether special government programs are put into effect to stimulate the growth rate, and they start and terminate in different years. The projected growth rates of output for the decade of the sixties generally fall within the range of 3½ to 5 percent per year.

The Commission has not made an independent estimate of the growth rate for the decade ahead. If we maintain a level of aggregate demand to assure low-level unemployment and reasonably stable prices, it appears reasonable to expect a growth rate of real GNP averaging somewhere between 3½ and 4½ percent per year. If government takes specific actions to encourage and stimulate the forces for growth and to reduce the impediments to growth in the economy, it also appears reasonable to expect a somewhat higher rate. A growth rate below that which is obtainable in an economy operating at a high level of employment of our human and physical resources and at reasonably stable price levels is clearly not adequate.*

Relationships among the Three Goals

The other sections of this chapter have examined the major factors which affect unemployment, the rate of growth of output, and the rate of change of prices. In this section the effect upon one goal of measures aimed at another and the relationship among policy measures to attain these goals are discussed. The relationship between levels of unemployment and price stability, between levels of unemployment and growth, and between price stability and growth are discussed in turn.

---

* H. CHRISTIAN SONNE—How can growth best be supported and encouraged in both the private and the public sectors?

Most likely this will be done by initiating a series of semi-public, semi-private long-range programs organized through semi-public authorities, financed by their own securities (they should earn enough to pay interest and amortization) possibly with a federal guarantee. For example, the biggest domestic task, which is urban renewal, could absorb by itself all available additional resources for many years.

The federal government should buy these securities during slack periods and sell them on the open market during times of high employment.

While these operations could reinforce the Federal Reserve System's open market policy, the main counter-cyclical effect would result from changes in the financing and debt management of these semi-public, semi-private long-range programs.

UNEMPLOYMENT AND PRICES

The relationship between unemployment and changes in the price level is fairly well understood in a general and qualitative way. An increase in the demand for a given supply of labor tends to increase wages and prices in both organized and unorganized industries. In the absence of any important elements of market power, wages tend to rise faster when there are more unfilled job vacancies (demand for labor) relative to the amount of unemployment. There is no universally applicable guide indicating the amount of wage and price increase, if any, which is likely to be associated with a specified increase in demand for labor or how much unemployment, if any, is likely to be associated with a particular wage increase.

The amount of additional aggregate demand needed to create a given number of new jobs, and hence a given reduction in unemployment, tends to be greater as unemployment declines. At some high level of unemployment, perhaps 8 percent, there is almost no pressure exerted on wages from aggregate demand. An increase in demand which then opens up 100,000 new jobs will reduce unemployment by almost 100,000 because workers of almost every skill category will be available in almost every local area. If unemployment falls because of further growth of demand, labor surpluses will tend to disappear in those skill categories and geographical areas where unemployment was initially smallest. Still further increases in demand will result in labor shortages and pressures for wage increases in these areas and skill categories, even though substantial unemployment may exist elsewhere. Each further increase in aggregate demand will reduce unemployment and will give rise to consequent pressure for higher wages. It is reasonable to expect that when unemployment has been reduced to 4 percent the pressure for wage increases will be much greater than when unemployment was 6 percent, and that by the time unemployment has fallen to 2 percent, unfilled vacancies will be widespread and the demand for labor will bring strong pressure for wage increases.

At some level of unemployment, which will vary with the changing structural and other characteristics of the labor market, further measures to reduce unemployment by stimulating demand will probably be more costly in terms of other goals than other measures which can achieve the same reduction.

If the number of unfilled job vacancies is about the same as the number of unemployed, then unemployment cannot be said to stem from inadequate aggregate demand. Rather the unemployment would be primarily structural, seasonal, and frictional in character. Under these circumstances there would still be many unemployed, and there would probably be some upward pressure on wages and prices. Such a situation constitutes an appropriate target of low-level unemployment for monetary, credit, and fiscal measures.

The remaining unemployment and upward price pressures could be eased by governmental measures to improve the functioning of labor and product markets. While the costs in terms of government expenditures of such measures might be substantial, it is preferable and probably less costly to bear them rather than to require policy makers to choose between the costs of rising prices or greater unemployment.

Unfortunately the data are not now available to estimate the current number of job vacancies and the proportion of unemployment attributable to inadequate demand as compared to structural, frictional, and seasonal causes. While it may not be possible to attain precise quantitative measures of these magnitudes, it is imperative that far greater effort and funds be devoted to acquiring better information. The government should institute a major program to identify the precise kinds of unemployment information needed as an adequate guide for policy decisions and then to acquire the data on a timely basis.

Neither the crude data for the years since 1952 when unemployment averaged nearly 5 percent and the Consumer Price Index rose at an average rate of 1.4 percent per year nor the more elaborate statistical studies of past relationships of prices and employment are a firm guide for the future. The underlying conditions and the complex of factors affecting the relationship are continuously changing. It does appear, however, that attempts to reduce the level of unemployment below 4 percent by stimulating aggregate demand through monetary, credit, and fiscal measures *alone* will result in an increase in the Consumer Price Index. Attempts to remove the last percent increase in the price index by dampening demand *alone* would probably lead to an unsatisfactorily high level of unemployment. If the only policy measures available were those relating to total demand, the alternatives would probably be a measure of persistent inflation or an unsatisfactory level of unemployment.

There are, however, many other measures for fighting inflation and reducing unemployment simultaneously. Among them are ways of improving the effectiveness of labor markets to reduce the amount of unemployment associated with a given amount of tightness in the labor market. The government could provide better information for matching men and jobs through an improved employment service, eliminate discrimination against particular groups of workers, provide retraining opportunities for workers displaced by technical change, and help move workers out of, or industry into, depressed areas. These measures should improve labor mobility and should reduce localized shortages of labor at a given level of unemployment. This would lessen inflationary pressure from wages.

Similarly labor unions and business could reduce unnecessary barriers to mobility and efficient production. Such impediments include racial, age, and religious discrimination, nontransferable pension and welfare accumulations, feather-bedding, restrictive trade practices, unduly long periods of apprenticeship, and restrictions on entry into certain trades. Other measures would aim at increasing the effectiveness of competition in product markets. A continued vigorous antitrust policy is desirable to encourage competition and to encourage great price flexibilities. A low tariff policy and minimum use of quotas are called for if the United States is to benefit from foreign competition.

Changes may also be possible in those government policies which prevent reductions in individual prices, such as farm price supports, some practices relating to stock-piling activities, and other procurement practices.

Business and labor statesmanship might be encouraged by educational programs regarding the causes of inflation. Business must not be asked to lay aside the profit motive or labor unions asked to refrain from attempting to raise the income of workers. But it is not unreasonable to ask labor and management to temper their demands by consideration of the longer-run economic consequences of their actions on themselves and on the community. The President's Advisory Committee on Labor-Management Policy should be helpful in promoting such statesmanship.

Monetary, credit, and fiscal measures aimed at reducing fluctuations in income will tend to stabilize both employment and prices. Sequences of recovery, boom, and recession involve rapid changes in the volume and composition of demand and rapid changes in profit rates. These changes in the upswing lead to pressures for price and wage increases, but in mild recessions the opposing pressures have had little effect in causing prices to fall. By reducing fluctuations in income and by moderating fluctuations in output, inflationary pressures in the upswing will be reduced.

If monetary, credit, and fiscal measures are supplemented by these other measures, then reasonable stability of the price levels and a low level of unemployment can be achieved simultaneously.

UNEMPLOYMENT AND GROWTH

The role of aggregate demand in promoting growth has been widely discussed in recent years. Some writers suggest that the rate of growth of output will increase automatically if the demand for goods and services grows at least as long as there is some unemployment. Others imply that the rate of growth is independent of the degree of utilization of the labor force and of available industrial capacity. These positions would appear to be extreme. While the level of demand has an important influence on the rate of growth, it cannot be controlled by merely affecting demand.

Discussion in this section focuses on the following questions: what is the influence of levels of aggregate demand on the level of unemployment and on economic growth, and is growth maximized by reducing unemployment to the lowest possible level? Because the rate of increase in total real GNP and in real GNP per manhour have been used as measures of growth, they are discussed in turn.

In considering the relationship between the level of demand, the level of employment, and the rate of growth of output, it is desirable to distinguish between the short-run effect of a *change in the level* of unemployment and the effect of a *continuing difference in the average level* of unemployment. If the unemployment rate falls from 5½ to 4 percent as a result of an increase in demand, output will increase because more men are at work and fewer of them work part time, and because of greater utilization of plant capacity. As long as this lower level of unemployment is maintained, the *amount* of GNP will be higher year after year because of this lower rate of unemployment. The increase in the *rate of growth* of GNP from this source occurs only in the period in which the unemployment is being reduced.

In addition to the immediate gain in output from increasing employment of the existing labor force, there will be a further gain for several years from an increase in the size of the labor force. New workers will enter or re-enter the labor force because jobs have become readily available. Continued low unemployment also puts pressure on employers to hire women and older workers. These changes result in sustained increases in the rate of growth of the labor force; they are more than one-shot affairs and should increase the rate of growth of total output. Finally, continued high employment may reduce the pressure for a shorter workweek and thus help forestall a factor leading to a decrease in total manhours.

There are no firm data on the relationship between the level of unemployment and the rate of growth of the effective labor force. However, when unemployment is in excess of 5 percent, there are likely to be general labor surpluses. Farm workers may find it more attractive to remain on the farm than to take a chance on being unemployed in the city; women who do not need to work may not find it worthwhile to seek work; older workers when laid off may retire earlier; and demands for a shorter workweek may become more widespread, particularly in those industries with greatest employment.* Moreover special programs for

---

* WILLARD L. THORP—A shorter work week might well be an appropriate objective in its own right and not necessarily a condition to be forestalled.

Mr. LUBIN and Mr. RUTTENBERG wish to be associated with Mr. THORP'S comment.

increasing the utilization of the labor force would probably become ineffective. While each of these factors by itself would have a relatively small effect on the growth rate, taken together they might affect it significantly. It has been estimated that if unemployment were at 4 percent rather than at $5\frac{1}{2}$ percent, the growth rate in the labor force might increase for a considerable period by as much as $\frac{1}{2}$ percent per year.

If special measures were adopted to deal with depressed areas and with social and age discrimination in employment, the level of unemployment at high levels of demand might be reduced to perhaps 3 percent.* While further gains in output could be achieved by a reduction in unemployment from 4 percent to 3 percent, they would be much smaller than those resulting from the reduction of unemployment from higher levels. When job vacancies approximate the number of unemployed, those who wish to work can secure jobs without too much difficulty; higher employment will not make people who do not want to work change their views. While favorable employment conditions will retard the tendency for the work week to decline, a still higher demand for labor is likely to create a demand for longer hours only through a limited increase in average overtime hours. Under present structural and frictional conditions a level of unemployment of about 4 percent should stimulate most of the potential growth in the labor force; the gains, if any, in output from generating a still higher demand for labor would be small.

What is the relationship between levels of unemployment and productivity? The high level of aggregate demand for goods and services necessary to ensure low-level unemployment should encourage capital formation, thereby providing both a larger stock of plant and equipment with a lower average age. On this account the rate of growth of productivity would be stimulated by demand measures which reduce unemployment.

This tendency may be offset by the use of older, less efficient units which are brought into production when demand is at high levels. Similarly, as unemployment falls to low levels, there is the likelihood that the additional workers employed will be less productive than the average of all workers. In addition, high profits and high employment may cause some decline in the efficiency of both management and labor. High plant utilization also tends to produce bottlenecks and rising prices for some materials. In the past some innovations in technique have resulted from attempts to eliminate those problems, yet high plant utilization may also reduce the competitive pressure to innovate.

No firm conclusion can be reached as to the effect of high employment and capacity utilization on the growth of productivity. Productivity falls or grows slowly in the early phases of a downswing, apparently because

---

* See Mr. RUTTENBERG'S comment on page 28.

of the difficulty of making rapid adjustments in overhead costs. Productivity usually begins to rise near the bottom of a downswing and rises rapidly during the early phases of an upswing. This rise may be due to delayed adaptation of reduced overhead costs, to the sharp increase in the use of existing facilities and overhead staff, and to the effect of other economies undertaken under the pressure of falling profits. The growth of productivity is usually rather slow in the latter part of the upswing when output is growing slowly and when plant utilization declines as new capacity comes into operation.

The rate of growth of productivity can be increased by special actions such as research that aims directly at production problems, by incentives to speed the replacement of obsolete equipment, and by a concerted effort to bring about labor–management cooperation to increase efficiency in the use of labor. Such programs are likely to be more effective when the rate of unemployment is low. Increasing productivity reduces the number of workers required to produce a given output; thus some are released and made available to produce more output. Their re-employment usually requires movement of workers from job to job and industry to industry. Although the workers displaced can be compensated, the process would meet with resistance unless they think it will be easy to get jobs elsewhere. And this condition will exist only if the level of unemployment is low.

The maintenance of a level of demand to achieve low-level unemployment will increase the rate of growth in several ways. First, as the economy moves to a low level of unemployment, there will be a rapid rate of growth during the period of change simply from hiring more workers. Second, the rate of growth of the labor force will be higher, and hence output will be higher, when unemployment is maintained at a low rather than a higher level. Finally, although a continuing low level of unemployment appears to involve little direct gain in productivity, the higher levels of demand permit other programs aimed at raising productivity to become more fully effective, and these effects may be substantial. Conditions of general labor surplus would impede the introduction of such programs. Thus, measures to stimulate aggregate demand to attain low levels of unemployment are basic to an adequate rate of economic growth.

PRICES AND GROWTH

There is considerable dispute about the impact of price-level changes on the rate of growth. Some contend that inflation is by itself a stimulus to growth, others argue that inflation is an inevitable concomitant of growth, and still others assert that continued inflation will preclude sustained growth.

Those who maintain that rising prices as such stimulate growth do so on the ground that inflation makes borrowing more profitable, creates an optimistic climate for expansion, and reduces the financial risks of investment. Those who argue that inflation hinders growth maintain that it encourages wasteful, speculative activity, frees inefficient firms from the discipline of possible financial failure, curtails the volume of saving necessary for investment, and may bring on a recession and ultimately a major depression as a result of a collapse of speculative activity engendered by inflation. These two views represent different aspects of the same phenomenon. When carried far enough an optimistic spirit which encourages investment can be an invitation to wasteful speculation. If rising prices reduce financial risks and encourage investment, they may also relieve inefficient firms from the discipline of the prospect of financial failure.

The evidence covering a wide range of periods and many countries shows that with price increases from zero to 6 percent per year, there is no appreciable association between the rate of growth and the rate of price change. As a broad generality, countries with declining prices or with rates of price increase greater than 6 percent appear to have lower growth rates than those operating within those limits. This record does not mean that there is no relationship between economic growth and rate of price change. It does mean that within the range indicated the relationship is not sufficiently strong or stable to stand out against the variety of other factors affecting the rate of growth.

Both general considerations and the empirical evidence lead to two conclusions. First, there is no basis for believing that inflation is needed to stimulate growth. Second, although every inflation does not lead to a speculative boom which collapses into a major depression, the risk of collapse is sufficiently real that we must strive to avoid the inflation. The last consideration suggests that rising prices in a general boom are a matter of particular concern.

A serious conflict between price stability and growth is likely to develop during wars, when every effort is made to achieve maximum output. This forced-draft growth has invariably created tremendous inflationary pressures which have been repressed by price and wage controls, allocations and rationing, and other direct controls. Even a milder form of forced-draft growth, stemming from direct government competition for resources with private producers under conditions of high employment, would probably generate similar, though less strong, inflationary pressures. And to contain the inflation, more direct controls might be required. The price of such growth would be inflation, or less freedom for individual decision, or some combination of the two.

The Commission concludes that all three goals—an adequate rate of economic growth, low levels of unemployment, and reasonable price stability—can be achieved simultaneously, and that they are fundamentally compatible if we do not expect the impossible for each. While conflicts may arise under certain conditions between reasonable price stability and low levels of unemployment, there are no conflicts between low levels of unemployment and economic growth, and between reasonable price stability and an adequate rate of economic growth. Moreover, monetary, credit, and fiscal measures to influence the level of demand are essential ingredients for the attainment of these goals, even though not sufficient by themselves. Both labor and management must cooperate to make our enterprise system work effectively. Other government measures are required to supplement monetary, credit, and fiscal measures.

The Commission believes that under such conditions an appropriate combination of both monetary, fiscal, credit, and other economic measures should resolve potential conflicts among goals when they arise, and lead to their attainment simultaneously.*

---

* MARRINER S. ECCLES—I feel the Commission has done as good a job as could be expected considering its size and the complexity of the objectives.

In general, I subscribe to the recommendations of the report. However, I have grave doubts that it will prove adequate to achieve the national economic goals which it seeks.

The special weakness in the report is that it fails to give adequate consideration and weight to the unstabilizing effects of the monopolistic power exercised by organized labor. It is unrealistic to gloss over the effects of its actions on prices, imports, exports, employment, rate of growth, and the deficiency in our international balance of payments.

Wages and fringe benefits of Union labor in this country are from two to five times that of other industrial countries. Thus, organized labor not only draws from the economy benefits in excess of increased productivity, but undermines our ability to compete in world as well as domestic markets.

Until the Government recognizes the seriousness of this situation and passes legislation which adequately deals with it, as it has with business, there is, in my opinion, not much chance of meeting the national economic goals which it seeks.

Mr. YNTEMA wishes to be associated with Mr. ECCLES' comment.

CHAPTER THREE

MONETARY
POLICY

Control over conditions governing the quantity of money is inevitable in a modern industrial society. As the nation has adopted more positive economic goals, it has become interested in how and to what extent monetary control can be used flexibly to influence the behavior of expenditures, output, employment, and prices.

Monetary policy is directly concerned with the provision of money, defined to include currency and demand deposits at commercial banks. In the United States, monetary policy is essentially Federal Reserve policy, which operates primarily through the System's exercise of conscious and continuous control over the reserve position of commercial banks. The reserves of commercial banks serve as the basis for expansion or contraction of their loans and investments and the consequent creation or reduction of demand deposits.

Changes in the degree of restraint or ease in monetary policy have an effect on the total flow of expenditures and in turn on output, employment, and prices. Because the link between the initial actions taken by the Federal Reserve to influence bank reserves and these variables is general, pervasive, and indirect, and because no attempt is made by the monetary authority to allocate credit among specific users, this approach to monetary policy is frequently referred to as *general* monetary control.

General Monetary Control

The Federal Reserve uses three major instruments of general monetary control. It sets the ratio of required reserves member banks must hold. It engages in open market operations, which alter the volume of actual reserve balances available to banks. And it changes the terms on which commercial banks may borrow from Federal Reserve banks to meet a deficiency in required reserves.

Monetary restraint reduces the availability of credit and increases its interest cost, thus retarding the flow of expenditures, output, employment, and income. Monetary ease makes credit more available and reduces its cost, and thus encourages an expansion in these flows.

The primary and most predictable effect of monetary measures is its impact on the "net reserve" position of member banks. All three instruments of policy, however, have direct impacts on other economic variables as well.

For example, the Federal Reserve may try to restrain economic activity by engaging in open market sales of Treasury bills. These sales influence at least six elements in the economy: net bank reserves are reduced; the money supply falls; the price of government securities tends to decline and yields to rise; the money value of total assets tends to fall; the overall liquidity of financial portfolios is reduced; and the ability and willingness of banks to lend is reduced.

The initial impact of a decrease in bank reserves falls on specific institutions and specific interest rates. Market forces of arbitrage and substitution then spread the effects of restraint. Short-term interest rates in general change in the same direction as the yield on Treasury bills, though usually not to the same extent. Rising yields on short-term Treasury securities are transmitted, but not fully, to the longer maturities. Long-term corporate yields tend to move with long-term governments. Thus, the initially localized consequences of changes in monetary policy spread to all holders of marketable financial assets because the market value of these assets falls as their yields rise. In addition to changes in interest rates, rationing of credit, that is, allocations by other measures than interest rates, will become more stringent.*

Changes in monetary policy influence expenditures through their effect on decisions made by lenders and through their effect on the decisions of spending units—households, business firms, and governments. The discussion covers the impact of monetary policy on the lending policy of commercial banks and then of other financial institutions. It then turns to the effects of changes in monetary policy on spending units.

---

* STANLEY H. RUTTENBERG—Contrary to views presented in many places in this Report, the money market is not a free competitive market in the classical sense. As the largest buyer and seller in this market, the federal government has substantial influence. When prices follow those of the leader, it is fiction to pretend that the market is free and competitive. The money market is no more an example of pure competition than are most key product markets. The reason that yields on private securities tend to move with interest rates on government issues is that the federal government dominates, in the main, the money market.

EFFECTS OF A POLICY OF RESTRAINT

A change in monetary policy may take the form of positive actions, such as open market sales, increases in required reserve ratios, or increases in discount rates. But, a shift to a restrictive policy is often passive; it takes the form of failing to increase reserves in the face of a rising demand for credit.

When the commercial banking system loses reserves as a result of open market sales by the Federal Reserve, or is faced with an increasing demand for loans by its customers while total reserves remain constant, some adjustments in bank portfolios must be made. If there are no excess reserves in the system, banks must either borrow additional reserves from the Federal Reserve or must restrict their earning assets either by curbing loans, disposing of security holdings, or both.

Although individual banks may borrow the excess reserves of other banks in the federal funds market, the amount of excess reserves in the system at any time is limited. Borrowing from the Federal Reserve is also limited and may be discouraged further by discount rate increases. Thus, even though earning assets may fail to contract immediately in response to an active restrictive policy, eventually they will if the restrictive pressure continues.

Banks have expanded their loans during periods of monetary restraint by selling off U.S. Treasury securities. Such sales soften the impact of monetary restraint on bank lending. Nor is this wholly undesirable, because the sale of securities helps to spread the effect of monetary restriction from the banking system to other sectors. In effect such sales absorb part of the money balances (cash reserves) of other lenders and the public and reduce their ability to extend credit and make expenditures. Also, the shift of part of the impact of a restrictive monetary policy to other sectors of the market does not imply that a restrictive monetary policy lacks a significant effect on bank lending.

During periods of credit restraint, bond prices generally fall as interest rates rise—partly because banks are selling securities, partly because demands for credit are increasing. Banks can sell off their short- and intermediate-term securities with little or no loss. But because they are concerned about their liquidity position, banks do not wish to dispose of all of their shorter-term investments. They will retain enough readily saleable assets to provide the funds to meet potential withdrawals of deposits. Banks are also generally willing to sell some long-term securities at a loss, particularly since the loss can be deducted from income for tax purposes. Yet many banks want to limit the loss recorded in any year, because they are under pressure to show earnings in order to justify dividends. Still others wish to limit losses to the amounts of their valuation reserves; and some banks may believe that taking a large loss on a long-term bond to switch into higher-yielding, short-term loans may not be profitable.*

Long before they have exhausted their liquid assets and longer-term investments, most banks take measures to restrain the growth of their loan portfolio. Most banks wish to be able to satisfy requests for loans by good deposit customers with whom they have a continuing relationship. These measures include reduction of the maturity of term loans granted, stricter application of standards of credit worthiness, and granting less than the full amount of the loans requested. Thus for all the reasons enumerated, the Federal Reserve can restrain bank credit.

Effects on nonbank lending

The rise in short-term yields from sales of shorter-term securities by banks will tend also to force up long-term bond yields. If private flotations of securities take place at the same time, the rise in long-term yields is further accelerated. The pressure on long-term interest rates will also be increased by the partial withdrawal of banks from the mortgage and municipal security markets. In addition, when banks restrict their lending to customers, some of those unable to obtain credit from banks seek it in other markets; this reinforces the rise in the general level of interest rates.

With interest rates higher, some individuals and businesses reduce their demand deposits and purchase securities or shift to interest-bearing thrift deposits. The demand deposits are made available to other individuals and businesses who wish to increase their expenditures or to financial institutions which make loans to such individuals and businesses. Thus even though the money supply has not expanded, the mobilization of idle balances will finance more expenditures, and there will have been a partially offsetting rise in the velocity of money. It is frequently argued that this rise in the velocity of money resulting from monetary restraint frustrates monetary policy.

Actually, part of the upward trend in velocity, as well as part of the cyclical movements, has resulted from increases in interest rates. But this does not mean that a restrictive monetary policy does not have a restrictive influence on nonbank lending. It means only that to restrict lending by a given amount, the growth of the money supply must be more limited than if velocity did not rise. The increase of velocity need not negate the effectiveness of monetary policy.

---

* STANLEY H. RUTTENBERG—The Commission should have recommended that banks be required to offset capital losses against capital gains, rather than the present practice of offsetting losses on long-term securities against operating income. Banks should be treated no differently in this regard from other taxpayers.

Nonbank financial institutions find their investment decisions complicated by the increases in bond yields at a time when there is an increase in the demand for funds. Also, the inflow of new funds available to some of these institutions may decline as some households choose to invest directly in higher-yielding securities. Mutual savings banks and savings and loan associations may reduce their mortgage lending commitments as the rate of inflow of new funds falls. In addition, if their mortgage placements are not reduced as much as the flow of deposits, the pressure on the bond market is increased by reduced purchases or by sales of corporate and other bonds. This additional pressure will tend to cause further increases in bond yields.

As the yields on bonds rise, insurance companies tend to reduce their commitments for Federal Housing Authority, Veterans Administration, and conventional mortgages because the yields on mortgages do not increase as much as market yields on other securities. The reduction tends to be greater for government insured mortgages because the ceiling rates do not increase enough and because there are limits to the discounts at which they will purchase them.

When the demand for credit is strong, most nonbank financial institutions may sell Treasury or other securities to supplement the inflow of new funds. The relatively small holdings of governments or other securities of some institutions may preclude substantial reductions because of the consequent impairment of liquidity positions, and even those institutions with adequate liquidity have only a limited willingness to accept capital losses on sales of longer-term securities. As it becomes increasingly possible to place all available funds in good quality securities at attractive yields, these lenders, like the banks, tend to raise interest rates, to tighten quality standards, to shorten maturities, and to refuse or to reduce loans to less credit-worthy applicants.

Thus monetary restraint causes a reduction in the willingness and ability of nearly all institutional lenders to meet the expanding credit demand. While it is difficult to make any precise assessment of the volume of loans refused or reduced during recent tight money episodes, it appears to have been substantial.

Effects on spenders

Insofar as monetary restraint does succeed in inducing lenders to reduce the rate of expansion of loan funds to borrowers, either absolutely or in relation to demand, it reduces total expenditures, though not necessarily by the same amount. In some cases expenditures may be financed by drawing down liquid assets. In others the expenditures curtailed may exceed the amount of borrowing withheld. For example, an indivisible project, for which borrowed funds would have provided a partial but essential segment of the total required financing might be completely abandoned. The general atmosphere resulting from credit restraint may also generate attitudes that discourage expenditures for which finance was already available.

Through the changes monetary restraint brings about in the rate of interest in the market value of income-yielding assets, and in the liquidity of the public's wealth holdings, it also affects the desire of the public to spend.

Opinions differ widely on the sensitivity of expenditures to changes in interest rates and other manifestations of credit restraint. The observable sensitivity varies among different sectors of the economy and from one situation to the next, depending on other significant variables that determine demand.

In general, the sensitivity of demand for real assets to a change in interest rates and credit terms depends on the relative importance of interest charges and amortization payments in the total cost of the project. Interest is a large element of cost in most home purchases, and the demand for housing shows marked sensitivity to changes in mortgage interest rates and credit terms—expanding significantly during periods of easy money and contracting sharply when money is tightened. Part of this observed sensitivity is due to the reactions of demand to the terms—interest rates, down payments, maturity of loans, and so forth—on which credit is available, although, as observed earlier, part is due to changes in the supply of funds available for mortgage lending.

Borrowing by state and local governments for capital expenditures has also tended to increase when credit was easy, and to decrease when credit conditions were tight. Data for the postwar period suggest that about 10 percent of total bond sales were shifted from the later phases of a boom to the following recession and recovery periods, partly because of the higher interest costs, and partly because funds were less available. While the sensitivity of permanent forms of borrowing need not mean a corresponding sensitivity of actual expenditures, outlays also have been somewhat sensitive. Estimates of the percentage of state and local construction expenditures shifted from the later phases of a boom to the following recession range from 2 to 5 percent.

There is less agreement about the sensitivity of business investment spending to changes in credit terms. Traditional monetary theory assumed a high degree of sensitivity, but this has been disputed both on theoretical and empirical grounds. The observed dollar volume of business investment has shown little apparent sensitivity to interest rates, and businessmen have said that they are not influenced by changes in interest rates.

It has been contended that an increasingly large proportion of business investment is financed with internal funds, and that the return required on these funds is not directly related to changes in interest rates. In addition, changes of interest costs are often said to have a negligible influence on business investment when compared with the uncertainties regarding future sales, profits, costs, and capacity requirements.

These arguments seem overstated. Internal financing may reduce the effect of changes in the rate payable on borrowed funds, but that effect is by no means eliminated. The higher the proportion of borrowed funds used, the greater will be the effect of changes in credit costs. Furthermore, even though corporations are able to rely largely on internal funds during recession and early recovery periods, the proportion of external financing generally rises during late recovery and boom periods, thereby increasing the influence of monetary policy at those times.

What little relation there might be is reduced by the tax deductability of interest payments, which, at present corporate tax-rates, more than halves the after-tax effect of a given change in the interest rate. The argument respecting the tax effect on net interest costs is incomplete. The incentive to invest depends on the relation between costs and returns. Income taxes reduce the after-tax cost of all expenses, including interest, but they also reduce the after-tax flow of revenues on an investment. A change in interest rates thus does change the incentive to invest regardless of whether it is computed on a before-tax or after-tax basis.

Unfortunately studies of the actual behavior of business investment and interest rates have not reliably isolated the effect of monetary policy from shifts in other determinants of investment. Fragmentary evidence, however, indicates that some kinds of investment are sensitive to changes in interest costs. High-leverage speculative investments, for example in real estate, are sensitive. Investment in long-lived assets, which are financed largely by external funds, and investments for modernization and cost reduction, which can be postponed until easier credit conditions prevail, also tend to be sensitive. And if price increases are not anticipated, investment in inventories seems likely to be somewhat sensitive to interest rates and credit terms.

The evidence indicates that changes in credit terms have some, but only a slight, direct effect on consumer expenditures for other than residential construction.

Despite some sensitivity of borrowers to higher interest rates, the direct effects of a restrictive monetary policy appear to work mainly through the reduction in the availability of funds to would-be borrowers. Mortgage borrowing will be clearly limited by the supply of mortgage funds. Lending to commercial, industrial, and finance company customers by banks and insurance companies will also be restricted by shortening loan maturities and raising quality standards.

Indirect effects on expenditures

Changes in monetary policy have other and less direct effects on the rate of expenditures in addition to their effects on the cost and availability of credit. The very announcement or recognition of a change in monetary policy may contribute to changes in attitudes and expectations as to the future rate of growth of demand, sales, income and profits, and the future level of prices. These attitude changes may have a substantially stabilizing effect on investment expenditures and consumer durable goods purchases. Changes in interest rates and expectations may also influence the movement of stock prices.

Also, business investment in equipment and inventory and credit-financed consumer expenditures are observably sensitive to the *secondary* effects of credit restraint on aggregate demand. A direct restraint in state and local construction, in residential construction, and in some categories of business investment tend to reduce the flow of new orders to a wide range of businesses. Business expectations may then change with respect to product demand, and this downward revision may reduce the urgency and profitability of business investment for short-lived equipment and inventories. Job uncertainty for employees may also be increased, and consumers may become less willing to incur new indebtedness.

EFFECTS OF AN EXPANSIONARY POLICY

A policy of monetary ease to stimulate an expansion of expenditures will operate through the same processes as a restrictive policy but in the reverse direction. Such an expansive policy will tend to increase the net reserve position of member banks, to increase the prices and reduce the yields on Treasury securities, to improve the liquidity of banks and other lending institutions, to enhance the wealth position of all holders of financial assets, and to increase the money supply. At times, however, these changes may not be as effective in stimulating economic activity as the reverse measures can be in restraining it.

As the reserve positions of commercial banks are improved, as interest rates and bond yields fall, and as liquidity positions of all lending institutions improve, both bank and nonbank lenders are decidedly more able and willing to extend additional credit. There is a definite increase in the availability of credit on more liberal terms and at lower costs to the borrower. But, whereas further restrictive actions can definitely restrain the volume of actual lending in boom times, further easing actions may in slumps bring about credit availability which is excessive in relation to the demand for it by spenders.

For credit ease to be effective, the demand for borrowing must be large enough to use the additional supply made available. Under given conditions of prospective product demand and profitability of expanded capacity to produce, any reduction of credit costs should increase the attractiveness of new investment. But during recessions the prospective profitability of added investment may already be so low that the reduced credit costs provide an insufficient stimulus to borrowing and to capital formation.

This is in contrast to the opposite case, when the underlying demand for investment is strong. At such times, a policy of credit ease is very likely to be effective in stimulating increased borrowing and capital expenditures.

In the same way, improved liquidity positions of households and businesses make possible and provide an incentive to increased expenditures. But whether that incentive is strong enough will depend on their attitudes toward their income prospects.

Thus, while the processes and channels through which monetary measures operate are the same for a policy of ease as for a policy of restriction, an expansionary policy may be less effective than a restrictive policy. Monetary ease is an essential part of a broad recovery policy; but measures in addition to those of general monetary policy will usually be necessary.*

Monetary Policy and Cyclical Stabilization

There is fairly general agreement about the nature of the processes through which monetary policy affects economic activity. Some experts contend, however, that monetary policy does not have large enough effects to be useful, and others contend that an active monetary policy works too slowly to be useful. These two contentions will be considered in turn.

---

* STANLEY H. RUTTENBERG—Monetary policy as a means of encouraging expansion is less effective than restrictive monetary policies because of the stickiness of long-term interest rates. As pointed out above, "further easing actions may in slumps bring about credit availability which is excessive in relation to the demand for it by spenders." However, if efforts were made directly at reducing the long-term interest rates, increased credit availability could be turned into a successful expansionary technique by making not only more credit available, but available at lower long-term interest rates. In other words, monetary ease is "an essential part of the broad recovery program," but must be combined with an effort at affecting the interest rates not only in the short-term, but in the intermediate- and long-term markets as well. This is why it is important for the Federal Reserve Board in its open market operations to be buying and selling across the entire maturity of government securities and not just "bills only."

VOLUME EFFECTS

The effectiveness of countercyclical monetary policy must be considered in relation to the objectives it seeks to achieve. The purpose of restraint during prosperity is to exert a moderating effect on total spending so as to prevent unsustainable boom conditions; its purpose is not to extinguish a large proportion of demand. Even a relatively small stimulus to spending can be helpful during a decline in business activity. The changes in the degree of monetary restraint or ease appropriate to the conduct of countercyclical policy do not have to have a controlling impact on any specific type of expenditure, but the pervasive and cumulative combination of a number of small effects does make flexible monetary policy a useful instrument of stabilization policy.

The power of the Federal Reserve to check the growth of the money supply or to cause it to contract must be exercised with caution. In the past the pressure has generally been exerted rather gradually. The rapid decline in bond prices which would follow if Federal Reserve action were very drastic imposes a limit on that action, because such a decline may lead to very adverse business expectations and in turn to a severe decline of expenditures and output.

Such adverse reactions have probably been exaggerated, and in any case, if inflation became pervasive, it would be necessary to take strong steps. A preventive policy of gradual monetary restraint could in combination with other restrictive stabilization measures prevent the conditions that might require drastic action by the Federal Reserve.

The Commission believes that the restrictive monetary policies in 1955-57 and again in 1959 demonstrate that monetary policy can have a very substantial effect on the level and rate of growth and of demand. In both periods monetary restriction seemed to induce a decline in the annual rate of residential construction of $3 to $4 billion. Business investment was lower than it would have been if credit had been freely available at low rates. If allowance is made for the indirect effects that the restraint on some investment had on consumption and on types of investment not directly affected, monetary restraint seems to have had an important effect on the level and rate of growth of economic activity.*

---

* CHARLES B. SHUMAN—Reducing a particular activity in a single year does not necessarily mean that there will be less of this activity over a longer period. Could the more rapid rate of construction and investment that might have occurred in periods of restraint be maintained; or would it have led to overexpansion and a serious slump at some later time? This point is made on page 59.

WILLARD L. THORP—To the extent that monetary restriction is implied to be the result of active monetary policy, the influence of monetary policy tends to be overvalued in this and other points in the Report. Presumably in a boom period, there will be increased demands and shifts in credit to more profitable uses so that to some degree the restrictive effects would be felt even if there were a passive monetary policy.

Moreover, during the postwar period, the monetary authorities have not exerted the maximum practicable degree of restraint within their power. If it had been considered desirable, the severity of monetary policy could have been somewhat greater without the danger of exceeding the practicable limit.

SPEED OF EFFECTS

Some experts have argued that monetary policy works so slowly that its effects become perverse, because the effects of a restrictive policy are not felt until after the start of the ensuing downswing and the effects of monetary expansion until the next boom.

In the postwar period, somewhat less than a year has elapsed before a change in the direction of monetary policy—from tightness toward ease or vice versa—has been followed by a change in the direction of movement of expenditures on residential construction. Even more time elapsed before the change in monetary policy had its full effect. However, because commitments on new mortgages and new orders for houses change earlier than expenditures, the stimulus to economic activity came earlier than that revealed by the relationship to expenditures.

The evidence available on the timing of monetary policy's impact on other types of spending is sparse and inconclusive. There is no clear indication that it has affected other types of expenditure any earlier than residential construction. But again the effect on attitudes and on new orders for capital equipment and goods for inventories may influence economic activity in less than a year.

It is true that a policy of monetary restriction has at times been carried on for too long, and that at other times the expansion of bank reserves or reduction in reserve requirements in a recession has created problems in controlling the ensuing upswing. These weaknesses reflect not inherent defects of monetary management but rather the inadequacy of the techniques employed and the criteria used for the timing of the changes in monetary policy. Also, certain actions can be taken which will speed up the effects of monetary policy.

Measures which restrain the growth of commercial bank assets have an impact on both bank and nonbank lending. But the speed of the impact will vary depending on the asset positions of lending institutions and the public, what types of borrowers are seeking credit, and how the maturity composition of the publicly held Treasury debt has changed during the upswing. When banks hold a large amount of relatively short-term securities and have excess reserves, when other lending institutions have comfortable liquidity positions, and when individuals and businesses hold a substantial amount of idle cash and liquid assets, then a policy of monetary restraint will not affect credit extensions for some time. But if bank liquidity is relatively low, at the time the Federal Reserve initiates restraint, and the idle cash holdings and liquid positions of the public are also relatively low, the impact of credit restriction on bank lending will come much sooner. In addition, a more direct and immediate pressure on long rates can be brought to bear by both Treasury and Federal Reserve sales of the long-term securities.

Monetary restraint on the upswing will be more effective if idle cash in the hands of the public is at a minimum, if excess bank liquidity at the start of the upswing is minimal, and if the Federal Reserve and Treasury together work to increase the long-term federal debt in the hands of the public, normally reducing short-term debt at the same time.

The effectiveness of monetary policy on the downswing will be increased if the Treasury and the Federal Reserve take direct action to reduce long-term as well as short-term interest rates. If excessive liquidity positions of banks, other lending institutions, and the public are not allowed to develop, and if the Federal Reserve and the Treasury take direct action to speed the adjustment process of long-term as well as short-term interest rates, the impact of monetary policy should be felt sooner.*

The monetary authorities should make full use of the fact that monetary measures can be varied continually in either direction and reversed quickly at their discretion. These properties make it possible to change monetary policy gradually in the restrictive direction before the economy has generated excessive demand, and to ease restrictions gradually before aggregate income has actually declined.

The Commission does not advocate placing sole reliance on monetary policy for stabilization purposes. Because of its reversibility and the possibility of changing policy by small steps, monetary policy can be used in many circumstances when discretionary fiscal policy changes should not be used because the need for so powerful an instrument has not yet become clear. In summary, the Commission believes that monetary policy is a valuable and effective instrument of stabilization policy.

DIFFERENTIAL EFFECTS

Another objection to the use of monetary measures for stabilization is that it is discriminatory in its application, with its restrictive effects falling particularly severely on investment in housing and on small business. Large businesses, which depend more on internal sources of financing and which have long-term relations with lending institutions, are held to be far less affected.

The available data which pertain mainly to the 1955-57 experience

---

* See Mr. SHUMAN'S comment on page 64.

show that bank lending to large business increased relatively more during the cyclical upswing when money was tight than to small business. However, to a large extent the differences in the rates of growth of lending reflect cyclical differences in *demand* for credit. Industries in which large firms predominate were growing at a faster rate than industries with mainly small firms. In addition, small retail firms normally rely on trade credit more than on bank loans; and large corporations did increase their lending to small corporations and to noncorporate firms faster than their own sales increased.

Bank credit rationing did occur and was not uniform. But the criterion for rationing did not appear to be size of firm. The two criteria which prevailed for loans other than mortgage and consumer installment loans were credit-worthiness and the value to the bank of obtaining or retaining the borrower as a depositor. Banks tightened their credit standards and refused to make loans to marginal borrowers who might have been accommodated in an easy money period. They also shortened maturities on term loans. Customers with large compensating balances found it easier to obtain credit than those with small balances and equivalent credit ratings. Many banks reduced or were unwilling to expand credit lines to sales finance companies on that ground; however, these companies often obtained credit from nonbank sources. Similarly some types of construction loans were rationed, and promoters of new buildings sometimes had to pay high rates to obtain funds from nonbank sources. But because small banks, all of whose customers are small, were generally less loaned-up than large banks, small businesses with good credit ratings and good bank connections may have often had less difficulty in obtaining loans than some large businesses.

Firms with poor credit ratings and poor banking connections appear relatively more often in the category of small businesses. Firms with low credit ratings may have either inexperienced management or insufficient equity capital, frequently both. To the extent that well-managed firms have weak credit ratings, they often cannot get bank accommodation because they lack sufficient equity capital. The gap in the equity capital could be helped by a more realistic attitude on the part of the owners and by further development of specialized institutions, including small business investment corporations.

The operations of monetary policy have had a greater direct impact on the availability of mortgage credit for residential building than on any other major type of credit, in large measure because of the interest ceilings on low-down-payment mortgages insured or guaranteed by the federal government. Because mortgage lending rates are unlikely to move quickly enough to make mortgage loans fully competitive with bonds, the mortgage market would probably be more sensitive to credit restraint even without this feature. Moreover, interest charges are a large part of carrying costs on housing, and increasing costs cut demands for housing.

Because residential construction tends to move inversely with the business cycle, it tends to stabilize the economy as a whole. The residential construction industry has been destabilized by variations in monetary policy. It does not follow that residential construction would have been more stable if monetary policy had *not* been varied cyclically. Variations in *total* construction employment have followed general business cycle movements. The countercyclical behavior of residential construction only partially offset the cyclical variations in total construction. Taking all these factors into consideration, the Commission believes that the cyclical impact of monetary policy on residential construction has not been undesirable.

It is also claimed that monetary restraint affects adversely the distribution of income among individuals. This income distribution effect, however, is difficult to measure. On the assumption that employment will be the same if any of the following three measures is used, monetary restraint may be considered an alternative to outright inflation or as an alternative to control of demand by fiscal policy.

Clearly those who are net creditors will fare better with monetary restraint than with inflation. They avoid a reduction in the real value of their net assets, and they obtain a higher interest income. Who are the net creditors? Though the data available are neither accurate nor complete, apparently, on the average, persons with incomes below about $6,000 are net creditors, those in higher income groups are net debtors. These figures include the debt of corporations in which the individuals hold shares and further assume that their share of the debt of the federal government is proportionate to their federal tax payments. While the very low income families are net debtors, a small proportion, mainly retired persons, are net creditors. It is this group which loses most by unforeseen inflation and gains from higher interest rates.*

At any level of government expenditures, a given level of demand may be achieved with a restrictive monetary policy and relatively low taxes or with an easier monetary policy and higher taxes. The use of restrictive monetary policy will tend to improve the position of net creditors and worsen the position of net debtors. How tax increases will affect them will depend on the character and composition of the increases. In general the Commission sees no reason to object to the use of

---

* STANLEY H. RUTTENBERG—This reasoning is tortured and the assumptions are unrealistic, although the arithmetic may be correct. The groups that benefit from a restrictive high interest rate policy are those whose annual incomes are derived in a significant part from ownership of debt securities and bank equities. These are not the low- and middle-income groups generally.

monetary policy relative to tax policy on account of its differential impacts among sectors of the economy or size of business, or its direct income distribution effects.

Long-Run Monetary Policy

Countercyclical monetary policy tries to time net injections or withdrawals of bank reserves so that they will best dampen fluctuations in the level of economic activity. Long-run monetary policies on the other hand must provide a monetary climate consonant with an adequate and sustainable rate of growth and over-all price stability. This climate should permit the banking system to expand its loans and investments and concomitantly the supply of money at a rate commensurate with the economy's underlying growth potential. Since the quantity of money needed to permit economic growth will depend on a variety of elements, including changes in the stock of money substitutes, the money supply need not always increase at the same rate as the increase in the economy's growth potential.

Since the end of World War II, the money supply has grown by less than 2 percent per year. The money supply in real terms has declined since 1947. Some authorities have contended that the failure of the money supply to grow in pace with our productive potential is responsible for retarding the rate of growth of output. It is important to note some special circumstances which have influenced policy governing the growth of the money supply.

The conduct of long-run monetary policy since the end of World War II must be interpreted against the background of depression and war finance. Between 1930 and 1946 the money supply increased much more rapidly than did the gross national product in money terms. Both the absolute supply of money and the ratio of money to GNP were at all-time highs in 1946. Possessing the money and liquid assets to make their pent-up demands effective, consumers and business firms in this country and abroad increased their purchases to unprecedented levels. These demands resulted in inflationary pressures during the early postwar years.

Money incomes rose by over 100 percent between 1946 and 1951 while money supply rose by only 17 percent, but there was relatively little increase in longer-term interest rates. Because of the growth in incomes, the relationship between the money supply and the volume of transactions had been restored to more normal levels by the end of 1951. From the end of 1951 to the end of 1959 the money supply continued to rise at a relatively slow rate, about 2½ percent per year. From 1951 to 1959 the ratio of GNP to the money supply rose from 3 per year to approximately 4. Part of the increase in this ratio would have taken place without a rise in interest rates, but part of it was a by-product of general monetary policy. As has already been shown, a restrictive monetary policy may consist of limiting the growth of the money supply to an amount less than that required to satisfy all demands for credit at the interest rates ruling when the policy decision is made. The resultant shortage of credit led to rising interest rates and induced a reduction in money holdings relative to economic activity. The relatively slow growth of the money supply since 1951 was in considerable measure a reflection and embodiment of the generally restrictive tone of monetary policy.

The average rate of growth of the money supply should reflect the rate of growth of real output at high employment and stable prices. However, the exact rate of growth of money supply will have to depend on the strength of private demand and the character of fiscal policy in that these will affect the demand for money. If private demand and fiscal policy together tend to push up aggregate demand at a high rate, a greater degree of monetary restriction will be necessary to maintain adequate but not excessive levels of demand. Since monetary control is achieved through control of the money supply, the rate of growth of the money supply must reflect our choice of a combination of monetary and fiscal policy as well as the strength of private demand.

The Commission urges that the average rate of growth of the money supply should be consistent with the continued maintenance of high employment at stable prices and adequate economic growth, but it recognizes that it may be appropriate for the money supply to grow more or less rapidly than the output of the economy at high employment.

Monetary Policy and International Balances

One function of Federal Reserve action is to take account of seasonal and random movements in factors affecting the level of bank reserves. Among these are seasonal shifts in the demand for currency and in the level of "float" arising from the clearance of checks, periodic flows of funds into federal government deposit accounts at Federal Reserve banks, and changes in the nation's stock of gold. Unless offset, these movements would cause serious and unnecessary disturbances in the money market.

The large reduction in the U.S. gold stock since 1958 has raised two basic questions. The first concerns the proper relationship of domestic monetary policy to gold outflows, which is discussed in Chapter Eight. Here it is merely commented that Federal Reserve policy should continue to consider the needs of our international balance of payments, but should be governed primarily by domestic economic needs.

The second issue relates to the desirability of the present 25 percent gold reserve requirement against Federal Reserve note and deposit liabilities. The Federal Reserve System can incur note and deposit liabilities only to four times the value of its gold certificate holdings. And while its free gold holdings are still large enough so that the Reserve System has freedom of action in a technical sense, the continued gold losses of the last three years have raised doubts as to whether further reduction in free gold reserves might lead to the adoption of restrictive measures solely to conform with the gold reserve requirement. Yet the requirement would certainly be adjusted whenever necessary to preserve the necessary latitude for the operation of monetary control to meet our domestic policy objectives. Its removal at this time would make it certain that the full amount of the U.S. gold holdings is available for settling international balances and dispel any uncertainties over what actions might be adopted if the free gold ever became exhausted while $12 billion of gold was tied up to meet the reserve requirement. This action would greatly strengthen the international position of the U.S. dollar and would give the United States a longer period in which to adjust its balance of payments position. A recommendation to eliminate the gold reserve requirement is made in Chapter Eight.

Measures for Strengthening Monetary Policy

INSTRUMENTS OF GENERAL MONETARY CONTROL

The major instruments of general monetary policy are the power to buy and sell securities in the open market, the power to fix discount rates and regulate other conditions of member bank borrowing, and the power to alter the reserve requirements of member banks within limits specified by the Congress.

Open market operations

Open market operations constitute the primary instrument of monetary control. These operations are flexible with respect to timing and magnitude, and the initiative for their use lies with the Federal Reserve. The major issue on the conduct of open market operations is the policy followed by the Federal Reserve from 1953 until early in 1961 to confine such operations to short-term government securities, generally to Treasury bills.

Between 1951 and 1953 the directive to the manager of the open market account included the instruction to "maintain orderly conditions" in the government securities market. In 1953, the Federal Reserve made explicit its philosophy of favoring free and unpegged markets. It directed that henceforth open market operations would be confined to affecting bank reserves as economic conditions warranted; that this was to be accomplished by operations in short-term securities, except to correct already disorderly markets; and that support of the market by buying new or maturing issues during periods of Treasury financings would be discontinued. This policy has become known as the "bills-only" or more recently the "bills-preferably" policy.

The argument advanced in support of the bills-only policy is that it minimizes the *direct* influence of open market operations on the structure or pattern of interest rates without sacrificing any of the total impact on these variables, because such impacts flow principally from the effect on reserves. Investors and dealers in Treasury securities are thus assured that "free market forces" will determine the structure of security prices, and this, in turn, will improve the "breadth, depth, and resiliency" of the market. The influence of Federal Reserve policy actions on intermediate-term and long-term yields takes place indirectly—as the forces of arbitrage and substitution transmit the effect of changes in bank reserves and bill yields to all maturities.

The bills-only policy has been a subject of controversy ever since it was adopted. Many critics have argued that the potency of Federal Reserve is reduced. They believe it is preferable to operate on occasion in the long-term market to correct incipient disorderly market conditions rather than to wait until they become worse. The assumption that rate changes in the short end of the market are transmitted rapidly and completely to intermediate and longer maturities has been questioned.

In the next chapter use of debt management policy as one countercyclical measure is advocated. The Treasury can affect the availability of credit and the structure of interest rates in various segments of the financial market by altering the maturity composition of its publicly held debt. The Federal Reserve can do the same thing by varying the maturities it buys and sells in its open market operations. Moreover, it can operate more continuously, more delicately, and more flexibly than can the Treasury, because the latter has an impact only when securities are issued or retired.

The crucial question is the actual difference in the effect on long-term rates from open market sales or purchases of bills versus bonds. The evidence shows that there is a difference, but that the difference is small. Open market operations achieve their principal effect on yields by altering bank liquidity. The impact on the short-term yields is far greater than that on long-term yields regardless of the maturity of the instrument used. Nevertheless, the differential effects and their timing are important, and the bills-only policy reduces the effectiveness of open market operations to alter the structure of interest rates. Much larger changes in Federal Reserve holdings of bills and thus in bank reserves may be necessary to effect desired changes in long-term rates indirectly than would be necessary to obtain the same changes by direct operations in longer-term securities.*

The Commission recommends the continued use of open market operations as the normal or usual instrument of general monetary policy. Instead of relying on a "bills-only" policy, the Federal Reserve should be willing, when domestic or international conditions warrant, to influence directly the structure as well as the level of interest rates in pursuit of countercyclical monetary policies and should deal in securities of varied maturities. This recommendation does not mean a return to a pegged structure of prices and yields for government securities. And the normal use of open market operations in bills to carry out technical and seasonal changes in bank reserves is appropriate.**

Discount policy

Under present arrangements, member banks may obtain bank reserves by borrowing from Federal Reserve banks. This privilege permits an individual bank to correct a temporary deficiency in its reserve position arising from unexpected withdrawals of currency or deposits. The discount rate is the charge on such borrowings, and this rate is altered from time to time as an instrument of monetary policy.

It is frequently argued that the discount privilege is no longer necessary and that during periods of restraint it provides a loophole through which the banking system is able to offset the effect of open market operations. The argument for retaining the privilege is that it provides a smoother means of adjustment to temporary and local situations than

---

* CHARLES B. SHUMAN—While conditions justifying open-market operations on long-term securities may arise, the case against a deliberate policy of operating in the long-term market is persuasive. Such a policy is only a short step from the price-pegging operations which preceded the Treasury-Federal Reserve accord. Thus, I subscribe to the "bills preferably" policy.

While the Treasury can, and does, affect the structure of interest rates by its management of the national debt, this is primarily a matter of adjusting the terms of security offerings to take advantage of market conditions. Open-market operations undertaken to affect the market are quite different in principle from Treasury operations undertaken to meet the government's financial requirements.

** STANLEY H. RUTTENBERG—I concur in the last two sentences of the recommendation, but I would strengthen the first sentence. The Commission should strengthen its recommendation on "bills only" by saying that the Federal Reserve Board should abandon its "bills only" policy and in its open market operations deal in securities of varying maturities.

Mr. NATHAN wishes to be associated with Mr. RUTTENBERG'S comment.

would be available otherwise, and that any slippage in the process of general monetary restraint can be easily offset by open market operations.

The Commission concludes that the discount facility should be retained as a source of temporary credit. The Federal Reserve should provide liquidity directly to the commercial banks in times of general or regional economic distress. The Commission urges that the banking system be assured this will be done.

Changes in the discount rate are generally used to support and strengthen the effectiveness of open market operations. Under this general policy, changes in the discount rate tend to follow movements in market rates. However, because market rates move continuously whereas changes in the discount rate are made infrequently, the relationship between the discount rate and market rates varies. Changes in this differential often have effects that tend to counter those pursued by open market operations. During a period of restraint, the relative advantage of borrowing reserves increases as market rates of interest increase faster than the discount rate. Banks in tight reserve positions increasingly tend to borrow rather than to sell short-term securities, and this reduces the restraint until such time as discount rates are increased relative to market rates. When market rates fall relative to the discount rate, the advantage of using idle funds to repay indebtedness to the Federal Reserve increases over using them to buy securities. This lessens the easing of credit conditions being pursued by open market policy.

Numerous proposals have been put forward to eliminate the effect caused by a changing relationship between the discount rate and market rates. One proposal is for the Federal Reserve to change the discount rate much more frequently than it does now. Another is that discretionary changes in the discount rate should be abolished altogether and the discount rate should be determined automatically each week by the current rate on short-term Treasury bills. A third proposal is a compromise between the present discretionary procedure and the fully automatic rule. Changes in the discount rate would be tied to changes in the Treasury bill rate but the *spread* between the two rates would be changed periodically on a discretionary basis.

An objection to the proposal of frequent changes is that changes in the discount rate currently serve as a signal of a major shift in monetary policy, and this advantage would be lost if the changes occurred too often. Tying the discount rate to a single market rate holds the danger that that particular rate might move out of line with other short-term market rates and would pull the discount rate also out of line. The third proposal would provide nothing which is not equally possible under the present fully discretionary system. If the Federal Reserve chooses to do so, it can now change the rates weekly, and it can inform the public directly whenever a given change represents a basic shift in policy rather than a technical readjustment. The Commission favors the fully discretionary system and urges that it be administered to avoid effects counter to those sought by open market operations.

Discount rates are now set for each Federal Reserve bank by vote of its board of directors subject to the review and approval of the Federal Reserve Board. However, credit markets have become essentially national in character, and the possibility of utilizing differential regional discount rate policies is negligible. Regional differences in discount rates would be ineffective in view of the active market for federal funds and Treasury bills. Under these circumstances a national discount rate policy is appropriate to correspond with a national open market policy.

The Commission recommends that a fully discretionary, uniform rediscount rate be established for all Federal Reserve banks. *

The twelve Federal Reserve banks administer the function of lending to member banks in their respective districts. The principles used by each bank in judging an application for a loan are based on uniform regulations issued by the Board governing the discount privilege, and discount administration of the banks is examined periodically by the Board. Nevertheless, there are claims that administrative criteria differ somewhat among districts.

Clearly the intent of the Federal Reserve Board is to have discount administration relatively homogeneous among the twelve Federal Reserve banks, and the Commission urges continued efforts to assure uniform standards of discounting practice. Uniform standards, of course, mean that like circumstances result in like treatment, at the same time permitting differences in practice where regional differences in economic conditions or needs require.

Reserve requirements

The reserve position of the banking system depends on the relationship between the volume of reserves held and the volume of reserves required. Both factors can be controlled by the Federal Reserve, and countercyclical adjustments in the reserve position of member banks can be achieved either by changes in reserve requirements or through open market operations. Since 1951 the Federal Reserve had made countercyclical use of changes in member bank reserve requirements only during recessions. Requirements have been reduced to ease monetary conditions, but they have not been increased as a restrictive monetary measure.

---

* STANLEY H. RUTTENBERG—The third proposal on page 65 should be the Commission's recommendation rather than a suggestion that the Federal Reserve Board continue "the present fully discretionary system."

While changes in reserve requirements are a powerful instrument of credit control, they are awkward and cumbersome in comparison with open market operations and present difficult problems of adjustment for many medium-sized and small banks. Even the customary changes in required reserve ratios of $\frac{1}{2}$ of 1 percent supply or absorb a very large quantity of reserves. While smaller changes could be made, it appears that under normal circumstances changes in reserve requirements are less finely adjustable than open market operations.

It is argued that changes in reserve requirements have an advantage over open market operations because they affect all member banks directly and immediately, whereas the initial effects of open market operations are commonly concentrated in the major national money markets. There is little clear evidence to indicate that the effects of open market operations are slower than those following reserve requirement changes. Nor is it clear, in view of the other lags involved in monetary policy, that any difference in timing is large enough to be important.

The Commission believes that the power to change reserve requirements should be used only sparingly and favors major reliance on the use of open market operations for countercyclical adjustments. *

Numerous alternatives to the present system of relating reserves to the volume of net deposits have been proposed as a basis for setting reserve requirements. These include reserves against bank assets, reserves based on turnover of deposits, and special secondary reserves to be held as Treasury securities.

A system of reserves based on the volume and composition of bank assets would be a move toward selective control over bank credit. The degree of selectivity would depend upon the classes into which assets were divided for reserve requirement purposes. While this approach appears to provide a powerful tool of credit policy, it suffers from the same formidable administrative difficulties involved in other selective approaches to business credit regulation, principally the ease of evasion through relabeling the purposes of loans. Unlike the more conventional approaches to selective credit controls, the use of variable and differential asset–reserve requirements would apply only to commercial banks, thereby limiting the effectiveness of the device and also raising important questions of equity among financial institutions.

---

* STANLEY H. RUTTENBERG—I do not agree that "the power to change reserve requirements should be used only sparingly." It is not wise policy for the Federal Reserve Board to give up its use of reserve requirements as one of the three tools used to affect the level of money supply. I agree that major reliance should be placed on open market operations, but it is also wise to retain, for countercyclical purposes, reserve requirements as well as the discount function as a means of regulating the level of money supply.

Mr. NATHAN wishes to be associated with Mr. RUTTENBERG'S comment.

A system of reserves based on turnover of deposits has been advocated to give the authorities some automatic offset to changes in monetary velocity. This proposal originated with the Federal Reserve authorities many years ago and has been revived by others from time to time. It is not clear that this addition to general quantitative control would provide a better means of offsetting velocity changes than those already available. Different categories of depositors have rational grounds for using their deposits at different velocity rates. Reserves based on turnover would hit banks with high-velocity, though stable, rates for their deposits, whereas the objective of basing reserves on turnover would presumably be to regulate *change* in the rate of turnover. Such a system might not touch those banks which are responsible for activating idle balance through their lending operations.

A compulsory secondary reserve requirement was proposed in the early postwar years when reserve requirements were already at their maximum legal levels and open market powers were subordinated to the task of pegging long-term security prices. Under present conditions, a secondary reserve requirement can achieve little for credit control that cannot be accomplished equally well by instruments already available.

The present general form of fractional reserve requirements against net demand deposits is adequate for the purposes of general monetary policy and the Commission recommends that it be continued. *

Since 1913, members banks have been divided into three groups with respect to reserve requirements on demand deposits—central reserve city banks, reserve city banks, and country banks. According to legislation enacted in 1959, the first class of banks is to be abolished by mid-1962. Reserve requirements for central reserve city and reserve city banks were made identical on December 1, 1960. The act of 1959 also provided that the Federal Reserve may permit all or part of vault cash to be counted as reserves, instead of only deposit balances at Federal Reserve banks.

The geographical distinction was based on conditions prevailing almost a century ago when the National Banking Act was passed. The elimination of the reserve differentials would provide more precise control over the money supply than is now possible. Shifts of funds between country banks and reserve city banks change the total amount of required reserves and thus change the amount of excess reserves within the banking system. With identical requirements, such shifts of funds would be of much less significance in managing the money supply. Now that vault cash is included in reserves, equalization is more feasible than

---

* STANLEY H. RUTTENBERG—The Federal Reserve Board should have standby authority to impose secondary reserve requirements. They should be viewed as an additional and appropriate tool of monetary policy.

formerly, because banks in different locations or with different categories
of depositors have to carry differing amounts of vault cash.

**The Commission recommends that the demand deposit reserve re-
quirements for all member banks be made identical and that the
classification of banks into country banks and reserve city banks be
eliminated.***

Reserve requirements on time and savings deposits are already uniform for all member banks. The level of these requirements and the form
in which they must be held, however, is significantly different from those
required of competing thrift institutions. The Commission believes it
unnecessary to require statutory reserves against savings and time deposits in banks and competing institutions. Management and supervisory authorities are able to see to it that such liquidity as may be necessary with respect to such deposits is maintained.

**The Commission recommends that existing statutory reserve require-
ments against savings and time deposits be repealed, and that pending
repeal of such requirements, those banks and competing thrift institutions subject to them be permitted to hold reserves in the form of either
cash or Treasury securities with maturities up to five years. (For a full
discussion of this point see Chapter Six.)** **

The reserve base required to support a long-run expansion in the
stock of money can be supplied either through open market operations
or through a reduction in required reserve ratios. Which method is used
will affect the leverage with which monetary control operates, that is,
the multiple by which demand deposits can be increased or decreased for
any change in required reserves; net Treasury interest costs; and the
level of bank earnings.

Reducing required reserve ratios increases the leverage of monetary
control. Increased leverage has some advantages for economic stabilization. A given change in available reserves will induce a greater change
in total bank loans and investments and in the money supply, the lower

---

* STANLEY H. RUTTENBERG—When identical reserve requirements are established for all banks, it shall not be at a level lower than what is the current level of
average reserve requirements for the reserve city banks and country banks.

** STANLEY H. RUTTENBERG—I do not concur in the recommendation that
"statutory reserve requirements against savings and time deposits be repealed. . . ."
I think that statutory reserve requirements should be maintained as they are now
against savings and time deposits of commercial banks, and that the Federal Reserve
Board develop techniques to apply a similar type of reserve requirement on competing
thrift institutions.

CHARLES B. SHUMAN—I would delete all but the first part of this recommendation and recommend only that existing statutory reserve requirements against savings
and time deposits be repealed.

is the required reserve ratio. However, a lower reserve ratio may increase the difficulty of dealing with short-run variations in factors affecting bank reserves such as changes in float, currency in circulation, or the gold stock. These effects can be offset with a smaller amount of open market operations, but to the extent that they are not, their net disruptive effect will be larger when required reserve ratios are low and leverage is high.

A second consideration bearing on the level of reserve requirements is the interest cost on the Treasury debt. The same volume of demand deposits can be supported either by a relatively small volume of reserves and a low level of reserve requirements or a larger volume of reserves and higher reserve requirements. In the second situation the Federal Reserve Banks would have a larger amount of earning assets, and because these assets consist largely of Treasury securities, more of the Treasury debt would be held by the Federal Reserve and less would be in the hands of the public. And because the Federal Reserve pays over 90 per- cent of its net earnings to the Treasury, the net interest cost to the Treasury would be less. Treasury interest costs would also be lower be- cause less of the debt would have to be publicly held and lower interest rates on all new Treasury issues would be likely.

Another consideration affecting the growth of the money supply is the level of bank earnings, because if demand deposits are to grow, then commercial banks must also grow. A bank's ability to expand its loans and investments and its deposits is limited not only by the volume of its reserves and its required reserve ratio but also by the volume of its capital and its required capital–asset ratio.

Whether a bank will be able to expand to take advantage of an im- proved reserve position will depend on its capital position. If individual banks insist on maintaining or are required by supervisory authorities to maintain a specified capital–asset ratio as a prudent protection against losses, then a bank can expand its earning assets only if it can enlarge its capital at a corresponding pace. Increased capital depends on ade- quate earnings. If capital is built up from retained earnings, then total earnings must be large enough to permit this; or if capital is to be ob- tained from new stock issues, the earnings rate must be high enough to make this course attractive both to the banks and to investors.

The level of reserve requirements affect the level of bank earnings, because the required reserves of member banks are nonearning assets. The higher the required reserve ratio, the smaller the proportion of bank assets in the form of earning assets and the lower the level of earnings. Conversely, lower reserve requirements make possible higher bank earn- ings. If the current level of reserve requirements permits an adequate level of earnings to attract the necessary capital at current levels of in- terest rates and other bank charges, then the reserve base for an expand- ing money supply can be met through open market operations. On the other hand, if the required reserve ratio does not permit an adequate level of earnings at the existing levels of interest rates and bank charges, then either the level of interest rates and bank charges must rise or the reserve ratio must be reduced to permit the increased earnings necessary for the growth of commercial banks and the money supply.*

The Commission recommends that Congress continue to grant to the Federal Reserve Board a range within which reserve requirements can be set for demand deposits, perhaps from 8 to 18 percent, so that the Board can adjust the specific level to meet the needs of growth or to meet emergency needs.**

SELECTIVE CONTROLS †

One suggestion frequently made for strengthening the effectiveness of monetary policy is that more use should be made of selective monetary measures. The traditional and continuing focus of Federal Reserve policy on general monetary control exercised through changes in the over-all reserve positions of commercial banks does not attempt to direct the allocation of credit among competing uses. If selective controls were used, the authorities could alter the terms and conditions on which credit is made available for particular purposes regardless of the reserve position imposed by general controls. Today the only selective control available to the Federal Reserve authorities is the power to alter margin requirements on credit granted by any lender—banks and others—for the purpose of purchasing or carrying listed securities.

Proposals for selective controls over other specific uses of credit are usually directed toward controlling volatile sectors of spending, such as

---

* STANLEY H. RUTTENBERG—It does not follow, that in order to increase bank earnings, it is necessary to reduce the level of reserve requirements, increase the level of interest rates, or increase bank charges. The bank can increase its earnings by having its reserves increased by the Federal Reserve Board's open market operations. If it comes to a choice of higher interest rates or bank charge increases, I would choose the latter.

** WILLARD L. THORP—The reserve requirement is important in determining bank earnings and government interest cost, neither of which should be the responsibility of the Federal Reserve Board. Adjustments in reserve requirements to meet the needs of growth can be made infrequently by Congress. The Federal Reserve Board has ample power to operate monetary policy through other means, and therefore the Congress should fix a single required reserve ratio with all factors taken into account rather than a wide range with discretion in the hands of the Board.

STANLEY H. RUTTENBERG—I object to the phrase "perhaps from 8 to 18 percent." The present law provides for a range of 7 to 22 percent and I see no reason for this to be altered.

† FRED LAZARUS, JR.—I am opposed to any new selective credit controls except during times of grave national emergency.

Messrs. BLACK and YNTEMA wish to be associated with Mr. LAZARUS' comment.

spending on consumer durable goods, housing, inventory accumulation, and industrial plant and equipment. Expenditures for these depend heavily on the use of credit, but they do not respond rapidly to changes in general credit conditions. Thus they can be reached quickly through general monetary policies only by imposing credit conditions on the economy as a whole that might not be appropriate. Influencing these expenditures directly, through selective controls, would make monetary policy more effective. At least three related issues are involved in the question of selective credit controls: the degree to which government should intervene in the allocation of resources; the type of intervention; and the specific means available for intervention in particular types of expenditure.

The degree and type of intervention

The debate on the appropriate degree of government intervention is frequently conducted entirely on grounds of doctrine. Some hold that intervention in resource allocation is undesirable in itself, except in time of war. Others believe that intervention to achieve accepted goals that cannot otherwise be attained is legitimate and desirable. The important issue is not the choice between intervention and nonintervention but between one type of intervention and another.

Existing credit controls are already selective, partly by conscious policy and partly because of the differential effects flowing from general credit controls. In addition to the margin regulations designed to curb stock market speculation, general monetary measures affect short-term interest rates more than long-term rates, housing expenditures more than business expenditures for plant and equipment and inventories, and expenditures for consumer durable goods more than for nondurable goods. There are also other deliberate selective controls in force elsewhere in the government for altering resource allocation. Federal credit agencies redirect credit flows in favor of such sectors as residential housing, slum clearance, agriculture, transportation, small business, and exports. General and specific tax and expenditure policies affect the distribution of resources between public goods and private goods, between aggregate saving and spending, between investment in tangible goods and intangibles such as research and education, and among particular kinds of consumer goods and services.

Selective credit controls attempt to influence the level and composition of output by regulating the volume and terms of lending for specific purposes. The effectiveness of such selective credit controls depends primarily on whether the purpose of the loan can be identified accurately by the collateral offered as security or by other means. Mortgage and consumer credit for the purchase of houses or automobiles and credit granted to purchase securities generally meet the test of loan identification by purpose through the collateral offered. It is not possible to identify the purpose of business borrowing by the collateral offered. To control such lending another type of identification device than any thus far used would be required. Unless private lenders can identify the purpose of the loan readily, evasion of control may be so easy as to make the control ineffective.

Whether the Federal Reserve should be granted additional powers to alter the pattern of credit and resource allocation through the exercise of new selective controls is a practical matter. It hinges largely on whether particular types of changes in the composition of spending among broad classes of output not readily affected by general controls can be identified *at the time* as being so destabilizing as to threaten the achievement of major economic objectives, and on whether there are efficient means to affect these types of spending and output in the desired directions.

Consumer credit

One opinion that has been expressed on the long-run impact of consumer credit on the economy is that the demand for installment borrowing has been so strong that it has diverted loan funds to consumption from business investment possibly to the detriment of economic growth. Another opinion has been that consumer credit has grown so fast and on such easy terms that overburdened consumers are dangerously vulnerable to any decline in income receipts.

In spite of the large increase in outstanding consumer credit in the postwar period, the evidence does not suggest that consumers, in the aggregate, are now overburdened with debt, although specific families may be. Many low income families are devoting a fifth or more of their income to installment payments. If these families should suffer a modest decline in income, the burden of existing debt could become too heavy. However, this problem of individual overindebtedness is likely to continue even with selective controls over credit terms.

A more frequently expressed concern about consumer credit and particularly installment credit is that it is a source of cyclical instability. The demand for consumer durable goods has been cyclically volatile, and the use of credit to finance purchases has aggravated an already unstable situation. Net extensions of credit, the excess of new extensions over repayment, has added significantly to durable goods purchases in cyclical upswings. The need to continue payments on the downswing has deprived consumers of purchasing power when incomes were falling and has intensified the fall-off in durable goods sales. And changes in general credit conditions have not had any prompt or discernibly significant effect on cycles in consumer credit.

The difficulty of efficient administration of selective controls over consumer credit is a major argument against them. Past experience shows that evasion is a constant problem. A minimum ratio of down payments on some durable goods, such as automobiles, have been by-passed by changing ostensible trade-in allowances. The growth of leasing could permit consumers to acquire cars on terms which might differ significantly from those being imposed by the credit authorities.

Regulation of consumer credit terms might contribute to cyclical stability, but it would require a large and complex administration to be fully effective. The benefits to stability promised by such a system must be weighed against the cost and inconvenience of installing and managing it.

During wartime emergencies, direct controls over the output and sale of consumer durables probably would be imposed, and if so, consumer credit control would be redundant.

During more normal periods, it might be useful to discourage undue loosening of credit terms when the demand for durables is an important source of inflationary pressure. But as a regular countercyclical tool of stabilization its practical possibilities are limited.*

The Commission is almost evenly divided as to the desirability of granting standby authority to the Federal Reserve Board for consumer credit controls. In the absence of a consensus, no recommendation is made except to urge an investigation of better forms of such controls which could be administered more effectively if they should be needed.**

Residential housing credit

The arguments for variable controls over the terms of housing mortgages are similar to those for consumer installment credit controls. But because the exchange of existing houses for new houses is not common, many of the administrative difficulties of evasion do not arise.

However, setting appropriate goals for the desired volume of residential construction presents a difficult and serious problem. The elimination of the interest rate ceilings imposed on Veterans Administration and Federal Housing Administration mortgages, which is recommended

---

* WILLARD L. THORP—It should be noted that control of consumer credit terms has a more rapid impact on private expenditures than most other devices, assuming that stand-by authority already existed so that this element of delay were removed.

  Mr. LUBIN wishes to be associated with Mr. THORP'S comment.

** See Mr. RUTTENBERG'S comment on page 76.

in Chapter Seven, would remove one cause of the present countercyclical variation of housing construction. The imposition of selective controls, however, would permit a restoration of all or part of such countercyclical variation that might be lost through the removal of interest rate ceilings.

In Chapter Seven the Commission recommends that the terms of housing loans insured or guaranteed under VA and FHA programs be varied in support of the countercyclical and price stabilization policies of the government. These changes would be administered by the VA and FHA. No further power to change credit terms on residential mortgages by the Federal Reserve Board is believed necessary.*

Business credit

The instability of business spending for inventory accumulations and for plant and equipment purchases has contributed significantly to cyclical fluctuations. General monetary controls do not appear to have rapid effects on either, and it is argued that selective controls might have.

Setting and altering the terms of lending for specific uses of credit might have little effect. Businesses could employ internal funds for the uses carrying the most onerous terms and borrow for those uses which the control authorities were attempting to encourage the most or discourage the least. Thus, differential selective credit controls over business uses of funds would be difficult to enforce. And if the concept of different terms for different uses is sacrificed to close loopholes in enforcement, selective credit controls become virtually identical to general credit controls. A blanket classification for all loans to business would also virtually amount to general credit control, although it could vary the cost of business borrowing relative to other categories of borrowing.

Even noncredit controls pose serious administrative problems. Expenditures for business plant, equipment, and inventory are not homogeneous categories. There are important differences of behavior within a category among industries in the economy and among different companies in the same industry. These differences would inevitably call for an intricate network of administrative adjustments to make a selective control effective.

No seemingly effective selective credit control device has yet been devised for regulating these volatile business expenditures. It may well be that more effective controls of such expenditures than general credit measures will be necessary to achieve our major economic objectives, and the Commission suggests that possible methods of influencing inventory

---

* See Mr. RUTTENBERG'S comment on page 76.

and business investment expenditures on a selective basis be investigated by the government.*

THE SPAN OF MONETARY CONTROL

The Federal Reserve has direct control over the reserve position of the 6,000 commercial banks which are members of the System, although its influence is felt through the entire credit market. The fact that nonmember banks are not subject to the same reserve requirements as members, and the fact that the public holds a large volume of liquid assets at nonbank institutions, such as savings and loan associations and mutual savings banks, have been cited as potential and actual sources of escape from the impact of monetary control. This has led to suggestions that the direct reach of Federal Reserve control should be extended to cover these institutions.

Nonmember banks

The existence of about 7,000 nonmember commercial banks creates a number of problems. Reserve requirements for nonmember banks are established by states and frequently are lower than requirements imposed on members, which gives nonmembership a competitive advantage. This weakens the incentives to join the Federal Reserve System and provides a potential inducement for member banks to withdraw. This situation may, at times, inhibit Federal Reserve action.

---

* STANLEY H. RUTTENBERG—An effective stabilization effort requires that there be standby authority to use selective controls on consumer and housing credits. The development of effective standby credit controls on business investment expenditures and business inventories are also needed. The absence of selective credit controls over all of these areas, including the very volatile areas of inventory and investment expenditures, dooms monetary policy in a complex economy to excessive general restraint during inflationary situations.

FRED LAZARUS, JR.—The attempt to control business investment in inventories and in plant and equipment would lead to a government-controlled economy and the end of private enterprise as we know it today. I am opposed to any such action.

Messrs. BLACK, SHUMAN, and YNTEMA wish to be associated with Mr. LAZARUS' comment.

ROBERT R. NATHAN—Measures to affect aggregate demand are obviously essential and important. However, instability in our economy stems in an important degree from divergencies in various classes of expenditures. The aggregate approach may often be less effective and more costly than selective controls. It may be much more costly in terms of unemployment suffered in the fight against inflation, or inflation encountered in the pursuit of low unemployment, or inadequate growth resulting from fighting inflation through aggregate demand measures. Selective controls must be pursued with care but it is my belief that the Commission report is too cautious with respect to the use of selective controls.

Mr. LUBIN wishes to be associated with Mr. NATHAN'S comment.

A more important problem is that the present basis for nonmember reserve requirements permits some escape from the influence of monetary policy. Finally, many nonmember banks make an exchange charge in settling checks drawn on them, and this constitutes an imperfection in the payments mechanism. None of these problems is serious, principally because the total volume of deposits held at nonmember banks amounts to less than one-sixth of the national total, though nonmember banks are more important in some regions than in others. However, the Federal Reserve must always bear in mind the danger that a particular policy that might otherwise be appropriate will increase the relative share of deposits in nonmember banks owing to withdrawals from the System or an increase in their relative growth.

Reserve requirements for nonmember banks differ from those imposed on member banks both in level and in the assets permitted as reserves. Nonmembers may count and deposit balances with other banks as reserves, and in some states specified amounts of federal, state, and local government securities may also serve as reserves. In one state no legal reserves are required.

In practice, the expansion of credit and money by nonmember banks is limited by two factors. Increases in vault cash needs, which accompany deposit expansion, must be obtained directly or indirectly from the Federal Reserve, and this absorbs basic reserve funds from the entire banking community.

The problems presented by nonmembership have long been recognized and several proposals have been repeatedly put forward. The broadest proposal would require all commercial banks to become members of the Federal Reserve System. A second proposal would require all banks wanting insured status under the Federal Deposit Insurance Corporation to become members of the Federal Reserve System. This would cover all but three or four hundred nonmember banks. A third proposal would require that all commercial banks, whether members or not, be subject to similar reserve requirements both with respect to quantity and form while permitting the present right to nonmembership. This would overcome the slippage in monetary control and the principal potential inducement for present members to withdraw. The Commission believes that either this or the preceding proposal is a feasible and desirable solution and that one or the other should be adopted.

The Commission recommends that all insured commercial banks should be required to become members of the Federal Reserve System. *

---

* STANLEY H. RUTTENBERG—I agree with the comment that "the broadest proposal would require all commercial banks to become members of the Federal Reserve System." I see no reason why this should not be the recommendation of the Commission.

Nonbank intermediaries

The more rapid growth of nonbank financial intermediaries than commercial banks has focused attention on the question of their significance as a potential offset to monetary policy because of the consequent rapid increase in the public's holding of liquid assets. Because of their closeness to money, changes in the volume of these near-money assets may have an important effect on the demand for money balances and hence on the velocity of money. Yet cyclical and secular changes in the volume of these liquid assets and in the lending practices of the institutions which create them now lie beyond the direct control of the monetary authorities. This, it is alleged, represents a potentially serious obstacle between Federal Reserve policy and the goals it seeks to achieve which should be remedied by an extension of direct Federal Reserve control to such institutions, particularly to savings and loan associations and mutual savings banks.

The effect on the total flow of spending resulting from the availability of a wide variety of money substitutes may be thought of as operating through their influence on the velocity of money. Money proper is held not only to carry out transactions but also as an asset which provides the holder with a fixed-value and easily negotiated claim, a store of value. When monetary policy is being tightened and interest rates are rising, holders of idle money balances may be induced by the increasing yields available to switch to savings and loan shares, savings deposits, Treasury bills, or some other form of interest-bearing liquid asset. For example, the holder of a checking account in a commercial bank may decide he will gain by switching to savings and loan shares. The commercial banking system's reserves are not diminished by this operation, so its loans and investments need not be reduced. The savings and loan association, however, now has the funds with which to extend more mortgage loans. The money supply is unchanged, but part of it becomes more active as spending rises and the velocity of money increases. During recessions, when monetary policy is eased, the reverse situation may prevail. Available data indicate that income velocity moves with and not against the business cycle, increasing when the monetary authority is restraining the economy and decreasing when it is easing credit. This movement would weaken the effects of countercyclical monetary policy actions, unless open market sales were adjusted to take into account and offset this change in velocity.

The velocity effects attributable to movements of funds out of currency and demand deposits into claims on nonbank financial intermediaries do not appear to be great. Although claims on nonbank financial institutions are often defined to include reserves of life insurance companies and pension funds, there is a good case for omitting these less liquid assets. These reserves are long-term and contractual in nature, and because individual savers are motivated primarily by the desire for family financial protection, these sums are ordinarily expected to be left intact until retirement or death. Moreover, it is not likely that funds move into and out of life insurance reserves in response to changes in interest rates as they do into and out of savings accounts. Only the evidence on switches between demand deposits and savings accounts in mutual savings banks, commercial banks, and savings and loan associations is relevant for the present argument.

The major holders of demand deposits are households and nonfinancial corporations, and it is their shifts from demand deposits which significantly affect velocity. However, shifts by corporations are largely into and out of short-term Treasury securities rather than into or out of savings and time deposits. Control over private nonbank financial institutions would not affect this important influence on velocity.

As for households, recent evidence suggests that the only important swings of fund flows towards savings institutions occur during recessions and consist principally of funds diverted from investment in securities when bond yields are falling and the course of stock prices is uncertain. Investors who move out of the securities markets at such times are either the income-minded ones who have no definite reinvestment plans or those who expect to reinvest shortly. The first group moves current accumulations of cash and some old balances into savings institutions; the second tends to stay in cash. In the upswings rising yields on savings deposits have not pulled household funds out of demand deposits in sufficient quantity to produce discernible effects on the rate of growth of savings accounts. If this evidence is correct, the cyclical effect of the flow of funds into the savings institutions is more likely to increase velocity in recessions than in booms and thus to assist rather than offset the effect of monetary policy.

In general, the argument that the cyclical behavior of velocity has been caused by systematic shifts of individual and business funds out of money assets into near-money thrift deposits during periods of monetary restraint is not supported by the facts. The velocity increases that do occur during booms have other causes, principally the shift of corporate balances into earning assets and the reduction of household balances to purchase goods and services.

Financial institutions, including banks, also influence velocity in other ways. When money is tight they may economize on their own cash balances. Moreover, they may sell liquid assets such as Treasury bills in order to make more remunerative longer-term loans. If the purchasers of these securities had used their previously held deposits less actively than the new holders, velocity would increase. However, the evidence, although fragmentary, suggests that portfolio adjustments by private nonbank financial institutions do not contribute significantly to the cyclical variations in velocity.

To what extent are nonbank financial institutions responsible for trends in velocity as distinct from the cyclical movements? Here, too, the evidence is fragmentary. It suggests that money substitutes play some role in secular velocity movements, but not an important one.

Factors such as the growth in real per capita income and the accumulation of real wealth tend to increase the community's demand for cash balances in relation to income over the long run, and this tends to reduce income velocity. Other factors, such as a greater volume and variety of money substitutes, expectations of price increases, and continuous institutional progress in economizing on money, tend to lower the requirement for cash balances secularly in relation to income and to increase the income velocity of money. Long-term movements in interest rates also play a role. Over much of our history, income velocity has gradually declined, suggesting a dominance of the former factors. Since the war, however, the rising trend in income velocity has focused attention on the latter forces, particularly on the growth of money substitutes.

The evidence of the postwar years indicates that the increase of money substitutes has played a role in the rise in velocity, but there is disagreement as to its relative importance. There is also little agreement as to whether money substitutes are likely to have a significant role in influencing the trend of velocity in the future.

Even though nonbank financial institutions may not greatly influence the secular trend of income velocity, their direct control has been advocated on the ground that continued growth of these institutions relative to commercial banks would endanger the safety of banks, especially if the Federal Reserve should have to cut down severely on the growth in the money supply to compensate for secular increases in velocity. In the past commercial banks have declined in importance relative to private nonbank financial institutions when velocity was falling secularly as well as when it was rising. There are no satisfactory predictions as to which way velocity will move in the next few decades. If it resumes its secular decline, the Federal Reserve will need to increase the money supply for growth purposes at a higher rate than in the postwar years. In addition, there is no reason to believe that banks will not continue to grow absolutely even though their relative position may decline.

The evidence, for either the cyclical or the secular periods, does not support a case for an extension of the direct monetary controls over nonbank financial intermediaries. Their contribution to cyclical changes in velocity appears to be too small to warrant such an extension. Their effect on velocity over the long run can easily be taken into account in regulating the long-run money supply.

The Commission recommends that there be no extension of direct Federal Reserve controls over nonbank financial institutions. *

However, one kind of control over banks that is not imposed on nonbank financial intermediaries deserves attention. This is the control of interest payments payable by commercial banks to depositors. At present, interest payments on demand deposits are prohibited, and interest payments on time and savings deposits are subject to ceilings imposed by the Federal Reserve. The ceilings restrict the freedom of commercial banks to compete for savings deposits with nonbank intermediaries which are not subject to similar control over the rates they may offer.

This topic is developed at greater length in Chapter Six. There recommendations are made to continue the prohibition of interest payments on demand deposits and to revise the present statutes authorizing regulation of interest rates on savings and time deposits for commercial banks, to convert the present power into a standby authority rather than continuous regulation, and to permit differentiation among types of deposits, including between foreign and domestic deposits. Recommendations are also made to have the same type of regulation cover similar liabilities of other thrift institutions and that the regulations be imposed only when in the opinion of the appropriate authorities further interest rate competition for deposits is deemed not in the public interest.**

Organization of the Federal Reserve System

The Federal Reserve System is charged with the formulation as well as the execution of monetary policy. Its mandate and structure are therefore of first importance in appraising governmental means of achieving national economic goals. A reorientation of the System's objectives in a freshly defined legislative mandate is proposed in Chapter Ten. This section deals with its structure, which is a joint product of legislation and practice.

The basic questions are both administrative and political. They center

---

* STANLEY H. RUTTENBERG—I dissent from this recommendation. Some means must be developed for bringing non-bank financial institutions directly under the nation's central bank. Nonbank financial institutions are continually increasing in size and relative importance in the American economy. The monetary authorities' problem of affecting the level of money supply would be considerably eased if direct Federal Reserve controls were extended to nonbank financial institutions.

Mr. LUBIN wishes to be associated with Mr. RUTTENBERG'S comment.

** STANLEY H. RUTTENBERG—See my comment on page 167.

on the degree of independence of the System from the other organs of the government on the one hand, and from the banking community on the other.

THE PRESENT STRUCTURE

The System has a regulated private base, a mixed middle component, and a controlling public apex. The mixture of public and private elements is unique among the closely regulated sectors of our national economy, and unique too among central banking systems around the world. It reflects in part the changing conceptions of the role of central banking over a half-century and in part the shift in interests and influences that has attended the System's evolution.

At the apex stands the Board of Governors (FRB). Its seven members are appointed by the President with the consent of the Senate for 14-year terms, one term expiring on January 31 in each even-numbered year. Members may be reappointed, and they are removable "for cause"; but the removal power has not been exercised. Because of the length of the term, most new appointments are to fill vacancies in unexpired terms. In making appointments the President must give due regard to "fair representation of financial, agricultural, industrial, and commercial interests, and geographical divisions of the country," and not more than one member can be appointed from any one Federal Reserve District.

The Chairman and Vice Chairman of the Board are designated from among the Board members by the President for four-year renewable terms which do not, unless by accident, coincide with the President's.

The independence invited by long, staggered terms is reinforced by the System's complete exemption from the controls of the budget and congressional appropriations. Board operating funds come from semi-annual assessments on the twelve Federal Reserve banks; the assessments, like the operating expenses of the banks, are a prior charge on their earnings before surpluses are transferred to the Treasury. Nevertheless, Board members' salaries are fixed by law and the Board in practice observes government salary scales for its staff in Washington.

At a level of authority equivalent to the Board's, but in the public-private category, is the Federal Open Market Committee (FOMC), by law composed of all seven FRB members and five of the twelve Federal Reserve bank presidents. The President of the Federal Reserve Bank of New York is always one of the five; the others serve in annual rotation. In practice, all twelve Reserve bank presidents regularly attend FOMC sessions and participate in the discussions, though only five of them vote.

The Presidents of the Reserve banks are not government appointees; they are elected for five-year terms by the boards of directors of their respective banks, subject to the approval of the FRB. Their compensation is fixed by their boards of directors, again subject to FRB approval. In the early years they were usually commercial bankers, but as the System has developed, recruitment from within has become more characteristic. The positions have attracted capable men.

The annual reports of the Board of Governors, in setting out the minutes of meetings, decisions, votes, and reasons therefor, as the law requires, record FOMC and FRB proceedings in separate sequences. This appearance, however, scarcely mirrors the realities, for FOMC and FRB actions are regularly discussed together.

The twelve Federal Reserve banks are "mixed" institutions. Their capital stock is subscribed by the member banks at the statutory rate of 6 percent of each member bank's capital and surplus. Only half of it has been required to be paid in, and this amounted, in 1960, to an aggregate of about $400 million. A surplus, fixed at the Board's discretion and presently equalling the amount of subscribed, that is, twice the paid-in, capital or about $800 million in 1960, has been built up from retained earnings. Member-bank stock of the Federal Reserve banks cannot be hypothecated or transferred, and is entitled only to be retired at par in the event of liquidation or dissolution. By law, Reserve bank stockholders are limited to a 6 percent cumulative dividend, which in 1959 and 1960 was earned more than 30 times over. Combined Reserve bank earning assets, mostly holdings of government securities, amounted in 1960 to upwards of $27 billion. Earnings beyond the dividend and the maintenance of the surplus are paid over to the Treasury as a matter of policy, under the label of "interest" on Federal Reserve notes. Combined Reserve bank earnings have mounted rapidly since the war, from $92 million in 1945 to $963 million in 1960. The dividend to stockholders in 1960 was $24 million and the payment to the Treasury $897 —about a tenth of the interest cost of the public debt.

Very tangibly, then, as well as legally, the Reserve banks are public service institutions, run at a profit but not for a profit. Their private "ownership" is a highly attenuated right. On the other hand, the salaries of the Reserve bank presidents and their staff salary scales are set at going market rates rather than government levels; the Reserve bank officers are not public servants in the usual sense. One more item is pertinent: the Reserve banks, their earnings and property, are exempt from all taxation, federal and state, except real estate taxes.

The public-private mixture characterizes the Reserve bank boards of directors too. Each Reserve bank has a board of nine. Six of them, Class A and B directors, are elected by the member commercial banks of the district, and the three Class C directors, including the chairman and the deputy chairman, are appointed by the FRB in Washington. Class A directors are bankers; Class B are men active in commerce, agriculture or "some other industrial pursuit"; Class C appointees must only have been residents of their districts for two years; the chairman must be "a person of tested banking experience." In order to insure the representation of small and medium-sized as well as large banks, and of small town as well as city banks, the electoral method for choosing Reserve bank directors classifies the member banks into three size categories, according to their capitalization. Banks in each group vote separately— one bank, one vote—for one director in Class A and one in Class B.

The final element in the statutory organization of the System is the Federal Advisory Council (FAC). Composed of one representative elected annually by the board of directors of each Reserve bank, the FAC meets quarterly with the FRB to discuss business conditions and is authorized to make recommendations to the Board on any matter of Federal Reserve policy. By custom, members are commercial bankers, for the Council originated as a concession in the original Federal Reserve Act to compensate for the denial of direct banker representation on the FRB itself.

THE DISTRIBUTION OF POWER

Of the System's three instruments of general monetary policy—changes in member bank reserve requirements, changes in the rediscount rate, and open market operations—the first is lodged clearly with the FRB. The second, the rediscount rate, is "established" every two weeks by each Reserve bank, but "subject to the review and determination" of the FRB. In practice this appearance of a measure of regional autonomy has largely yielded to the national nature of the money market. But the Board explores regional sentiment in discussions of possible changes in the rate at meetings of the FOMC, and conclusions usually emerge from discussion and consensus. By determining changes before their announcement the FRB avoids occasions when it might have to disapprove regional preferences publicly.

The control of open market policy, the third and most flexible instrument, is formally vested not in the Board but in the FOMC. The meetings of the FOMC, held at least every two or three weeks, have become, in Chairman Martin's words, "a forum, a clearing-house for all the aspects of policy determination in the System, not failing to recognize the statutory responsibility of the Board of Governors for reserve requirements." The System coordinates its policies and actions, that is to say, in sessions that intermingle its public and private elements completely, and fuses all its powers in support of decisions reached there.

In concluding this description it is appropriate to notice that things have not always been as they are. In a half-century the size and composition of the Board have undergone several changes. It began with five appointed members (two of whom had to be experienced in banking or finance) providing representation of industrial, commercial, financial and regional interests (but not agriculture or labor), together with two *ex-officio* members, the Secretary of the Treasury and the Comptroller of the Currency. The term of office was 10 years. In 1922 the Board was enlarged to bring in an agricultural representative, while the requirement of financial experience for two members was dropped. The term of office was extended in 1933 to 12 years, and again in 1935 to 14 years. At that time, at Senator Glass' insistence, the *ex-officio* memberships were terminated, and the appointive members increased to seven. At that time too, the Board was given a majority of the membership of the FOMC, which had first been given statutory recognition in 1933. Two trends are discernible in these changes, notably in the 1935 legislation: one toward centralization of control over banking and monetary policy through the System, and the other toward increased independence of the System from the rest of the government.

Independence and decentralization remain matters of dispute. What is beyond dispute is the change in the primary function of the System, and in the general awareness of that function. What was thought of in 1913 as essentially "a cooperative enterprise among bankers for the purpose of increasing the security of banks and providing them with a reservoir of emergency resources" has not ceased to be that. But it has also become one of the most potent institutions involved in national economic policy.

FEDERAL RESERVE BOARD CHANGES

It is a matter for argument and judgment whether and in what directions, and how far, the System's governing structure should be altered in the national interest. The basic issue is the degree of independence of the Federal Reserve from other parts of the government and from the banking community it both serves and regulates. A strong advocate for the claims of monetary stability is needed within the government, and the central bank is the natural home of such advocacy. A measure of independence from the Treasury with respect to support of the Treasury securities market is a requisite too, if the central bank is to exercise effective monetary control. Disagreements turn on how far insulation from the President and Congress and from the other agencies concerned with economic policy helps or hinders the expression of the central bank's viewpoint; and on whether a clear locus of authority is needed to secure coordination and prevent conflicts from deteriorating into stalemates.

Some arguments for independence are more or less frankly antidemocratic in their premises. For example, it is said that anti-inflationary measures are unpopular though necessary, and therefore the best assurance of their being taken is by "endowing the Board of Governors with a considerable degree of independence," or that "hard" decisions are more acceptable to the public "if they are decided by public officials who, like the members of the judiciary, are removed from immediate pressures." Others assert, instead, that the accountability of the System is achieved through its responsibility to Congress, and call the Federal Reserve an "agent of Congress," invoking then the doctrine of the separation of powers to argue that this requires independence for the Federal Reserve from the executive. It has been argued, however, that the FRB is less accountable to Congress than the line departments in the presidential hierarchy. It does not depend on appropriations for its funds and so is freed from the most potent of congressional controls over administrative agencies. And Congress has been notably circumspect in even suggesting its policy views to the Board, let alone incurring responsibility for its decisions. All agencies, line departments like the Treasury no less than the FRB, are "creatures of Congress" in the sense of owing their existence and powers to legislation. And agencies with single heads are more easily held accountable by Congress or by anyone else than those with boards at the top.

No doubt there are occasions and types of pressures that need to be guarded against. But the telling arguments for independence are less protective than positive: independence spells opportunity; it is an invitation to vigor; it attracts able people.

The need for coordination, however, is very important. Isolation may mean weakness, and presidential support can be very helpful at times. The real ability of the System to influence national economic policy might well be increased rather than diminished if its ties to the President were closer. The Commission believes that somewhat closer ties are advisable.

Of the means to this end, one has already been tried and discarded: the *ex-officio* memberships of the Secretary of the Treasury and the Comptroller of the Currency on the Board. This tended rather to subordinate the System to the Treasury, and it is not simply a Treasury view but an over-all perspective that is wanted.

A presidential power to issue published directives to the Board has also been suggested, on the principle that if presidential influence is to be brought to bear, it had better be out in the open. The objection to this is not its visibility but the clumsy nature of the instrument. No one wants every Board action to require presidential clearance. Nor is a mechanism desirable that would tend to dramatize differences in views. The need is for closer working relationships and greater unity of purpose and outlook.

The mildest suggestion, amounting to no change, was urged by Chairman Martin in 1952, after the "Accord": he granted the need for coordination but argued that it could be met through informal consultation. If congeniality of temperament and outlook among agency and department heads could always be counted on, the Commission would have looked no further for solutions. But in the interests of government-wide coordination of economic policy the Commission in Chapter Ten recommends some steps to provide a consultative forum and to increase the incentives toward concert. To the same end, and because of the exceptional degree of the FRB's independence, the Commission makes the following recommendations here.

The FRB Chairman and Vice-Chairman should be designated by the President from among the Board's membership, to serve for four-year terms coterminous with the President's. *

This strikes a balance in formal status between tenure at the President's pleasure, which some of the Commissioners would prefer, and no change, which other Commissioners advocate.

The FRB should consist of five members, with overlapping ten-year terms, one expiring each odd-numbered year; members should be eligible for reappointment.

This would assure the President of one vacancy to be filled shortly after his inauguration, while retaining the general stability of Board membership. The reduction in numbers should enhance the status of members, and the ten-year term combines a sufficient protection for independence, with some safeguard against superannuation.

Apart from the instruments of general monetary policy, the Board has important regulatory powers over member banks and some other financial institutions—for instance in the administration of the Bank Holding Company Act and of the anti-trust laws as applied to banks, in the approval or disapproval of applications for branches, mergers, and the like. These powers are vested in the Board, and the Board appears to treat them as non-delegable. Their exercise is exceedingly time-consuming and will become considerably more so, if the Commission's recommendations in Chapter Six regarding the consolidation of functions of the Comptroller of the Currency and of the FDIC into the FRB are adopted. In this aspect of its work the Board has suffered from a malady that has

---

* JESSE W. TAPP—The implication here is that the chairman may dominate the Board. If the recommendations of the paragraph on qualifications are followed, this would certainly not be the situation.

Mr. FLEMING wishes to be associated with Mr. TAPP'S comment.

STANLEY H. RUTTENBERG—While this recommendation does strike a balance between the various positions of the members of the Commission, I want to associate myself with the position that the Chairman and Vice-Chairman of the Federal Reserve Board shall serve at the pleasure of the President.

Mr. NATHAN wishes to be associated with Mr. RUTTENBERG'S comment.

plagued the other independent regulatory commissions, a congestion of detailed business at the top, to the detriment of the time and energy Board members can devote to the broad issues of monetary policy.

The FRB Chairman should be the chief executive officer of the Board, empowered to handle administrative matters. The law should be clarified to authorize the Board to delegate to Board committees, or to Board members individually, or to senior staff officers of the Board, any of its functions in the administration of its powers in regard to the supervision of the banking structure, such as the Bank Holding Company Act, the anti-trust laws in regard to mergers, and applications for charters and branches. Any actions so delegated should be subject to review in the Board's discretion. The first sentence strengthens existing language in the statute slightly and makes clear that the Board as a whole is not to be encumbered with routine administrative matters. The remainder of the recommendation would give the Board an authority similar to that vested in other independent regulatory commissions, to conserve its members' time and to arrange for the more expeditious dispatch of its case load business.

Occupational and geographical qualifications for Board members should be eliminated. Instead the statute should stipulate that members shall be positively qualified by experience or education, competence, independence, and objectivity commensurate with the increased responsibilities recommended for them in the achievement of low levels of unemployment, an adequate rate of economic growth, and reasonable stability of price levels in the economy. Salaries of top officials throughout the government should be sharply increased, and in view of the gravity of their responsibilities, FRB members should be compensated at the highest salary level available for appointive offices in the government. *

---

* EMIL RIEVE—In connection with the composition of the Federal Reserve Board, I would add that due regard be given to membership on the Board of Governors of competent individuals from various economic groups in American society. The intent of the Commission's recommendation, as it now stands, may be to broaden the base of the Federal Reserve system's contact with the community as a whole. The language of the recommendation, however, is not clear in this regard, particularly in the light of the present statutory requirement for occupational representation and charges concerning the system's unrepresentative character.

This same comment, in support of statutory changes for a broadly representative Federal Reserve system, applies to the Commission's omission of any recommendation at all concerning the composition of the governing structure of the twelve district Federal Reserve Banks. The statute should be amended, with the aim of making the entire Federal Reserve system broadly representative of the American people.

The problem of responsiveness in the Board is closely connected with the problem of representation. From the beginning the Federal Reserve Act has contained varying provisions stipulating occupational and geographical qualifications of one sort or another for Board members. None of these has noticeably improved the calibre of the Board, and their tendency is to imply a responsiveness to parochial interests. Whether or not this is the fact in particular cases, the status of members and the chances of coordination with the rest of the executive branch should be improved if Board members understand that the President's selection is based on their personal qualifications rather than on any representational ties they may bring with them. In addition, the listing of some interests to be recognized produces claims for recognition from others. There cannot be places enough to go around for all claimants. The present geographical restriction also limits the President's choice of a Board Chairman, if he selects a new member, to districts not already represented on the Board.

The present statutory Federal Advisory Council should be replaced by an advisory council of twelve members appointed by the Board from nominees presented by the boards of directors of the Federal Reserve banks. At least two nominations, not more than one of them from any single sector of the economy, should be presented by each bank. The Board should make its selection, one from each district, in such a manner as to secure a council broadly representative of all aspects of the American economy. Council members should serve for three-year terms, not immediately renewable. The council should meet with the Federal Reserve Board at least twice a year.

The channels of outside advice to the Board need broadening, and one obstacle to this is the present statutory position of the Federal Advisory Council. Custom has confined the membership of the FAC to commercial bankers. The Commission thinks the mandate to consult should embrace a wider range of interests, and that the means, beyond a reconstituted council, should be deliberately left open-ended.

An important internal source of advice should be further recognized and strengthened. The law should formally constitute the twelve Federal Reserve bank presidents as a conference of Federal Reserve bank presidents, to meet at least four times a year with the Board, and oftener as the Board finds necessary.

The Board is already authorized to appoint and consult such other continuing or *ad hoc* advisory committees as it finds proper in the furtherance of its work, and this authority should remain.

The determination of open market policies should be vested in the Board. In establishing its open market policy the Board should be required to consult with the twelve Federal Reserve bank presidents.*

The determination of the rediscount rate (the same for all Reserve banks) should be vested with the Board. In establishing this rate the Board should be required to consult with the twelve Federal Reserve bank presidents.

The determination of reserve requirements should continue to be vested in the Board. In establishing these requirements the Board should be required to consult with the twelve Federal Reserve bank presidents.**

As to the Board's powers, three points should be made. First, the distinction between the Board and the Federal Open Market Committee has outlived its usefulness. The exercise of the System's three main powers should be complementary and governed by the same considerations, that is, by the same people in the same forum. This has come about in practice and is desirable. Second, the decisions of the Board are exercises of public regulatory authority, and there should be no ambiguity about where the responsibility for them lies: it belongs exclusively in the hands of public officials. Third, the quality of the deliberations over the use of these powers gains from the advisory participation of the Reserve bank presidents in the discussions. Their experience and counsel are needed and should continue to be available. There may well be others whose advice would be helpful too, and the channels of access to the Board can be profitably extended.

---

* STANLEY H. RUTTENBERG—In order to clearly avoid any confusion, I think the Commission's recommendation should be that the present open market committee be abolished and that the functions of the open market committee be placed in the hands of the Federal Reserve Board directly. I am sure this is the intent of the recommendation, but I prefer to see it stated more affirmatively.

Mr. NATHAN wishes to be associated with Mr. RUTTENBERG'S comment.

** EMIL RIEVE—I disagree with the compulsory nature of the requirement that the Federal Reserve Board of Governors consult with the twelve Federal Reserve Bank Presidents in establishing open market policies, rediscount rates and reserve requirements. The Commission recommends, in the previous paragraph, that the district bank presidents should meet with the Board at least four times a year. It is unnecessary to require additional consultation. The determination of open market policies, rediscount rates and reserve requirements should be vested in the Federal Reserve Board, and the Commission's recommendation should be direct and clear, without the limitation of compulsory consultation with the district bank presidents in the establishments of such policies.

FEDERAL RESERVE BANK CHANGES

The changes already recommended—compulsory membership in the Federal Reserve System for all insured banks, a nationally uniform rediscount rate, and concentration of all System powers in the publicly appointed Board, as well as the altered relationships of the Board to the President and the other agencies of the executive branch—taken in the light of the changes in the role of the central bank in our present-day economy, call for a reconsideration also of the governing structure of the twelve Federal Reserve banks. The Commission has examined that structure and sees no compelling reasons for recommending changes in it, except for the stock ownership of the Reserve banks by the member banks.

The Commission recommends that the present form of capital stock of the Federal Reserve banks should be retired. Instead, membership in the System should be evidenced by a noncarning certificate of, say, $500, the same for each member bank. *

Member-bank stock in a Federal Reserve bank today and for the foreseeable future is a riskless and virtually guaranteed 6 percent investment. It would impose no hardship on the many thousands of nonmember banks to subscribe for their quota of stock upon joining the System. But stock subscriptions are no longer needed for Reserve bank working capital and the Reserve banks are public service institutions whose operations are governed by policy considerations beyond profit. Neither the Reserve banks nor the member banks have anything to gain from the continuance of an arrangement that leaves them open to the charge that they have too direct an interest in each others' profits. The concept of member bank representation, however, is legitimate and worth preserving, and this can be accomplished as well through a nonearning certificate of nominal value.

The agency–clientele relationship, between a government agency and the business concerns it both serves and regulates, is almost always, almost inevitably, close; and the more so after it has matured for decades. There are public advantages in this: regulation can be knowledgeable,

---

* H. CHRISTIAN SONNE—I agree with the desirability of removing any valid argument to the effect that member banks can profit by their stock ownership of the Federal Reserve banks; but I recommend that this be done by reducing the present investment of every member bank to the nominal sum of $500.00—limited—as now—to a maximum dividend of 6 percent.

In this way we can retain a structure which has stood the test of time while offering several advantages and which—once eliminated—it might be difficult to reinstate.

its inconveniences can be minimized, personal working relationships can be easy. But the hazards of too close a relationship are also well known; conflicts of interest tempt individuals on either side of the public–private line to consult private advantage too far; organized interests among the regulated may first infiltrate and then paralyze their public regulators; even legitimate transactions and contacts risk misconstruction; parties on both sides come to take too parochial a view of the national interest. The member banks of the Reserve System are alone among nationally regulated industries in technically "owning" the institutions that regulate them. It is better to end any vulnerable appearances forthwith. The member banks should welcome an opportunity to clarify their status in the System in this manner.

FEDERAL RESERVE REPORTS

More complete information on monetary and credit flows is given to the public in this country than elsewhere. The same is true of official explanations of policy decisions and actions, but they are still sparse in content and usually occur long after the event. The most complete explanations are made in the annual reports of the Board. Many have argued for more complete and timely explanations from the Federal Reserve for its major policy moves.

The case against more complete and timely disclosure is partly that the central bank is likely to be misunderstood if it says anything, and partly the fear that its statements may generate destabilizing expectations in the community. Language is far from a perfect instrument of communication, and Federal Reserve officials seem to feel that there is a great possibility of misinterpretation if statements are made concerning current policy.

The case for more complete and timely disclosure is partly that accurate information would perhaps be less dangerous than the rumors that are continuously circulating about what the Federal Reserve policy is today or is likely to be next week. In the absence of adequate knowledge, those interested in such matters have a tendency to seize upon even the most outlandish rumors as significant. Good reporters do ferret out information, and one is never sure whether a particular news report is rumor or is reliable. Another argument for more complete disclosure is that monetary policy represents one facet of national economic policy, and in a democratic society public policies should be subject to current debate.

Although there is no easy solution to this issue, the Commission believes that the Federal Reserve should follow the general rule that the public should be kept informed with reasonable promptness and with reasonable detail of the reasons for its major policy decisions and actions in order to avoid misunderstanding and misinterpretation.*

---

* J. CAMERON THOMSON—The Federal Reserve should accept as a primary responsibility improving information as to the causes of cyclical recessions and communicate such information to government officials and the private economy so that these may share the responsibility for reducing number and extent of cyclical recessions. The Federal Reserve should also give their analysis of the economy actions taken by them to offset adverse trends during cyclical recessions and the reasons for such actions so that citizens may be better able to appraise the results and value of money and credit policies in maintaining economic stability. Such understanding is necessary as a protection to the Board in meeting its responsibilities."

Mr. LUBIN wishes to be associated with Mr. THOMSON'S comment.

CHAPTER FOUR

T H E
P U B L I C
D E B T

The problems of the public debt and its management are closely linked to those of monetary policy. Both monetary policy and debt management policy affect economic activity by altering the liquidity of the economy and the level and structure of interest rates. The discussion begins with some pertinent facts about the public debt.

The direct and fully guaranteed debt of the federal government as of June 30, 1960, the end of the fiscal year 1960, was $286.5 billion (Table 1). More than nine-tenths of this debt arose from deficit financing in World Wars I and II and the Korean conflict, while most of the remainder was created in the thirties. Although the debt is at a peak, it has grown very slowly relative to all other debt in the postwar years. In consequence, the federal debt now comprises less than a third of all public and private debt in the United States, compared with nearly three-fifths in 1946.

There is no one statistic that measures unambiguously the size of the federal indebtedness. The figures on the federal debt may be reported gross or net of claims between agencies of the federal government itself. Alternatively the report can be the debt gross or net of contingencies and guarantees. One can also report the federal debt gross or net of financial claims by the federal government on other sectors of the economy, since the government holds financial assets, such as mortgages, which constitute liabilities of other sectors to the government.

The data in Table 1 exclude the contingent liabilities of the federal government, a huge sum whose size would vary depending on how one measures these contingent obligations. Some would include the obligations of federally sponsored agencies, the contingent claims arising from

Table 1

COMPOSITION OF THE DIRECT AND GUARANTEED DEBT
OF THE FEDERAL GOVERNMENT, JUNE 30, 1960

(par values; billions of dollars)

Type of Debt	Held by Government a	Privately Held	Total
Total debt	81.9 b	201.5 b	286.5
Issues available to public	37.0	201.5	238.5
Marketable c	34.4	149.6	184.0
Nonmarketable	2.6	51.9	54.5
Convertible bonds d	2.5	3.8	6.3
Savings bonds e	0.1	48.1	48.2
Special issues	44.9		44.9
Matured debt and debt bearing no interest			3.1

a Held in U.S. government investment accounts and by the Federal Reserve System.
b Excludes matured debt and debt bearing no interest.
c Includes Panama Canal bonds.
d Investment Series B bonds.
e Includes $.6 billion of other nonmarketable bonds.

SOURCE: *Treasury Bulletin,* September 1960.

the insurance or guarantee of private mortgage and other private debt, and the obligations of the social security system; others would go further and suggest that the contingent obligation of the federal government to support the insurance of deposits in commercial and savings banks and insured savings and loan associations should also be included.

Of the $286.5 billion total of direct and guaranteed federal debt outstanding at the end of June 1960, about $82 billion was held by U.S. government agencies and trust funds and the Federal Reserve banks; the remainder was held by the public, including financial institutions. It is this portion of the federal debt which is important to debt management policy because only changes in the composition of the publicly held debt have a direct effect on the liquidity of private investors. Of the debt held by the public, nearly three-fourths was in marketable form; the remainder was largely in nonmarketable issues redeemable on demand.

In 1946 federal debt was approximately 58 percent of the total debt outstanding (Table 2). By the end of 1959 it accounted for 29 percent of the outstanding debt, compared with 9 percent in 1929. It should be evident that since World War II the federal debt has been contracting as a share of total debt outstanding because it has remained relatively constant while other sectors of the economy have been borrowing heavily. Since 1946, state and local debt increased nearly 4½ times, and private debt rose somewhat less than fourfold.

Table 2

NET PUBLIC AND PRIVATE DEBT IN RELATION TO GROSS NATIONAL PRODUCT,
DECEMBER 31, 1929, 1940, 1946, AND 1960

	1929	1940	1946	1960
		(billions of dollars)		
Gross national product	104.4	100.6	210.7	503.2
Total debt	190.9	189.9	397.4	882.9
Public debt	29.7	61.3	243.3	301.0
Federal a	16.5	44.8	229.7	241.0
State and local b	13.2	16.5	13.6	60.0
Private debt	161.2	128.6	154.1	581.9
Corporate	88.9	75.6	93.5	295.0
Other	72.3	53.0	60.6	286.9
		(as a percentage of GNP)		
Total debt	182.9	188.8	188.6	175.5
Public debt	28.4	60.9	115.5	59.8
Federal a	15.8	44.5	109.0	47.9
State and local	12.6	16.4	6.5	11.9
Private debt	154.4	127.8	73.1	115.6
Corporate	85.2	75.1	44.4	58.6
Other	69.3	52.7	28.8	57.0

Details may not add to totals because of rounding.

a Federal government securities including those held by the Federal Reserve System but excluding those held by federal agencies and trust funds; and the guaranteed and nonguaranteed securities of federal government agencies excluding those held by the Treasury and other federal agencies.

b As of June 30.

SOURCE: *Survey of Current Business,* July 1960, and May 1961.

Economic Effects of the Debt

The size of the debt has long been a major issue of public policy because it has been considered a burden for present and future generations. Before discussing debt management—the control over the composition of the publicly held debt outstanding—some of the basic issues of the economics of the debt are considered. This discussion is in two stages: first on the assumption of no change in the size of the debt and second on the economic effects of changes in the amount of outstanding debt.

What are the implications of the existence of a given federal debt? Interest must be paid. To pay the interest, taxes must be collected. During the fiscal year 1960, these payments amounted to about $9 billion, about a ninth of total federal budget expenditures of $77 billion. Expenditures for interest payments, to be sure, do not transfer an equivalent amount of resources from private to public uses; they represent a transfer of funds from taxpayers to bond holders. But all taxpayers are not recipients of interest. Consequently, there does occur some redistribution of income from taxpayers to debt holders. It is frequently assumed that this redistribution is strongly in favor of the upper income groups to the detriment of the lower income groups. In fact, the debt has come to be fairly widely held, and the federal tax structure is fairly progressive. Consequently the transfer of income from taxpayers to debt holders resulting from interest payments appears to have no significant effect on the distribution of income by income group.

Nevertheless, taxes must be levied to pay the interest charges, and taxes may affect adversely the incentives of taxpayers, thereby discouraging production. This effect cannot be measured, but if it exists, the debt may impose a burden because production is lower than it would be if no interest had to be paid, and therefore taxes could be lower.[1]

The relation of interest payments to gross national product is one measure of the economy's capacity to pay taxes. The present ratio is relatively low. Interest charges on the public debt rose from 1.0 percent of GNP in 1939 to 2.3 percent in 1946 and then declined to 1.8 percent in 1960. Since World War II, the rise in interest payments has been more than offset by the rise in the money value of the GNP. To the extent that this rise in value was due to inflation, the resulting easing of the debt burden was at the cost of the lenders and must be distinguished from the desirable easing of the debt burden which results from a growth in real output. If the economy grows and if the dollar amount of interest payments remains constant, the ratio of interest payment on the debt to GNP will decline. And the higher the rate of growth, the greater will be the decline in this ratio. While it is true that the need to finance interest payments pre-empts our ability to raise taxes for other purposes, the financing of current interest payments does not pose a serious problem in a growing economy.

The debt may also be considered a burden if it reduces the effectiveness of monetary policy. This may occur if the monetary authorities find it necessary to modify a policy of restraint in order to assist the Treasury in a refunding operation. Or it may occur if the Treasury allows the debt structure to shorten continuously when a policy of restraint would be appropriate. In such circumstances the monetary authorities are confronted with excessive liquidity in the economy, which reduces the effectiveness of monetary restraint. However, the debt may be managed to

---

[1] The alternative to debt financing would be either to continue the federal expenditure and finance it by taxation in which case tax rates must be raised, or to eliminate the expenditure and the need to finance it by borrowing, thereby removing the need to finance interest payments on the debt. Both of these could adversely affect total output.

assist monetary policy. A widely held public debt may increase the effectiveness of monetary policy by providing a better network for its swift transmission throughout the economy. The net effect of the existence of a public debt on the effectiveness of monetary policy depends on how stabilization instruments are used.

On balance, the existence of the public debt contains some features which are burdensome and some which are helpful. But even if the existing debt is held to impose a net burden on the economy, one cannot conclude that it should be reduced without fully accounting for the effects of such reduction on current economic conditions. This leads to consideration of the question, under what conditions are *changes* in the size of the debt harmful or beneficial?

The public debt must be viewed as a part of the total financial structure of the economy. As economic activity expands and private capital formation takes place, savers acquire title to this newly acquired wealth; thus their holdings of private debt or private equity increase. If private capital formation fails to absorb the flow of potential saving generated by a high-employment, high-level-of-income economy, then economic activity will decline. To prevent the latter, some offset to saving (budget deficit) on the part of the government will be necessary. Thus, increases in government debt will be needed to ensure that the saving is returned to the income stream. Conversely, if potential private capital formation exceeds the supply of private saving at high levels of economic activity, some public saving (budget surplus) and government debt reduction will be called for to check inflationary pressures and to facilitate the growth in private capital formation.

For these reasons, budget policy should be countercyclical, moving toward a deficit during periods of potential unemployment and a surplus during periods of potential inflation. The level of a budget deficit or surplus—and hence the resulting changes in the level of the debt—called for by a stabilizing budget policy depend not only on prevailing economic conditions but also on the effects of other policies. If a policy of budget surplus combined with tight credit would lower total demand too much, a budget surplus combined with easier credit conditions might be appropriate. Similarly, if saving is not being readily invested and a budget deficit is needed to maintain an adequate level of demand, the required deficit may be less if taxes bear more heavily on saving than on consumption. Or the required deficit may be less if special incentives can induce more private investment on a sustainable basis. Thus a change in the size of the debt should be determined in the light of stabilization requirements.

An economic policy for growth, given ample investment demand, may make use of budget surplus and debt retirement to increase the supply of saving available for private capital formation. This procedure involves considerations of both monetary and fiscal policies. If monetary policy is relatively easy, maintaining an appropriate, noninflationary level of aggregate demand will call for a tighter budget policy—a larger surplus in prosperity and a smaller deficit in bad times. In order to further growth, this combination of policies may be desirable if it allocates more resources to private capital formation. In this sense, public debt reduction is a desirable part of economic policy for growth, provided that the combined effects of monetary and fiscal policies ensure low levels of unemployment and reasonable stability of the price level.

The Commission concludes that none of the difficulties posed by the existing debt are so great as to justify giving priority to a policy of debt reduction if such a policy would interfere with a stabilizing fiscal policy. A gradual reduction in the debt can be effective as a stimulant to sustainable economic growth, however, if combined with other measures which maintain low levels of unemployment and reasonable price stability. In short, the debt should be permitted to fluctuate in response to the policies required for economic stability and growth.*

Debt Management Policy

Management of the federal debt involving changes in its amount is exercised through two general types of debt operations. There are the decisions and operations regarding the timing and type of securities to be sold to finance budget deficits and to be retired from the proceeds of budget surpluses. These also include debt operations to effect a basic change in the Treasury's cash balance and to provide extra-budgetary

---

* CHARLES B. SHUMAN—I disagree very strongly with the casual treatment in this chapter, and especially in this paragraph, of the serious effects of the large public debt on efforts to maintain stable prices, a high level of employment, and satisfactory rates of growth. Interest costs on this debt add materially to the tax load of individuals and businesses. High taxes discourage risk investment and innovation, thus limiting growth and employment.

Granting that we may be able to carry the present debt without serious difficulty, it does not follow that there are no dangers in an ever-expanding public debt. Given the present tendency for the debt to grow in recessions, and the possibility that the international situation may some day lead to a real emergency, I believe we should follow a positive policy of gradually reducing the debt in prosperous periods.

Mr. FRED LAZARUS, JR. wishes to be associated with Mr. SHUMAN'S comment, and adds the following: The federal budget should include an item showing either a reduction or addition to the debt as part of governmental expenditure programs so that the matter of debt is debated by the Congress at each budgetary session.

financing for certain federal agencies. The economic effects of the expenditures and revenues on the flow of national income and expenditure are discussed primarily in Chapter Five, but additional economic effects stemming from changes in the structure of the debt are considered here.

Second, there are debt operations which arise from refinancing the debt. Refinancings occur frequently and account ordinarily for the bulk of all debt operations. Unlike budget deficits and surpluses, refinancings involve no change, except for short periods, in the size of the debt, although they may influence importantly the debt structure.

Debt management policy as discussed in this section is concerned largely with the structure or composition of the *publicly held* debt. This debt, which excludes Treasury securities held by the federal agencies and investment accounts and by the Federal Reserve banks, amounts to $202 billion. Since national stabilization policy is designed to influence the private sector of the economy, it is the management of this portion of the total public debt which affects business and consumer behavior and has a direct relevance for the attainment of our economic objectives.

VOLUNTARY VERSUS COMPULSORY HOLDING

The federal debt is now managed on the premise that the public must be induced to buy and hold Treasury securities by their attractiveness relative to opportunities to buy goods and services or competing investments. The terms of issue of the public debt, including interest rates, maturity, and other features, must be sufficiently attractive to persuade holders of public debt in the aggregate to refrain from acquiring private interest-bearing securities the proceeds of which are used to finance private expenditures or to limit their expenditures on goods and services.

Instead of offering this inducement, the government could create money to pay off its debt. This, however, would obviously be inflationary under conditions of high employment.

A quite different and highly controversial approach to debt management involves compulsory holding of federal debt. From the view of the Treasury, debt management would be easier if investors (individuals, businesses, commercial banks, or other financial institutions) were required to hold a minimum volume of Treasury securities. The interest cost of the debt would be reduced, and the ability of the Treasury to market the debt during periods of rising interest rates would be enhanced. With regard to interest costs, it is evident that compulsory holding is a means of funding the debt while avoiding the interest cost which would be required if this were done on a voluntary basis. If the interest cost of a voluntary debt funding policy is held unacceptable, required holding may be the only way of avoiding debt shortening or monetization. Such a requirement might be limited to certain types of investors and might stipulate minimum holdings. Though not applied to all investors, such controls could still restrict liquidity, in the same way though not necessarily in the same degree, as lengthening the debt would in a voluntary market.

Compulsory holding of Treasury securities—under the title of security reserve requirements—also has been supported as a device for increasing the effectiveness of monetary policy. The objective is to immobilize Treasury securities in the portfolios of owners and thereby to prevent their sale in periods of economic expansion. The purchases at that time frequently are financed from idle cash balances and contribute to a rise in the income velocity of money, which in turn counters a monetary policy of restraint. Compulsory holding could be made to apply to all debt holders, including individuals and nonfinancial corporations. These latter groups hold perhaps two-fifths of the marketable debt, and studies indicate that these groups are responsible for much of the shifts into and out of Treasury securities in response to changing interest rates on those securities and other financial assets. While it should not be difficult to administer controls over financial institutions' holdings of government debt, it would not be easy to exercise such controls over individuals and nonfinancial corporations.

Regardless of their specific form, these special reserve proposals have a common feature. They all provide strong inducements or requirements to lend to the government. If the requirements are effective, therefore, some investors hold a greater volume of Treasury securities than they would otherwise hold at prevailing interest rates on these securities. Such a program involves the insulation of Treasury securities from market forces in the sense that it supplies a built-in demand for them and thereby protects them from the usual competitive pressures of other capital market demands. Security reserve requirements have been defended on the basis that they might contribute to a lower interest cost in servicing the debt.

To the extent that such requirements provide a demand for Treasury securities at lower interest rates, some interest savings will be effected. This saving, however, must be set against the increased cost of private debt that will result as private debt is displaced through compulsory holding of public debt by financial institutions.

The Commission concludes that the advantages of compulsory holdings of debt are not sufficient to offset the disadvantages that may result from complicating the reasonably smooth operations of the money and capital market in response to free choices by investors.* The Treasury

---

* ROBERT R. NATHAN—With the increasing institutionalization of savings and the corresponding increase in the investment role of financial managers of large accumulations of savings, serious consideration should be given to some compulsory holdings of Treasury securities. The institutions which might be subjected to such

should continue to induce purchases of its securities on the basis of their attractiveness relative to competing uses of funds.*

THE MATURITY STRUCTURE

The marketable debt in the hands of the public at the end of the fiscal year 1960 was $150 billion, approximately three-quarters of the total publicly held federal debt. With the passage of time and the quite limited issuance of long-term securities, the maturity of this debt has shortened substantially during the postwar years. The average maturity decreased by more than half between 1946 and 1960, and the marketable debt maturing within one year increased from 33 to 38 percent. Debt maturing in one to five years increased as a share of the total from 13 to nearly 40 percent. Debt maturing beyond five years fell from 54 to 22 percent. Unless maturing issues are replaced by longer-term issues, or unless advance refunding into longer maturities is employed, this process will continue. The Commission believes the shortening of the debt should be arrested for various reasons.

Further shortening of the debt results in increased liquidity. To be sure, no investor can turn his securities into cash, irrespective of whether they are short-term or long-term issues, unless someone else wishes to surrender cash; and the Treasury can always replace maturing issues with new long-term issues if it meets the terms of the market. This suggests that the *basic* difference in liquidity is between debt instruments and money and not between debt instruments of differing maturity. However, short-term issues can be more readily converted into cash than long-term issues because they mature sooner and can be sold more readily at less risk of capital loss. Because of these features, a large volume of

---

requirements and the amounts or proportions to be held would have to be given careful study. It might be desirable to attach a price escalation provision to special securities issued for such compulsory holdings.

Mr. RUTTENBERG wishes to be associated with Mr. NATHAN'S comment.

* CHARLES B. SHUMAN—A far more serious objection is that insulating Treasury securities from the market would make it easier for the government to follow inflationary policies. At the same time artificially depressed interest rates on federal borrowings would stimulate demands for the federal government to supply an ever-increasing proportion of the economy's capital needs.

Compulsory holding of the public debt at an arbitrary interest rate is in effect a partial confiscation of the savings of individuals. If this policy were adopted, there would be no good reason for paying any interest on the forced holdings. I object to the extensive discussion of this completely unacceptable idea.

THEODORE O. YNTEMA—Compulsory holding of public debt is a form of taxation. Such taxation could not be based on any rational criterion of equity. It would be capricious and unfair in its incidence. In addition to the reasons advanced in the Report, compulsory holding of the debt is objectionable on grounds of gross inequity.

Messrs. SCHWULST and SHUMAN wish to be associated with Mr. YNTEMA'S comment.

short-term debt facilitates the activation of cash balances at times when restrictive monetary policy is employed.

As against this reasoning, it has been argued that the increased liquidity of a shorter maturity structure of the marketable debt may always be offset by a reduction in the money supply and that this action may be desirable in that it reduces the cost of the public debt. This argument may have merit when looked at from the point of view of the supply of financial claims, including money and all other debt instruments, in any given situation. However, the stabilizing or destabilizing effect with which a given financial structure responds to changing economic conditions must also be considered. The potential built-in instability introduced by the existence of an excessive volume of short-term debt is the more troublesome because this debt tends to be held precisely by that group of investors who are sensitive to interest rate changes in the financial market. By having so heavy a proportion of short-term debt instruments in our financial structure, we may already have gone too far in this direction. We should try to avoid aggravating the problem further.

The Commission concludes that sound debt management requires that we arrest the shortening of the outstanding publicly held marketable debt which has occurred since the end of World War II. The Treasury should pursue a program which, over a period of time, would lead to a more balanced maturity structure for the debt.

COUNTERCYCLICAL DEBT MANAGEMENT

Before considering the timing and speed with which the new debt structure should be approached, the role of debt management as a stabilization tool is discussed. This shifts attention from the built-in stability or instability of a given debt structure to the more immediate economic effects of policies to change this structure.

Countercyclical debt management would entail lengthening the debt structure during a boom because this tends to be restrictive, and shortening the debt structure during a recession because this tends to be expansionary. In booms, the budget surplus should be used to retire short-term debt, and new borrowing in recessions should be short term.

Opponents of countercyclical debt management hold that such a policy raises the interest costs of the debt and that these increases are substantial. It requires the Treasury to borrow long at precisely the time when long-term rates are high. It precludes a policy of borrowing long in a recession when interest rates are lower. Whatever choice is made, however, a difficult forecasting problem is involved. For example, at the time of refinancing, long-term rates may be lower than short-term rates. But soon thereafter short rates may fall. In this situation minimization over a period of time would call for current financing at the higher short rates than at the lower long rates. Another objection of the opponents of countercyclical debt management is that its stabilizing effects are so slight that little stabilization is gained, and that the destabilization effects of the interest minimization are also so slight that little is lost.

The economic effects of a countercyclical policy and the process by which these effects are brought about are best illustrated by examining the refunding of short-term securities into long-term securities during a period of prosperity.

The initial impact of issuing long-term Treasury bonds is in the capital markets. Here the debt management operation affects both interest rates and capital values by creating uncertainties in investor expectations as well as by changing the supply of various types of securities. Both the level and structure of interest rates may be influenced, although the more lasting effect is on the structure of rates. A reduction in the supply of short-term securities and an increase in the supply of long-term securities would tend to lower short-term interest rates and raise long-term rates.

The rise in long rates reduces the value of long-term private and Treasury debt and one part of the economy's assets. The holders of long-term assets, particularly debt securities, are especially affected. Those assets have become more concentrated in recent years in the portfolios of institutional long-term investors. Individuals also hold these assets, although they are not spread equally among income groups. Evidence suggests that the effect of lower capital values in expansion periods is to restrain lending and money expenditures.

This same operation has special significance, whether or not it reduces money expenditures directly, because it reallocates funds away from private and state and local long-term investments into Treasury securities. Long-term lenders in prosperity usually devote the bulk of their investable funds to the purchase of mortgages, corporate bonds, and state and local government securities. Funds drawn into Treasury bonds will be diverted from these sectors. Even if total money expenditures are not reduced at once, the momentum of expansion may be restrained. The potential economic consequences involved may be significant. The Treasury, in recent years, has often expressed concern about these effects.

The fall in short rates will raise the value of short-term debt. However, the rise in the value of short-term debt will be less marked than the fall in the value of long-term debt. Inventory investment, which typically relies on short-term financing, is dominated by factors other than *small* declines in short-term rates. Capital outlays which draw on long-term financing will be more sensitive to the increased costs and reduced availability of long-term funds. On balance, the effect of lengthening the structure of the debt is likely to be restrictive. Similar considerations, though in reverse, would apply to the effects of shortening the maturity of the debt in recessions.

The Commission concludes that countercyclical debt management can make some contribution to stabilization. It may also tend to affect interest costs. At the same time, it is important to point out that if the Treasury fails to issue long-term securities in the upswing, it must issue them in the downswing so long as it desires to prevent a secular shortening of the debt. Failure to use a countercyclical policy, therefore, not only involves the risk of losing a possibly helpful tool of restriction in the upswing; it also involves the risk of using a potentially harmful destabilizer in a recession.

The Commission concludes that once the shortening of the debt structure is arrested, management of the marketable debt can and should make some contribution to stabilizing the level of economic activity. However, the primary responsibility for achieving this objective must be borne by monetary and fiscal policy.*

TRANSITIONAL PROBLEMS

When should the transition to a better balanced debt structure be made? This will require a substantial flotation of long-term securities which will tend to have a restrictive effect. The over-all mix of stabilization measures must be adjusted therefore to provide an offset in a period of recession. That is, monetary policy must be easier and the budget surplus less large or the deficit larger if longer securities are issued than would be needed otherwise.

It is the Commission's view that the transition to a more balanced debt structure may be made more safely when general economic conditions are such that restrictive action is needed on balance.

---

* STANLEY H. RUTTENBERG—I cannot concur in the recommendation that debt management be used countercyclically. I feel that the need to minimize the cost of managing the federal debt must have top priority.

The contribution made by countercyclical debt management will be considerably less than the effect it will have on rising interest rate costs. My position is stated in the third paragraph of this section, where the Report sets forth the arguments of the opponents of countercyclical debt management. The advantages derived from the use of countercyclical debt management are not, in my judgment, outweighed by the increased cost to the federal government.

The appropriate tools for stabilization are fiscal, including tax expenditures, and monetary policies and should not include debt management.

ECONOMIC GROWTH

The preceding discussion of debt management was concerned with cyclical aspects. The growth aspects of debt management are also important.

In planning the debt structure so as to adapt it to the preferences of lenders, their future as well as their present needs are of concern. Economic growth creates demands for increased stocks of financial assets as well as for changes in the composition of these assets. Thus the Treasury should shape its debt management activities in such a way as to alter the portion of its debt which is in the form of short-term, intermediate-term, long-term securities, and savings bonds in response to prospective demands for these securities. As the economy grows there will be an increased demand for liquid assets including Treasury bills. In particular, the Treasury needs to take this demand into account and work in harmony with the monetary authority in the provision of money and short-term securities because to a degree, at least, one form is substitutable for the other.

There is another and less obvious relationship of debt management to economic growth. As explained before, the basic reason for not monetizing the public debt is that this would result in an excessive level of expenditures and inflation. To put it differently, the purpose of maintaining the debt in nonmonetary form is to hold down private expenditures. An economic policy for growth is not only concerned with the level, but also the composition, of expenditures. Once low-level unemployment is attained and maintained, increased growth is encouraged by allocating a larger share of resources to capital formation. The implication of this for debt management is that the debt structure should be designed to avoid heavy restraint on capital expenditures and to emphasize restraint on consumption expenditures. For this purpose, nonmarketable issues that are sufficiently attractive to divert additional funds from consumer spending should be preferred to long-term securities that would divert funds from private securities issued to finance capital outlays.

Lengthening the debt structure introduces rigidity into the management of the debt; this may prove undesirable if underlying conditions change. This disadvantage of rigidity in the debt structure may be overcome by using call provisions in long-term government debt instruments.*

---

* STANLEY H. RUTTENBERG—I regret to see that the reference to the use of call provisions in long-term debt instruments is not made as a positive recommendation. This is an important technique for the debt managers to have at their disposal and should be in the form of a recommendation instead of a comment.

Mr. LUBIN wishes to be associated with Mr. RUTTENBERG'S comment.

THE NONMARKETABLE DEBT

At the close of the fiscal year 1960, $52 billion, or a fourth of the publicly held debt, was nonmarketable, consisting of $48 billion in savings bonds, $4 billion in investment series bonds, and a small amount of depository bonds. In recent years the nonmarketable sector of the debt has diminished in size. The flexible use of monetary policy in the last decade has posed problems in adjusting the nonmarketable debt to fluctuating interest rates, and, in consequence, some types of these securities have been cashed in at maturity and not replaced.

Among the many public debt instruments, however, there should continue to be one appropriate to small savers. These investors lack the sophistication required for dealing in the security market and desire an investment not subject to fluctuation in market value. The terms of the savings bonds are simple and can easily be fitted into a regular savings program.

Moreover, by fitting its offerings to the requirements of the investor the Treasury may be able to secure the basic objectives of debt management at lower cost. Savings bonds are redeemable at fixed prices, but many holders do not readily consider their holdings as equivalent to cash. The arrangement by which yields increase with the length of the holding period encourages retention and strengthens saving habits.

To promote the sale of savings bonds the Treasury may have to increase the rate of interest which it pays to savings bond holders. Yields must continue to be made competitive. However, the Commission is opposed to the introduction of constant-purchasing-power savings bonds as a means of encouraging the sale of savings bonds.*

The Commission recommends that the Treasury take measures to expand the proportion of the public debt in the form of savings bonds on terms which are competitive with yields of suitable alternative forms of investment for small savers.

Organization for Policy

There are compelling reasons why monetary policy and debt management must be formulated and executed in close relationship. Although

---

* STANLEY H. RUTTENBERG—I regret that the Commission sees fit to oppose even the experimental introduction of the idea of constant purchasing power bonds. Certainly the sale of savings bonds could be significantly improved if the saver were assured of some security. These bonds being nonnegotiable place them in a different category than the other negotiable securities issued by the Treasury.

these policies are in the charge of different authorities, there is great similarity in the impact which they have on the economy and in the processes by which the effects are reached. Monetary policy and debt management both influence the level and structure of interest rates, the availability of loanable funds, and, through liquidity and asset changes, the velocity of money. Both open market operations and debt management can influence directly the maturity structure of the publicly held federal debt. This does not mean that the economic powers and effects of each agency are identical—they are not—but it does mean that a close relationship between debt management and monetary policies is essential in reaching our economic objectives.

In addition, there are potential points of conflict between the Treasury and the Federal Reserve which, without continued close cooperation, can easily cause difficulty. The Treasury's debt management can interfere with an appropriate monetary policy if by increasing the frequency and volume of refinancings it reduces the time for maneuver by the Federal Reserve. Also there may be some interference with monetary policy if the Federal Reserve finds it necessary to provide direct support to a refinancing. Similarly, Federal Reserve policy may interfere with debt management by its influence on the Treasury securities market.

Clearly there is need for close working relationships between these two agencies, and for a means of resolving policy differences when they arise. One structural approach to this end would confer on the Treasury greater powers over the formulation, and perhaps the execution, of monetary policy—in effect, a reversion to something like the arrangement before the Banking Act of 1935, when the Secretary of the Treasury was an *ex officio* member of the Federal Reserve Board. But against such a solution it can be persuasively argued that the decision in 1935 in this respect is politically irreversible and correct on larger grounds of public policy. As the largest single borrower in the capital market the Treasury has too strong and direct an immediate interest in minimizing the cost of public borrowing to allow it a deciding voice in all policy disputes over debt management and monetary policy. A close relationship should not imply Treasury dominance.

In the opposite direction, the suggestion has been more frequently advanced in recent years that the necessary intimacy should be legitimized by a marriage that would in effect transfer public debt operations from the Treasury to the Federal Reserve: let the Federal Reserve buy all new Treasury issues directly and in full and then distribute them to the market as it thinks economic conditions dictate. Such an arrangement would centralize in the Federal Reserve the control of at least the maturity structure, if not the coupon and other terms of the publicly held debt, though it would not avoid the need for offsetting operations to compensate for net fluctuations in Treasury borrowing or debt retirement. But unless the Federal Reserve adopted the Treasury's auction methods in place of its own day-to-day sales to and purchases from dealers, the change might seriously disturb the dealer market in long-term Treasury securities. For the knowledge that the Federal Reserve held a large block of long-terms awaiting distribution would have a depressing effect on prices and future commitments.

A more serious obstacle is the political unreality of the supposition that either the President or his Secretary of the Treasury would acquiesce in such a transfer of the borrowing power of the government—for that is what is basically at stake—to an independent agency, outside of administration control. If the Treasury is not to be permitted to dictate the terms of its borrowings, neither should it be deprived of its responsibilities and opportunities for making the best terms it can get in bargaining with the market.

Accordingly, the Commission does not favor so drastic a method as consolidation of the Treasury and the Federal Reserve as a means of coordinating debt management and monetary policy.

The need for coordination remains, and by and large has been readily acknowledged in recent years; Treasury and Federal Reserve officials recognize their complementary relationships and are not likely to fail in cooperation by accident. They know well enough how to work together when they are in agreement on objectives. The recent apparent abandonment of the Federal Reserve's bills-only policy extends the potential range of constructive collaboration. The problem is not the technical one of properly meshing an intricate set of interlocking administrative gears; rather it is the policy problem of making sure that the motivating forces in the two institutions are both driving in the same direction. There have been occasions, which may recur, of serious conflict between the Treasury and the Federal Reserve. When they occur, and especially when they do not yield to the influences of direct interagency negotiations, the important thing is that they be identified promptly and be brought to the President's attention. In the previous chapter a realignment of the Federal Reserve Board Chairman's relationship to the President was proposed, and in Chapter Ten improvements are suggested in the staff and advisory council methods of presidential coordination of economic policy. The Commission believes that Treasury–Federal Reserve disagreements, if any, should be resolved in the framework of these suggested arrangements.

The Commission has recommended that the Treasury give prompt attention to achieving a more balanced maturity distribution of the debt. It recommends further that this policy should be adopted at a time when underlying economic conditions call for a policy of restriction. It has also recommended that the Treasury undertake a countercyclical debt management policy once it has achieved a better maturity distribution of the debt. Since the Treasury is unlikely to pursue such a stabilizing policy on a continuous basis, it would be desirable for the Federal Reserve to conduct its open market operations on a more flexible basis throughout the maturity structure. These considerations lead to the conclusion that the Federal Reserve's apparent abandonment of its bills-only policy should be viewed as being in the interest of better coordination of monetary and debt management policy.*

The Congress is the final authority in matters concerning the public debt. Before World War I, Congress normally enacted new legislation setting forth the precise terms of the financing each time the Treasury needed to borrow money. But congressional determination of maturities and interest rates introduced rigidities that often proved costly because of swiftly changing business and capital market conditions. During and after World War I the Congress gradually expanded the authority of the Treasury to exercise discretion in the debt management area. Today the President and the Secretary of the Treasury enjoy a considerable degree of latitude in managing the debt. But there are still several serious obstacles to a desirable degree of flexibility.

There is, first of all, the limit on the public debt. On February 19, 1941, Congress combined its authorization for each type of security into a total debt figure. With this legislation, Congress introduced the present form of the federal debt ceiling. The debt limit had little effect until 1953. Since then, however, the federal debt has often bumped against the ceiling, and this has been a source of inflexibility and inefficiency in the management of the public finances.

The debt ceiling has been defended as a means of inducing fiscal responsibility. The ceiling has, on the contrary, served as a stimulus and a sanction for devious budgetary practices. These have included financing at higher interest cost through the Commodity Credit Corporation and the Federal National Mortgage Association and monetizing a portion of the small remaining balance of gold against which no certificates have been issued. Moreover, the debt ceiling on one occasion is reputed to have resulted in delaying payments of its bills by the government with the unfortunate consequence of destabilizing economic activity.

The debt ceiling has also been defended as a curb on federal spending. Within limits, the executive can slow the pace of federal outlays. On the other hand, the Treasury must eventually find the funds necessary to finance whatever Congress appropriates. If the ceiling prevents additional

---

* STANLEY H. RUTTENBERG—See my comment in Chapter Three, page 64.

borrowing, the Treasury must obtain funds indirectly through another federal agency rather than by marketing its own obligations. The result is added and unnecessary interest costs, because federal agency issues can be sold only at higher interest rates than those on direct obligations of the Treasury. Thus, as an expenditure control, the debt ceiling may be self-defeating.

Not only has the debt ceiling failed to promote fiscal responsibility and to control expenditures, but also it has restricted the Treasury's freedom in managing the debt. In 1957 and 1958, for example, the excess of the ceiling over the outstanding debt shrank to $0.8 billion and $1.8 billion, respectively. This was seriously below the margin considered necessary to permit the Treasury to maintain flexibility in its financing. If the cash balance is driven too low, the Treasury cannot vary the timing of its financing operations to take advantage of favorable market conditions. Moreover, some leeway is needed to take care of the sometimes volatile and unpredictable needs for cash from various government agencies such as the Commodity Credit Corporation, the Federal National Mortgage Association, and the Export–Import Bank.

The debt ceiling also hampers the ability of the Treasury to finance through "tap" issues, such as savings bonds. Because these issues are continuously on sale, the Treasury must resort to their use with caution for fear of unwittingly breaching the debt limit. Similarly the debt ceiling restricts the ability of the Treasury to carry out other debt operations. For example, the Treasury might wish to sell long-term bonds and accumulate cash balances as an anti-inflationary measure.

Another rigidity imposed by the Congress is the interest rate ceiling on bonds, established in 1918. The $4\frac{1}{4}$ percent ceiling applies to all new issues of Treasury bonds but does not apply to notes, certificates, or bills. Because only bonds may carry maturities equal to or in excess of five years, the ceiling affects only those security issues of five years or greater maturity. During the twenties when the debt was being reduced in size, and during the easy money periods of the thirties and World War II, the ceiling was ineffective. But recently, market yields on outstanding long-term Treasury securities rose above the $4\frac{1}{4}$ percent level.

The objective of the interest rate ceiling is to hold down the interest cost of the federal debt. But the ceiling may fail to achieve this goal. When the demand for capital has been strong, there have been occasions when long-term yields have been less than those on obligations with a four-to-five-year maturity. To avoid breaching the interest rate ceiling for longer-term bonds, and at the same time to avoid further shortening in the debt, the Treasury has found it necessary on a few occasions in the late fifties to refinance the debt at the higher interest rate permitted on securities with maturities of four but not five years. The Treasury could doubtless have sold some long-term issues at a lower interest cost if it had been permitted to offer these issues at a rate somewhat in excess of the 4¼ percent ceiling.[2]

On a few occasions in the late fifties the interest rate ceiling has also interfered with arresting the shortening in the maturity structure of the debt. It has sometimes precluded the use of advanced refunding techniques to lengthen the debt, and it has in the recent past prevented the issuance of long-term debt as a part of a program of countercyclical financing. But in much of the postwar period when the interest ceiling did not prevent issuing long-term securities, the average maturity of the debt also declined.

Congressional action in other areas has also intensified the difficulty of managing the debt. The market for Treasury issues has become increasingly competitive since World War II. In part, this reflects the improved quality of competing investments. Federal programs to stimulate home building have led to the growth in the supply of FHA and VA mortgages, and their federal guarantees and amortization features make them close competitors of Treasury obligations for some institutional funds. Federal insurance of bank deposits and savings and loan shares has increased their attractiveness relative to Treasury securities in the eyes of individual investors. The amelioration of the business cycle through built-in stabilizers and a more cyclically sensitive monetary and fiscal policy has contributed to the competitive improvement of corporate obligations by reducing the risk of business failures due to depression.

The desirability of these various guarantee and insurance programs or of the federal government's efforts to smooth out business activity is not questioned. The Commission wishes only to emphasize the competitive pressures to which the Treasury is now subject and the need for wide administrative discretion in meeting them.

The succeeding section discusses the possible advantages to the Treasury of seeking a periodic spacing of the debt. One of the objectives of this proposal is to increase the size of individual issues. To accomplish this objective will require reopenings of an issue. Such reopenings would involve offering the same security at a discount if current rates of interest are higher than they were when the security was originally issued, or at a premium if current rates are lower. Present tax laws, however, inhibit the reoffering of securities if the discount exceeds ¼ of 1 percent for each year of the life of the bond. At present the appreciation on such securities at maturity is not eligible for capital gains rates, while the appreciation on their outstanding counterparts is. The tax status of reopenings

---

[2] At the end of April 1961, the Treasury announced an interpretation by the Attorney General to the effect that the sale at a discount of a new issue of Treasury bonds carrying a coupon rate at the statutory interest rate ceiling would be permissible—that is, the yield on the security could exceed the 4¼ percent ceiling.

should be placed on the same basis as that of outstanding securities. Such a tax reform would involve a negligible loss of revenue, and it would facilitate Treasury attempts to achieve a better distribution of the debt.

The Commission favors broadening the range of discretionary debt management authority exercised by the executive branch of the federal government. Specifically, it recommends the abolition of the debt limit, the elimination of the interest rate ceiling, and the same tax treatment for reofferings as for outstanding securities.*

Debt Management Techniques

The techniques used to manage the debt may be important in determining the success of the Treasury in competing for funds in the capital market.

In arresting further shortening of the debt the maturity distribution should meet two requirements. The Treasury should, insofar as practicable, issue the variety of securities necessary to cater to the tastes and preferences of all potential purchasers of federal government debt. This would include issuance of securities in all broad maturity classes. By doing so the objective of a stabilizing debt management policy may be met at lower interest cost. At the same time, there may be an advantage in a fairly homogeneous debt involving fewer issues of varying maturities, each sufficiently large to encourage wide and more active trading in the secondary market.

Regularization of Treasury offerings would reduce the difficulty of refunding operations occurring at erratic intervals. It would broaden the interest in Treasury securities by encouraging the periodic allocation of funds for new Treasury issues by both individuals and institutional investors and by reducing uncertainty about the timing and maturity of new issues. Investors would also benefit from greater advance

---

* STANLEY H. RUTTENBERG—I concur in the recommendation that the debt limit be abolished and that the same tax treatment for re-offerings as for outstanding securities be adopted by the Congress. However, I cannot concur in the recommendation to eliminate the interest rate ceiling on long-term securities.

If I were convinced that the Treasury would proceed on the assumption of minimizing the cost of the debt to the federal government (which they cannot do if they follow a countercyclical debt management policy) and if I were convinced that the Treasury would actively engage in using auction techniques, advanced refundings, and call provisions in long-term bonds, I would be less inclined to oppose the elimination of interest rate ceilings. However, because the Commission strongly recommends the use of countercyclical debt management and only gingerly calls upon the Treasury to use call provisions and just urges further experimentation with advance refunding and auction techniques, I cannot concur in the recommendation to eliminate interest rate ceilings.

knowledge of Treasury financing plans which would permit more efficient portfolio planning. In addition, issuers of private long-term securities would be better able to arrange their financing so as to avoid conflict with Treasury offerings. The Federal Reserve would benefit because its policy would be less interrupted by refunding operations, and a well-spaced debt in the hands of the public would provide a more effective conduit for the communication of monetary policy to all sectors of the capital market.

An important reason for market resistance to new long-term issues is that they are typically offered in exchange for maturing issues often held by short-term investors. The advance refunding technique, by which holders are offered an opportunity to exchange present holdings for securities with a comparable maturity as their original issue, would increase the average maturity of the outstanding debt. More holders of the outstanding long-term securities would be interested in the new issues. In addition to encouraging a more favorable response, there would be less market "churning." But it would have less restrictive effects than refinancing short-term by long-term issues.

The Commission recommends that the Treasury continue to experiment with the use of the advanced refunding technique.

The Treasury also is making wider use of the auction method, formerly restricted to offerings of 90-day bills. Greater use of this technique would place greater reliance upon the market and relieve the Treasury of responsibility for a wide range of pricing decisions. This in turn would diminish confusion and avoid misplaced criticism to the effect that the Treasury, rather than the market, determines the level of interest rates.

The present auction procedure involves the payment of different prices by different purchasers. The bidder pays his bid price even though it is higher than the lowest price accepted. Another procedure would permit each investor to receive at the price set by the auction that amount of securities for which he expressed a willingness to pay a price equal to or greater than the stop-out price—the lowest accepted bid or the price necessary to sell the entire issue.

There are differences of opinion among experts about the consequences of these alternative procedures. Supporters of the present practice argue that the Treasury benefits because each issue is sold at a price above the stop-out price. And, it is argued, the present procedure works well. Others argue that it may tend to limit the market to specialists, because someone out of touch with market conditions may have to bid unnecessarily high for fear of losing out or may choose not to bid at all. More important, even for the specialists, uncertainty of market conditions causes them to be concerned about bidding too high since they may have difficulties in selling securities in the secondary market. Under such circumstances they tend to underbid rather than overbid with the result that the costs to the Treasury are increased. The risks become much greater, the longer the maturity of the issue.

Proponents of the alternative procedure mentioned above argue that if the securities were issued at the stop-out price for all, uncertainty for both dealers and others would be reduced. Hence bidders would be brought into the market who might otherwise remain out. In addition, small investors might be further encouraged if their non-competitive bids for limited amounts were awarded at the stop-out price rather than at the average price as at present. Others argue that this procedure would result in a higher interest cost to the Treasury.

The Commission has not investigated in detail these alternative techniques and takes no position in regard to this controversy.

Although the auction technique reduces the Treasury's control over allotments, less reliance upon administrative pricing is desirable. The Commission recommends, therefore, that the Treasury should continue to experiment further with the use of the auction technique.

Each year the Treasury must refinance roughly $75 billion in maturing issues. Even though new issues replace old ones, a debt digestion problem may arise because the new securities are frequently taken by different investors from those who hold the old ones and because market reactions to short-run developments may suddenly dampen the reception of a new financing. In consequence, a large block of new securities may temporarily strain the market's capacity to absorb it. Under such circumstances an underwriting fund to help smooth temporary market fluctuations and to facilitate distribution—a commonly used technique in private financings—might perform a useful function for the Treasury.*

The Treasury Securities Market

MARGIN REQUIREMENTS

Concern with the rapid advance in interest rates and rising bond yields which occurred in the summer of 1958 has prompted the suggestion that regulation of margin requirements imposed for loans against Treasury securities as collateral be reviewed and strengthened.

The Treasury, in effect, already imposes margin requirements on new cash offerings by insisting that subscriptions be accompanied by a down

---

* CHARLES B. SHUMAN—I question the wisdom of a Treasury underwriting fund. Treasury financing is not comparable to private financing. There is danger that an underwriting fund would become a first step toward a program of pegging bond prices.

payment in cash. This is not true in the case of exchange offerings, although the Treasury might require certification that the subscriber has a minimum equity in the maturing securities he is presenting for exchange, or it might cease making exchange issues in favor of issues for cash.

For their own protection, lenders also usually require margins sufficient to assure the credit soundness of each individual loan with Treasury securities as collateral. These margins are normally related in a general way to the range of possible price decline. The New York Stock Exchange, for example, requires its member firms to obtain a margin of at least 5 percent of the principal amount of all Treasury securities financed for their customers. Exceptions to this rule are made by special permission, however, for short-dated instruments. The Comptroller of the Currency, in April 1960, also directed the national banks to require as a general rule a 5 percent margin on their loans against Treasury securities. National bank examiners are allowed some discretion in deciding when the 5 percent requirement should apply. Loans to dealers in Treasury securities are exempt from this ruling.

No such uniform minimum standards exist, however, for nonnational banks or brokers or dealers not members of the New York Stock Exchange, nonfinancial corporations, or other lenders.

High initial margin requirements might be employed to limit more effectively the amount of speculation and to provide high enough margins to ensure that a price decline would not immediately result in margin calls and forced liquidation. Such margin requirements might be administered by the Federal Reserve System along the lines of Regulations T and U.

Or, if it appears that speculation in new issues is in greatest need of regulation, the Treasury might require high cash deposits with subscriptions for cash offerings and evidence of a corresponding amount of equity in the rights to an exchange issue. New legislation would be unnecessary, and requirements could be changed by administrative action as market conditions warranted. However, such Treasury controls might be inadequate in effectively curbing speculation since they would not cover purchases in the secondary market.

The Treasury now has substantial power over new cash issues. Broad control over the secondary market by other agencies might discourage initial subscriptions to Treasury issues and increase the interest cost of floating new issues, especially in recessions. Moreover some liquidation of Treasury securities will accompany the troughs of future business cycles regardless of margin requirements. When the business outlook turns from one of pessimism to one of optimism, individual investors in Treasury securities tend to unload their positions and build up their holdings of equities.

Although the Commission does not favor broad authority over margins for the secondary market in Treasury securities along the lines of Regulations T and U as applied in the stock market, it does urge, however, that minimum margins, such as now set by the New York Stock Exchange and the Comptroller of the Currency, be applied by various supervisory authorities to presently nonregulated lenders, including nonfinancial corporations.*

THE TYPE OF MARKET

The Treasury securities market is organized presently in two different ways: one a formally organized market on the floor of the New York Stock Exchange, and the other, the more informal over-the-counter market.

The over-the-counter market handles the overwhelming volume of transactions today. Bonds are the only federal securities listed on the Exchange, and even these are traded almost wholly in the over-the-counter market. The large transactions in Treasury bills also have increased the relative importance of the over-the-counter market. By 1960, federal bond trading on the Exchange had shrunk to practically zero as compared with $2.9 billion in 1919.

The over-the-counter market essentially comprises 17 Treasury securities dealers, 5 banks, and 12 nonbank securities houses. Many of the latter maintain branch offices in leading cities, but their trading offices are located in New York City. Three of the bank dealers are in New York City; two are located in Chicago. Trading activities are conducted primarily by telephone.

The over-the-counter market in Treasury securities has been subjected to criticism on the ground that it is highly concentrated, that the market is not supervised by a public agency, and that there is little information available to the public about activity in the market. For example, in the dealer market, the prices at which Treasury securities are bought and sold are not revealed to the public. An organized exchange, by contrast, regularly supplies the public with detailed information regarding its transactions. Transactions in Treasury securities are exempt from regulation by the Securities and Exchange Commission, whereas members of

---

* STANLEY H. RUTTENBERG—I regret to see that the Commission has not recommended that margin requirements in the secondary securities market be applied in the Treasury securities market. If margins are proper for the New York Stock Exchange, then they are also proper in the Treasury securities market. This issue cannot be dismissed as easily as the Commission does. Stand-by authority to impose effective and flexible margins on the secondary securities market would be helpful in preventing speculation and manipulation.

Mr. LUBIN wishes to be associated with Mr. RUTTENBERG'S comment.

an organized stock exchange are not. Since dealers trade for their own account, there is a potential conflict of interest between the dealer and his customer. On the New York Stock Exchange, no member acting as a broker may do business with an account in which he has an interest. Dealer operations also may contribute to cyclical swings in securities prices. On the Exchange, members are prohibited from making successive purchases at rising prices or successive sales at falling prices for the purpose of improperly influencing the market.

However, the present dominant form of market organization grew out of the needs of market participants. Essentially, the dealers were able to attract the business away from the New York Stock Exchange because they were willing to handle large orders at a fixed price. This redounds to the advantage of the customer, since he is not forced to push the price up or down on the Exchange by an amount sufficient to generate investor interest on the opposite side of the market at the time of the sale. By acting as a principal the dealer thus prevents the price from fluctuating as it would if trading were confined to the market on the Exchange floor. The dealer risks his capital by taking a position, and the investor is satisfied immediately rather than having to wait while a broker finds a matching order.

Recent studies have shown that the present over-the-counter market made by the 17 dealers operates efficiently. Short- and intermediate-term securities turn over rapidly at narrow price spreads. Active competition prevails, and dealer trading profits per dollar of sales are small. Fewer dealers, however, operate in the long-term markets, and often they act more as brokers than as dealers. Even if the market were broad and active, price spreads would be wider in the long-term market than in the short-term market because of the greater inherent risks in trading in long-term securities. The size of orders which can be executed at quoted market prices is frequently relatively small, and price spreads are wider than in the short-term market. This basic characteristic, however, appears to be more the fault of the structure of the debt itself—the large numbers of issues of small size. In any event, it does not appear capable of correction by changing the nature of the market; hence the Commission makes no recommendations in regard to the market's structure.*

While there are relatively few dealers, they transact business mainly with large investors who are actively engaged in trading in a variety of

---

*STANLEY H. RUTTENBERG—I do not know what the right answer is, nor do I know how the securities market for Treasury issues should be organized, but I cannot accept the recommendation of the Commission that it has "no recommendations in regard to the market's structure." I think that the least the Commission could say, is that the problem of the operations of the Treasury securities market needs to be continually reviewed with the aim of developing some means to broaden the operations of the market to middle income investors.

issues both as buyers and as sellers. This in itself provides a measure of insurance that competition prevails and price spreads are relatively narrow. Entry into the Treasury securities market is open. Moreover, certain large investors who are not now dealers could potentially trade among themselves rather than through dealers if marked deficiencies developed in present dealer arrangements.

Dealers operate on exceedingly low margins of equity capital, and among the factors which determine their willingness to take a position is the cost and availability of borrowed funds. There are two principal sources of these borrowed funds. There are the New York money-market banks, from which the dealers borrow on the basis of call loans, using their Treasury securities as collateral. Numerous other institutions—nonfinancial corporations, commercial banks outside of New York City, the states and their political subdivisions, and foreign agency banks—also provide the dealers with funds. With these lenders, the dealers typically engage in repurchase agreements, selling the lender the securities to be financed while agreeing to repurchase them at a specified price and date in the future.

The New York money-market banks are looked upon in good part as residual lenders. When the money market is relatively easy, dealers can usually secure financing at favorable rates from a wide variety of potential lenders throughout the country. But even during these periods, there are both regular and erratic changes in the availability of these sources of finance. At these times dealers fall back on the usually more expensive funds available from the New York money-market banks.

During periods of tight money, however, the banks increase the call loan rate sharply and funds are less readily available from other sources. The costs of carrying a portfolio are often higher than the amount the dealer earns on his portfolio. Moreover, other holders of Treasury securities are likely to be reducing their portfolios of these securities at these times. Thus when markets for Treasury securities are thin, dealers are discouraged from buying and holding them because of the increased cost and the reduced availability of financing. It is for this reason that attention has been given to improving dealer financing facilities.

Several suggestions have been made to rectify this problem. One is that the money-market banks be persuaded to provide the dealers with loan capital continuously at favorable rates. The banks would more readily provide such accommodation if they were normally permitted to borrow from the Federal Reserve a corresponding amount. Another suggestion is that it lend directly to the dealers at the latter's initiative. At the present time the Federal Reserve on its initiative does provide the dealers with occasional financial assistance on the basis of repurchase contracts.

The Commission does not favor direct access to the Federal Reserve by dealers on their own initiative because it may conflict with an effective monetary policy. Moreover, it has confidence that the central bank will take appropriate action to make funds available in periods of stress.

STATISTICAL INFORMATION

The Commission welcomes the publication of new weekly data on the Treasury securities market by the Federal Reserve Bank of New York on behalf of the System and the Treasury. It is now issuing data on the volume of transactions in Treasury securities, the extent of market business stemming from various groups, the net holdings of the 17 dealers, and the extent and kind of credit used by the dealers to finance their trading positions. In addition it is publishing daily quotations of closing bid-and-asked prices. Because the quotation sheets reflect the market close, they do not reveal unusual price gyrations during the day. It is hoped, therefore, that the Federal Reserve will expand its daily quotation sheet to include the day's high and low.

This reliable reporting of badly needed data on the activities of dealers in Treasury securities should improve the public's understanding of their role in the market, prevent irresponsible criticism, and satisfy more fully the need for information of investors, analysts, and students of the market. The information on dealer financing will be particularly helpful because the cost and availability of financing are important determinants of market performance. In addition it should throw more light on how the effects of monetary and debt management policy are transmitted throughout the money and capital markets.

Additional data are also required on the ownership of the federal debt. The excellent survey of ownership now provided by the Treasury should include finer breakdowns for classes of investors and for types of securities held. It should also be made more current. There is a particular need for better reporting of holdings by state and local governments, savings and loan associations, corporate pension funds, nonprofit institutions, private individuals, and dealers and brokers.

CHAPTER FIVE

FISCAL
POLICY

The contribution which fiscal policy can make toward the achievement of the three major national economic goals is examined in this chapter. In its most general sense, fiscal policy deals with the effects of changes in the level of government receipts and expenditures and with the effects of changes in the budget deficit or surplus on economic activity. Detailed fiscal policy analysis also involves consideration of the effects on the level of economic activity of changes in the composition of revenues and expenditures and the economic effects of differing fiscal policies at the different levels of government—federal, state, and local.

The Commission, however, did not undertake an exhaustive analysis of all fiscal policy effects primarily because it believed that the effects on money and credit were the major domain of its inquiry; there were also time and budgetary constraints. This chapter, therefore, is mainly restricted to fiscal policy in its most general sense, and to the policies at the federal level of government in particular. Any excursions into the more detailed considerations mentioned above are confined to a few specific situations.

The role of fiscal policy in economic stabilization is far better understood now than it was during the depression of the thirties, and it is now likely that the fiscal adjustments undertaken in major inflations or depressions will be appropriate in direction though perhaps not in magnitude. However, the challenge of the future is to improve the use of fiscal measures to level out lesser fluctuations of prices, output, and employment, and to promote growth.

The federal budget has served as a useful stabilizing force in the economy. In part this force is exerted through automatic changes in tax receipts and transfer payments as incomes rise and fall. In part it is the result of deliberate changes in tax and expenditure programs. The com-

121

bination of automatic and discretionary budget forces has generated surpluses in prosperity and deficits in recession. The surpluses were helpful in restraining inflation and the deficits in cushioning recession and aiding recovery. But neither the size nor the timing of fiscal policy changes has been appropriate to the movement of the business cycle. The Commission therefore examined what changes could be made in fiscal policy to further improve this record. Finally, it examined the role of fiscal policy in economic growth.

During the postwar period most changes in taxes and in transfer payments, such as unemployment compensation or other social security payments, were not undertaken by themselves for stabilization reasons. Except during the early part of the Korean War, any stabilizing increases in tax rates were offset by equal or greater increases in government expenditures, and tax rate decreases were offset by declines in expenditures. Also with the same exception, discretionary changes in tax or transfer rates, either taken or recommended, were tardy and inadequate. And high tax rates were generally retained during recessions.

Wide fluctuations in the level of government purchases have been a major factor in the fluctuations in economic activity in the postwar period. Some were stabilizing and some disrupting. Usually even the stabilizing changes could be called discretionary in only the loosest sense, for they were dictated by major shifts in social priorities. Following the demobilization after World War II, major changes in programs were those involving Marshall Plan aid, the Korean War, its termination, and the post-Sputnik expansion of the defense program. The development and growth of Marshall Plan aid, although not designed for stability, fitted well into the recession of 1948-49. The Korean War mobilization required and received stabilization action on all fronts to contain the inflationary pressures it generated. The demobilization that followed contributed significantly to the recession of 1953-54. The post-Sputnik expansion of the defense program raised the sagging demand of 1958. These longer-run modifications in governmental programs have, therefore, by no means uniformly upset the economy.

An examination of the postwar record reveals that discretionary fiscal policy, correctly timed, was hardly ever used independently as a stabilizer. Thus automatic fiscal stabilizers had to shoulder the major share of the stabilization burden appropriate for fiscal measures, and they were very helpful.

Automatic Stabilizers

With a given tax and expenditure structure, changes in total output and income result in automatic changes in tax yields and in certain outlays, the first changing in the same direction as income and the latter in the opposite direction. For example, as personal incomes fall, the yield of the personal income tax falls along with them, while payments for unemployment compensation rise. Consequently, the absolute decline in income available for personal spending is less than the absolute decline in national income. As personal incomes increase, tax yields rise, and unemployment compensation payments decline. These and other similar cushioning effects on fluctuations in the amount of income available to the private sector of the economy occur without legislative or administrative changes in tax and expenditure programs and are thus called *automatic stabilizers*.

The higher the tax rates, the more progressive the rate structure, and the more sensitive the tax base to swings in the cycle, the more will changing tax yields absorb variations in national income, and the smaller will be the remaining change in income available for private spending. The more closely unemployment compensation payments approximate the wage the employee loses, the less will unemployment reduce disposable income. But because tax rates are much less than 100 percent at the margin, and because unemployment compensation is less than the lost wages, changes in national income are only partially offset by the tax and transfer-payment changes. Nevertheless automatic fiscal stabilizers do cushion the fall in income. As a result, private expenditures fall less than they would otherwise. Thus, automatic stabilizers aid recovery by reducing the cumulative deterioration in economic outlook that would otherwise take place and facilitate the forces of recovery contributing to an early upswing. Although the built-in stabilizers are very useful when the economy contracts, they are a mixed blessing when it expands. When business conditions recover from a recession, the federal tax system automatically cuts the growth in private spendable incomes, and hence the expansion tends to proceed more slowly. If the recovery is strong, the automatic stabilizers provide an important and desirable curb to the inflationary pressures that may ensue.

The very size of government expenditures and tax receipts relative to gross national product today, compared with the period before the thirties, greatly increases the potential cushioning effect of the automatic stabilizers. Whatever the merits or demerits of large government expenditures and tax receipts may be on other grounds, it is clear that the larger they are in relation to the total level of economic activity, the stronger is the impact of the automatic stabilizers. If taxes are equal to 30 percent of GNP, it is apparent that the decline in tax yield with a given fall in GNP will be greater than when taxes account for 10 percent of GNP, and as a consequence the reduction in income available for private expenditures will be less severe. Correspondingly, the smaller the relative level of government expenditures to total outlays, the weaker will be the protection provided by the automatic stabilizers against wide swings in economic activity. This is the case because government expenditures are more stable than private expenditures and often move counter to private expenditures over the cycle.

The effectiveness of the automatic stabilizers does not, however, depend exclusively on the relative size of government expenditures and the level of tax rates. It also depends on the degree to which the tax base (the particular incomes or expenditures subject to tax) fluctuates with changes in the national income and on how tax yields vary with changes in the tax base. Broadly speaking, corporate income taxes are most sensitive to changes in national income because of the great sensitivity of corporate profits before taxes (the tax base) to changes in national income. The remaining major taxes can be ranked in order of sensitivity as follows: the personal income tax; sales and excise taxes (with the degree of their sensitivity depending on the commodity or service taxed and on whether the tax is specific or *ad valorem* in nature); payroll taxes; and, finally, the property tax.

The major portion of federal revenues is derived from the corporation and personal income taxes, both of which (especially the former) are highly sensitive to change in national income. In contrast, local tax receipts, primarily from property taxes, vary little with income. State governments have a wide variety of revenue sources, a large proportion representing general sales taxes or sales and excise taxes levied on particular commodities or services. State tax revenues are therefore much less sensitive to changes in national income than are federal revenues but more so than local revenues.

In addition, state and local governments are less able to borrow than the federal government. Thus, no individual state or local unit of government, acting by itself, has the same capability as the federal government to take countercyclical actions. In addition, since the effects of its fiscal actions are not contained within its own borders but spill over to other areas, they do not have the same incentives.

It follows from the above discussion that the task of maintaining the strength of the automatic stabilizers must be undertaken at the federal level. So long as the major fraction of total government expenditures continues to be made by the federal government, largely because of the size of national security and related outlays, the automatic stabilizers will remain relatively strong. If, however, an improvement in international conditions should permit a substantial reduction in the share of the gross national product required for defense and related purposes and hence a reduction in aggregate federal expenditures, the power of the automatic stabilizers would be weakened because of the diminished size of *total* government outlays. Also total federal revenues, which are sensitive to changes in income, would be smaller in relation to economic activity.

In this eventuality the strength of the automatic stabilizers could be partially maintained by modifications which would permit a substitution of the more flexible components of the federal revenue system for the less flexible components of the state and local systems. One means would be to expand the use of federal grants to state and local governments, thereby enabling taxes to be collected at the federal level and spent at the state and local level.*

It is impossible to estimate precisely the effectiveness of existing automatic stabilizers.** The best available evidence indicates that during the postwar period the built-in flexibility of the federal budget offset between one-third to two-fifths of the fall (or increase) in the gross national

---

* ROBERT N. NATHAN—In seeking means of strengthening the automatic stabilizers, it would be desirable if state and local government taxes were more responsive to changes in income than the present taxes. Personal income taxes qualify best for this purpose. A credit to individuals against federal income tax liabilities for income taxes paid to local governments is a possibility. An alternative might be a system whereby some proportion of federal taxes would be allocated to local governments.

Messrs. LUBIN and RUTTENBERG wish to be associated with Mr. NATHAN'S comment.

STANLEY H. RUTTENBERG—In addition to federal grants to state and local governments, the Commission should recommend the use of federal income tax credit as a means of encouraging state and local governments to raise revenue. Federal income tax credits could be based on the same general principle as the estate tax was when it was originally enacted in 1924. The federal income tax credit would not significantly increase the tax burden of the individual but it would increase the revenue potentialities of the states at the expense of reducing the revenue to the federal government.

J. CAMERON THOMSON—This general subject of federal grants and aids to state and local governments should be considered only in relation to a long overdue study of the relationship between federal, state, and local government expenditures budgets and their respective sources of revenue. Such a study should also take account of the desirability and practicability of having decisions regarding local government expenditure made at the appropriate local government level and under conditions which will insure such governments meeting to the fullest possible extent, their portion of total government expenditures.

Mr. SHUMAN wishes to be associated with Mr. THOMSON'S comment.

** THEODORE O. YNTEMA—The analysis in this chapter of the stabilizing power of the federal budget seems to me inadequate. A budget surplus decreases current incomes in relation to the value of goods and services currently produced; a budget deficit increases current incomes in relation to the value of goods and services currently produced. True, the automatic stabilizing effect is not big enough to offset sudden major fluctuations in inventories; but such fluctuations are short-lived. Once the bulge of inventory accumulation or liquidation is passed, the budget surplus or deficit will be a powerful and effective force to end a boom or a depression. My guess is that temporary changes in tax rates will rarely be needed to deal with business cycle fluctuations after the inventory bulge is passed and that changes in tax rates cannot be made quickly enough to deal with inventory fluctuations.

Mr. SHUMAN wishes to be associated with Mr. YNTEMA'S comment.

product. This is a sizable fraction, far greater than that prevailing before World War II. Recent experience with recurrent and moderately severe recessions raises the question whether the automatic stabilizers can and should be strengthened to play a greater role in reducing the amplitude of cyclical fluctuations.

The discussion, therefore, turns next to possible means of increasing the strength of the automatic stabilizers at given over-all tax and expenditure levels. These might take the form of greater reliance on more cyclically responsive types of tax revenue and a revision of unemployment insurance. Finally, the more novel proposal of "formula flexibility" is considered, a proposal that involves a change in tax rates.

CHANGES IN THE STRUCTURE

The Commission examined a variety of changes in the existing tax structure aimed at increasing its strength as an automatic stabilizer and came to the conclusion that no changes in the tax structure that would result in substantial gains for automatic stabilization are feasible. *

Among the measures at the federal level considered by the Commission were modifications in the level of exemptions, the starting rate, and the degree of progression in the bracket rates of the personal income tax; possible revisions in definition of taxable income and the timing of payment of the personal income taxes; a revised treatment of capital gains and losses; differing rate structures for the corporate income tax, the timing of tax payments and changes in depreciation policy, or the granting of investment credits; a revision of existing excise taxes, including the substitution of *ad valorem* for specific taxes; and other similar measures. Some improvements in automatic stabilization might be made by alterations in some of these areas, but they would not be large enough to affect significantly the over-all impact of the automatic stabilizers.

Increased reliance on the corporate income tax relative to other taxes, especially excises, could provide a significant increase in built-in flexibility, but it would not be desirable on other grounds.

---

* ROBERT N. NATHAN—Although changes in the tax structure cannot sufficiently strengthen automatic stabilizers to assure satisfactory economic and price stability, I believe this report understates the contribution that can be made toward automatic stabilization by changes in the tax structure designed to increase its sensitivity to changes in income. The increasing relative role of state and local taxes in the collection of total tax revenue and some erosion in the progressive and responsive character of federal taxes have tended to weaken automatic stabilizers based on the tax structure, which should be revised to counteract this tendency.

Mr. LUBIN and Mr. RUTTENBERG wish to be associated with Mr. NATHAN'S comment.

At the state and local level, the decreasing importance of the property tax as a source of revenue has resulted in a steady strengthening of the automatic stabilizers since the thirties. This tendency can be expected to continue in the future. However, there is little scope for rearranging state and local taxes to augment flexibility. Taxation of profits, for example, is necessarily limited at the state and local level. The major contribution to built-in flexibility at the state and local level, consequently, must come largely from expenditure variations. Built-in flexibility through expenditure variations, however, is more limited since access to the financial markets for state and local governments is more limited than for the federal government. Federal policy, particularly variable grants, could make an important contribution.*

REVISION OF UNEMPLOYMENT INSURANCE

Changing the present structure of unemployment compensation offers one of the more promising approaches to a strengthening of the existing automatic stabilizers, though once again only moderate improvements can be hoped for by action in this area. A primary reason for the attractiveness of a strong system of unemployment compensation as an automatic stabilizer is that such payments are related directly to employment rather than to income. Among the measures that may be taken to increase the countercyclical action of the system, the most important is an increase in the benefit level. The upper limit of benefits is set by the need to maintain adequate work incentives, but there is wide agreement that the present level is too low because the ratio of benefit payments to current wage rates has declined in recent years. An increase in benefit levels would thus be consistent with stabilization objectives and with social policy. However, the basic principle that insurance benefits should be materially less than the net money earned at full employment must be observed. Next, the practice of lengthening eligibility periods during the recession phase of the cycle should be regularized and might be rendered automatic. If this is done, however, the regulations should be reviewed and tightened to prevent abuses.**

The ceiling on covered wages should also be raised to a level more

---

* See Mr. THOMSON'S comment on page 125.
** CHARLES B. SHUMAN—I do not agree that the present level of unemployment benefits is too low. The objective of unemployment compensation should be to ease the hardships associated with unemployment, but benefits should not be so high as to discourage efforts to find work—even though available work may be less desirable than that at which the worker has been employed.

Rising wage rates do not necessarily justify a corresponding increase in unemployment compensation.

in line with the actual wages paid. Then the system would be able to support the increased benefit payments and the longer benefit periods on a self-financing basis, and the taxes would be more sensitive to fluctuations in the level of economic activity. In most states only the first $3,000 of a worker's earnings is covered. This tax base was also $3,000 in 1940, but then covered wages constituted 95 percent of total wages in covered employment. Today, the share has fallen to less than two-thirds.

A more technical proposal is one for revision of experience rating. During *short* economic cycles, an employer's contribution based on a rating of his unemployment record in the previous year may fluctuate countercyclically. In the early stages of a recession his tax rate tends to be low, reflecting the lower unemployment of the year before. If the economy recovers during the following tax year, his tax rate, which will now reflect the increased unemployment of the recession year, will rise. In *longer* economic swings, however, his contributions will be cyclically perverse, because experience rating tends to cause average tax rates to decline during prolonged periods of prosperity and to increase during lengthy recessions. To be consistent with long-term countercyclical policy, the period on which experience rating is based should be longer than a single year.

Finally, variations from state to state in eligibility, in the level and duration of benefits, in waiting periods, and in ceilings, weaken the stabilizing action of the system. Federal action should require that all states comply with at least uniform minimum standards.*

The essential purpose of unemployment insurance is to protect the unemployed. The contribution to stabilization of the present system of unemployment compensation is significant, and it can and should be increased, even though any addition to built-in flexibility will be limited.

---

*FRED LAZARUS, JR.—I am opposed to uniform federal minimum standards. These would greatly reduce the flexibility needed to meet the varying problems of each state and would be a large step towards complete federal control of these programs.

Messrs. BLACK and SHUMAN wish to be associated with Mr. LAZARUS' comment.

STANLEY H. RUTTENBERG—I would like to underscore the need for the adoption of uniform minimum federal standards in the field of unemployment compensation. I concur with the paragraph which urges an increase in the benefit level and in lengthening the period of eligibility.

These are important recommendations that can be accomplished only through the adoption of federal minimum standards. I would also urge, that rather than try to improve the merit rating system (which I do not think can really be done because of its perverse countercyclical character) it be completely abolished.

Mr. NATHAN wishes to be associated with Mr. RUTTENBERG'S comment.

CHARLES B. SHUMAN—I disagree. Conditions vary from state to state and industry to industry. I see nothing wrong with allowing the states to determine minimum standards.

FORMULA FLEXIBILITY

The limited possibilities of strengthening the automatic stabilizers of the conventional type led the Commission to explore the possibility of strengthening automatic stabilization through the device of formula flexibility. The introduction of some type of formula flexibility is probably the only feasible automatic method of substantially strengthening the built-in stabilizers. Indeed, if the principle of formula flexibility were adopted, the automatic stabilizers could be strengthened to almost any desired degree.

Formula flexibility implies provision for automatic changes in the level of certain tax rates whenever prescribed economic indicators change by specified amounts. If such flexibility were to be introduced, the most attractive possibility would be to provide that the first-bracket rate of the personal income tax should be reduced by a specified number of percentage points whenever these economic indicators suggested deficient demand, and conversely that the tax rate would automatically be raised to its old level when the indicators revealed the restoration of adequate demand. In a similar fashion the first-bracket rate of the personal income tax could be increased by a specified number of percentage points whenever the indicators suggested excess demands; conversely, the tax rate would be lowered automatically to its original level as excess demand was eliminated.*

At first glance, such a proposal may seem radical. Actually, however, it would do little more than make explicit what is now implicit in the conventional type of automatic stabilizers. The essential logic behind the proposal is the same as that underlying the existing automatic stabilizers; the problems, if any, arise in reducing the suggestion to workable terms, and in facing the question of by how much automatic stabilization should be strengthened.

If a formula approach is taken, it is of critical importance that the tax adjustment should be as simple and straightforward as possible. For this reason a change in the first-bracket tax rate is to be preferred to alternatives such as an across-the-board cut in rates or changes in exemptions.

---

* CHARLES B. SHUMAN—I do not agree that changes in the first-bracket rate of the personal income tax should be made either by formula or executive decision. It would be impractical to write a formula that would be equally appropriate in all situations. The proposal to give discretionary power to the President would further impair the system of checks and balances established by the Constitution.

The power to change tax rates is not comparable to the negotiation of changes in tariff rates or the reorganization of administrative machinery. If we are to continue to have government of divided powers, the Congress must retain its historic and constitutional powers to control the raising and expenditure of federal revenues.

The formula approach has much to recommend it. It would ensure that changes in tax rates, by their very nature, would work both ways. If rates were cut in a recession because of the formula adopted, the same formula arrangement would ensure that they would be raised again in the upswing. Thus, the formula approach would avoid any bias that might result from discretionary action. In making discretionary changes, the decision-making authority, either legislative or executive, might well be subject to heavier pressure to reduce tax rates in recession than to raise them back to normal during the subsequent recovery and to above normal in booms.

Another advantage of formula flexibility is that it would ensure prompt action by separating cyclical from basic structural changes in the tax law and might avoid some of the difficulties that could arise in attempting to secure greater flexibility in discretionary fiscal action. The formula arrangement could be prepared by the tax committees of Congress and legislated in the ordinary way, subject to subsequent revision as are any other tax provisions. It does not therefore require any surrender of authority by the Congress to the executive branch of the federal government.

A possible disadvantage of the approach is its unconventional nature, which may retard ready acceptance. Another criticism might be that it would be difficult to choose appropriate indexes to which changes in tax rates should be related. These considerations carry weight, but they are hardly decisive. More important is the question of whether greatly increased reliance upon automatic stabilizers is desirable. If the built-in effect is too strong, it may overshoot the mark and become destabilizing. Moreover, the nature of successive business cycles may well differ, and a formula suited to deal with one particular situation may not be suited to deal with another. Finally, formula flexibility can deal with changes in aggregate demand only, and cannot deal with changes in employment and the price level due to structural factors. For these reasons, destabilizing effects may arise if reliance on built-in stabilizers is carried too far, and the need for discretionary action is neglected.

The Commission believes that a strengthening of the existing degree of built-in stabilization would be desirable. This increase cannot be provided to any significant degree by changes in the structure of taxes or expenditures of the conventional sort. A promising approach that merits detailed investigation is formula flexibility wherein changes in the first-bracket rate of the personal income tax would be made automatically in response to changes in appropriate economic indicators. *

---

* FRED LAZARUS, JR.—I agree with the value of tax rate changes as a tool in dealing with cyclical fluctuations in the economy. However, I strenuously object to limiting such changes to the first-bracket of the personal income tax, favoring instead

Discretionary Fiscal Measures

Even if the automatic stabilizers can be improved, discretionary fiscal measures will remain an important instrument of stabilization policy. Consequently, the advantages and disadvantages of possible discretionary actions must be considered. Two major objections are commonly raised against discretionary fiscal measures.

The first is that economic forecasts are necessarily so inaccurate that there is always the possibility that discretionary action taken on the basis of such forecasts may do more harm than good. However this objection is applicable to all discretionary stabilization policies, monetary or fiscal. It is a serious objection, for much is yet to be learned before we can assess the economic outlook as well as we need to. Nevertheless, the Commission is convinced that judicious use of discretionary measures, including fiscal policy, cannot be dispensed with.

Secondly, it is frequently alleged that the time required by Congress to enact discretionary measures and by the executive to put them into effect may rule them out. For instance, the time required by Congress to enact tax changes is frequently alleged to rule out such changes as a desirable means of discretionary stabilizing action. It is claimed, for example, that the time necessary to enact tax reductions to combat a recession is so long that they are not likely to take effect until the subsequent recovery is well underway and that consequently these reductions, enacted to cut short a recession, may in fact feed a subsequent boom.

---

temporary across-the-board adjustments in rates. Under conditions of recession both consumption and investment need stimulation, and across-the-board changes would help to provide such increases in both segments of the economy. I also oppose delegating to the President, discretion in this field, preferring to rely on congressional action.

Mr. BLACK wishes to be associated with Mr. LAZARUS' comment.

J. IRWIN MILLER—With respect to "formula flexibility" I believe it would be well nigh impossible to select a single indicator or set of indicators to whose movements we could for any period of time safely entrust the determination of tax rates. The danger of destabilizing tax changes would be so great that any formula could not be permitted to operate automatically without executive review. The increasing rapidity of changes in the ebb and flow of our economy seems to call for the application of imaginative judgment within prescribed limits rather than automatic applications of a formula, for which reason the proposal to grant to the President limited discretionary authority to change tax rates has genuine merit.

Mr. TAPP wishes to be associated with Mr. MILLER'S comment.

J. CAMERON THOMSON—Eliminate the last sentence.

Messrs. BLACK, SCHWULST and SHUMAN wish to be associated with Mr. THOMSON'S comment.

The alleged inability of Congress to act promptly is usually based on the fact that the passage of major revenue legislation has been typically an extended process. This was true in the case of the Revenue Act of 1942, the Revenue Act of 1951, and the Internal Revenue Code of 1954, all of which took the major part of a year to enact into final form. These measures, however, dealt with complicated long-run structural reforms rather than with short-run problems of economic stabilization. In certain instances, when emergency conditions dictated a need for speed, even complicated reforms were put through in a shorter time. For example, the Revenue Act of 1950 was halted halfway through its passage as a tax reform measure and sped to enactment as a substantial tax increase in only 60 days. The Excess Profits Tax of 1950 was passed within 49 days of a special presidential message despite enormous complexities.

Of more relevance as a measure of congressional legislative speed are the simple tax extension measures, such as those in the postwar period covering the excise and corporate income tax rates. They have generally consumed less than a month's time from the initial action by the Ways and Means Committee. Even the highly controversial extension of the excess profits tax in 1953 required less than 50 days. The temporary extension of unemployment compensation in 1958 was enacted in 73 days, and its extension in 1959 took only 18 days. Debt ceiling increases are the same type of legislation. Prompt hearings and prompt reports could reasonably be expected because of the compelling nature of arresting a boom or stopping a recession.

In sum, when Congress has had straightforward changes before it which it wished to enact, ways have been found to accelerate the legislative process. Fear that action will be delayed by legislative lags, therefore, provides no valid excuse for executive failure to recommend action. These precedents indicate that there is no technical or institutional barrier to a discretionary fiscal policy designed to promote economic stabilization and growth *provided* that the need for such policy is recognized by Congress and the executive and that appropriate discretionary measures are proposed. This conclusion, however, rests on the acceptance of the following basic proposition.

Discretionary fiscal policy requires speed of decision and effect and can only be successful if temporary and reversible fiscal changes for stabilization purposes are dissociated from permanent and structural changes. Techniques should be developed by which taxation and expenditure policies can be applied more flexibly, and the first step in this direction lies in a sharp demarcation between short-run cyclical changes and long-run structural changes.

Thus, the Commission's recommendations for a stabilizing fiscal policy are based on the assumption that the basic tax structure and the basic government expenditure programs are not to be varied for stabilization purposes.

The tax structure and expenditure programs do change from time to time and must be changed periodically as the growth of the economy alters the tax revenue–expenditure relationship. The periodic reassessment of the relationship between tax revenues and expenditures is necessary. When reassessment indicates the need for changes, it would be helpful for stabilization purposes if these basic changes could be timed to coincide with stabilization needs. However, stabilization policies and programs must not be dependent on basic changes in tax and expenditure programs.

TAX POLICY CHANGES

What component of private demand should bear the brunt of fiscal adjustments to promote short-run stability? Should it be consumption or investment, and what kind of expenditures within these broad groups? It would be helpful if investment outlays could be pushed up in recessions and pulled down in booms, since they are the primary short-run destabilizer. Such a result would provide a more steady level of capital formation and more sustainable rate of growth. Yet this sector is probably more difficult to affect than any other. Consequently, it would appear that at present the best policy is to consider both investment and consumption as potential candidates for stabilization adjustments.

To be able to alter taxes or transfers for this purpose, they must meet certain criteria. Changes must be easy to make without creating uncertainty in the administration of, and compliance with, the tax law. They must be promptly effective and easily reversible. And they must not create uncertainty in business ouput, planning, and efficiency.

The personal income tax ranks high in satisfying these criteria, with cyclical varying of the starting rate preferable to varying personal exemptions. The tax is not a major factor in business planning; it is broadly based; and the rate can be easily varied and changes can take effect promptly through withholding. Variation in personal exemptions might create uncertainty from year to year for many taxpayers about whether they needed to file.

Excise taxes can be easily raised or lowered, but their initial effect on demand is perverse. Advance notice of changes must be given. Therefore, if rates are to be raised because demand is excessive, taxpayers are put on notice that their purchases will shortly cost them more. This encourages them to speed up purchases and increases demand. Similarly, if demand is deficient, a coming reduction in excise tax rates can lead to the postponement of purchases, further weakening demand. This perverse effect on demand would not be significant for all excises; for example, those on some of the nondurable goods and services—gasoline, admissions, telephone service. But for a large group of other taxed commodities, such as liquor, tobacco, and the durable goods, it might be substantial. Furthermore, increases in excise taxes, once imposed, would result in price changes because of the increase in cost, which in turn might lead to increased wage demands.

Temporary changes in social security contributions have some of the same advantages as changes in the starting rate of the personal income tax, but the employer contribution is a cost item and changes in it may disturb costs and prices. Furthermore, countercyclical variation in contributions may not be readily compatible with the nature of the old age insurance system; the government tries to maintain a schedule of contribution rates that matches actuarial estimates of costs in the long run. Also the unemployment compensation system is state administered and might not be readily subject to variation. The federal payroll tax for unemployment compensation might be varied, with excess collections going into a federal fund to provide emergency relief in recessions. Shifts in the tax would, nevertheless, still affect costs.

Countercyclical adjustments in the corporation income tax rate, the remaining important tax to be considered, would almost surely create the most uncertainty for business. This holds for changes in the tax rate, as well as for changes in depreciation allowances or in investment credits.

As in the proposal for formula flexibility, the most appropriate choice for short-run discretionary changes in taxes is the first-bracket rate of the personal income tax. They are least likely to open up controversial questions of income tax structure. The legislative and administrative problems in making such changes would be relatively simple. No uncertainty would be encountered in complying with such changes. They could be made effective with very short notice to taxpayers through the withholding mechanism. They would be easily reversible. They would have a minimum of adverse side-effects such as causing uncertainty in business planning or speculation in commodities. Moreover, small changes in the tax rate would provide large amounts of additional spendable funds to consumers. A 1 percentage point reduction in the tax rate would provide consumers with additional disposable income at an annual rate of well over $1 billion.

If this proposal were enacted, the 20 percent rate applicable to all taxpayers on their first $2,000 of income could be increased or reduced, but all other bracket rates would remain unchanged. If the first-bracket rate were cut by 1 percentage point for a full year, the Commission's proposal would work as follows. Under the present law a person with taxable income of $4,000 pays 20 percent on the first $2,000 of income (tax liability of $400), and he pays 22 percent on his next $2,000 of income ($440); his total tax liability is $840. If the first-bracket tax cut were enacted and a 1 percentage point reduction were effectuated, this same taxpayer would pay $380 on his first $2,000 of income and would continue to pay 22 percent on his next $2,000 of income. His total tax would be $820, $20 less than before the cut.

If this rate reduction were expected to continue in effect for some time, the best evidence indicates that consumer expenditures would rise by a very large fraction of the increase in disposable income, probably by upwards of 80 cents on the dollar within a year of the date of tax reduction. In fact, more than half this response would probably occur in the first quarter following the tax reduction. It seems reasonable to suppose that the response in spending would be somewhat lower if the tax reduction were clearly understood to apply for only a brief period of six months or less, but almost no empirical evidence exists on which to base a quantitative estimate for such tax reductions. Conversely, tax increases would cause a fall in consumption as disposable income was reduced.

A variation of this procedure would be to make a percentage reduction in all rates and thus a percentage adjustment in final liabilities. In principle this is the same kind of device as a change in the starting rate alone, but it would apply to upper-bracket rates as well as to the starting rate.

Clearly, as a stabilization instrument, the first-bracket rate adjustment is superior to proportional adjustments in the entire rate structure in stimulating consumption, since for each dollar of income tax reduction the lower income groups would receive a proportionately larger share of the reductions.

A change of this sort is also flexible and reversible. Withholding changes can be made promptly, regardless of their size. Congress and the administration have had experience with intra-year changes in withholding rates, for example in 1948, 1950, and 1951. The technique is readily and easily applicable. Declarations of estimated tax can also be promptly modified in line with the new tax liabilities.

The Commission therefore concludes that when discretionary tax adjustments are used to promote short-run economic stabilization, they should consist of variations in the first-bracket rate of the personal income tax.

Such variations should be regarded strictly as temporary departures from a permanent tax structure. Under such a plan the starting rate could be shifted to a temporary level, either up or down, for as long a period as is believed desirable, with a corresponding adjustment provided in the final tax liabilities for the year depending upon the length of time over which the temporary rate was in effect. For example, if the first-bracket rate were cut 2 percentage points to 18 percent for six months, the annual liability would be based on a 19 percent starting rate, rather than on the present annual rate of 20 percent. Obviously, there are many possible variants of this illustration.

The main point to emphasize here is that short-run stabilization adjustments are not the place to make basic changes in the tax structure. The permanent rate structure should be governed by such considerations as tax equity, investment incentives, and economic growth. Full consideration of all these factors is not really relevant to this section on short-run stabilization policy.

Because of the vicissitudes attending the consideration of ordinary legislation, the President's responsibilities for prompt and decisive action under the Employment Act—and the more so if that act is amended as recommended in Chapter Ten—warrant a limited delegation of power to initiate a tax rate change as an instrument of countercyclical fiscal policy. Any proposal to vest the President with stand-by power to alter tax rates for any reason under any circumstances runs counter to the long-established tradition, jealously guarded, that gives the House Ways and Means Committee exclusive jurisdiction to originate revenue measures. The Congress since 1934, to be sure, has acquiesced in a delegation of power to the President, within specified limits and conditions, to change tariff rates under the Reciprocal Trade Agreements Acts, but only because tariffs vitally affect our foreign policy—traditionally a primary concern of the President, and a field in which he is otherwise accorded a wide latitude of discretion—and because the trade agreements can hardly be negotiated without the offer of firm commitments. Even in this case the Ways and Means Committee, not the Committee on Foreign Affairs, initiated the basic legislation.

The delegation should specify the particular rate to be changed and limit the maximum amount and duration of the changes, as well as the conditions under which it is to be made. Finally, the delegation should be accompanied by an opportunity for a congressional veto of its application in particular cases, along lines currently employed when executive reorganization plans are authorized. This procedure protects the opportunity for timely action by assuring that a tax adjustment, once formally proposed, will not get lost in a shuffle of alternative proposals; it must be acted upon, in the form submitted, within a limited time. Moreover, it minimizes the disturbance in the balance of executive–legislative power.

The position of the Commission on discretionary changes in tax rates is summarized below.

1. One obstacle to stabilizing tax policy has been the failure to disassociate temporary and reversible changes for stabilization purposes from permanent and structural changes. It is the Commission's view

that techniques must be developed by which tax policy can be applied more flexibly, and that the first step in this direction lies in the separation of short-run cyclical tax changes from long-run structural changes in the tax system.

2. Among various alternative taxes, the personal income tax lends itself best to countercyclical variation, and adjustments in the first-bracket rate are recommended as the best type of change.

3. In order to provide maximum flexibility for stabilizing tax changes, the Commission recommends that Congress grant to the President limited conditional power to make temporary countercyclical adjustments in the first-bracket rate of the personal income tax, the grant to be accompanied by the following qualifications and safeguards:

a. The power should be available for exercise only when the President has issued a statement that in his judgment economic conditions are running significantly counter to the objectives set forth in the Employment Act as amended (see Chapter Ten for details of this procedure).

b. The range of permissible adjustment should be limited to 5 percentage points upward or downward, that is, one-quarter of the present 20 percent rate.

c. The duration of the adjustment should be limited to six months subject to renewal by the same process, unless Congress acts sooner by law to extend or supplant it.

d. The exercise of the conditional power by the President should be subject to a legislative veto by a concurrent resolution of both houses of Congress before any tax adjustment takes effect, in accordance with the procedures made familiar by the recent Reorganization Acts. To this end the President should be required to lay before the Congress any proposal to adjust the tax rate, the proposal to lie there up to 60 days, unless a concurrent resolution of disapproval is sooner voted on and rejected, and to take effect only if no such resolution is adopted in that time. In the same law that authorizes the adjustment, the parliamentary rules of the two houses should be amended ad hoc in a manner to ensure that a concurrent resolution of disapproval may be introduced and voted upon within a 60-day period.*

---

* J. CAMERON THOMSON—Eliminate section 3 and subsections a, b, c, and d thereunder.

Section 3 and subsections a, b, c, and d constitute a mandate to the President to put the full weight of his office behind an increase in purchasing power, credited by deficit financing, as the best means of offsetting adverse trends in a cyclical recession. This recommendation is to be made in spite of the inadequacy of our statistical in-

EXPENDITURE CHANGES

Discretionary expenditure policy can also be used to promote economic stabilization, though its potential is more limited than that of discretionary tax policy. The opportunities for expenditure variations for stabilization purposes may be greater for state and local governments than for the federal government. Limitations on the use of expenditure policy are imposed by two considerations. Only a portion of expenditure programs are sufficiently flexible to permit countercyclical timing, especially where the phases of the cycle are relatively short and not easily recognizable at an early stage. Beyond this, care must be taken so that countercyclical use of expenditure programs does not interfere with their long-run objectives and efficiency.

The immediate difficulties of countercyclical timing are technological as well as administrative. Certain projects, once started, must be carried through even if the projects extend into the high-employment phase. For example, buildings, once started, must be completed. Not all projects, however, are in this category. Some, such as highway programs, can be carried out in steps. Much the same division governs the administrative processes. Although it takes considerable time from the initial planning of a project, through the placing of orders, to the beginning of actual construction, this process may be speeded up if advance preparations

---

formation, and the wisdom, experience, and judgment required to meet a particular situation. I am opposed to section 3–a, b, c, and d because they tend to undermine the basic essential checks and balances in our federal government; such pressure on Congress is unnecessary because Congress has and will find means to accelerate their legislative procedure in a national emergency; and the remedy suggested may not be the best or necessarily the exclusive means for meeting the problems of a particular recession. The real problem involved in attaining the Commission's objectives is not providing crisis remedies such as 3–a, b, c, and d. It is rather in finding the methods for developing understanding, discipline, and cooperation among the principal groups in our private economy, which will insure their cooperation together and also with the federal government in attacking problems relating to the Commission's objectives. Their help is essential, in cooperation with government, if we are to reduce or eliminate the primary cause of cyclical recessions, periodic overexpansion in credit inventories, and capital goods, both producers and durable. Other measures which require cooperative analysis and study are increasing the possibilities for labor mobility, reduction in structural and chronic unemployment, particularly in distress areas, reducing wage price rigidities caused by self-interest groups, and accomplishing the Commission's objectives by means consistent with our free competitive enterprise system. The Commission has rightfully concluded if the required nonmonetary measures are not put in effect, then monetary, credit and fiscal measures will not be able to attain all these goals simultaneously.

Messrs. SCHWULST and SHUMAN wish to be associated with Mr. THOMSON'S comment.

See Mr. SHUMAN'S comment on page 129.

have been made. Also some projects already authorized and scheduled for later starts can be accelerated. Those projects already under way can be speeded up or retarded.

A more basic objection to expenditure variation as a vehicle for short-run stabilization is the view that the government should shape programs according to the economy's long-run requirements for public services independent of short-run stabilization considerations. Moreover, some believe that the use of changes in expenditures for short-run stabilization will result in an undesirable increase in the level of government purchases of goods and services because programs instituted in recessions will not be stopped in prosperity.

Appraisal of this position cannot be well documented, because there has been little or no postwar alteration of expenditures for short-run stabilization. Further study of this purported inflexibility is urgently needed. The character of a program determines its inflexibility, both technically and politically, and ways may be found to achieve a higher degree of flexibility without incurring the waste of ill-conceived and poorly executed projects. These possibilities must be seen against the background of an expanding economy. New activities started during a recession may only anticipate future requirements. Such new expenditures should be viewed as cyclical adjustments consistent with long-run expenditure plans.

In addition, for programs which, over the years, are to be financed in given proportions by taxation and borrowing, cyclical variations in sources of finance can be used to assist stabilization without altering the proportions over longer periods. For example, a road-building program which over its life is to be financed half from taxes and half by borrowing may for limited periods be wholly financed from borrowing in a recession or from tax sources in periods of boom.

For countercyclical decisions, projects and programs should be ranked both according to the social priority of the expenditures and the length of time necessary to complete the project, as well as according to its time pattern. The social priority test ensures that only the most useful expenditures will be made; it would be foolish to undertake low-priority expenditures simply to stimulate the economy when the same result can be achieved through tax reductions or other means. Subject to the social priority test, the most desirable expenditures from the standpoint of combating a recession are those in which a high ratio of spending will take place within a brief time span when it can safely be assumed that the expenditures undertaken will be cyclically stabilizing.*

---

* CHARLES B. SHUMAN—The "social priority test" does not assure that only the most useful expenditures will be made. The expenditures made will be those that are thought to have the greatest political appeal.

Changes in planning and budgeting techniques would also help to make expenditure policy more flexible. The possibility of advance appropriations for public expenditure programs should be considered. If Congress approved a capital expenditure budget for a number of years in advance, the program of the government might be seen in better perspective, and the executive might be given more flexibility in timing particular projects. Congress might require the executive to show cause whenever the conduct of the program exceeded or fell short of what would be a constant annual rate. Capital budgeting of this nature, involving the planning of capital outlays over a relatively long period, would be highly desirable. It should be noted, though, that such capital budgeting carries no necessary implication that capital outlays should be financed differently from current outlays.*

The distribution of expenditure functions between levels of government is such that state and local expenditures should play a crucial role in any countercyclical expenditure policy. Efforts should be made to provide incentives for state and local governments to modify their expenditures in a countercyclical direction. A program of emergency short-run grants or loans, which would expire if not used within a specified time, could be used to accomplish this objective. New grants or loans or increases in existing ones could be initiated in a recession and terminated or decreased in boom periods.** Such a program would also contribute to the stability of state and local finances.

The Commission's recommendations on the use of public expenditures for countercyclical purposes are summarized below.

---

* ROBERT N. NATHAN—Our failure to distinguish between current and capital expenditures by the government is unrealistic and subjects the choices between public and private capital formation to arbitrary and unrealistic influences. Consideration should be given to dividing the present budget into a capital budget and a current budget. In the current budget, expenditures would be shown on one side and the current tax revenues used to finance them on the other. In the capital budget, expenditures would be shown on one side and on the other both the current tax revenue and the borrowing used to finance them. A part of the current revenue allocated to the capital budget would have to cover the depreciation and amortization of the capital assets of the government. Such a presentation of the federal budget should help the public to a better understanding of the nature of the federal debt and its analogy to private debt. Thus an increase in the public debt backed by real assets would correspond to an increase in private debt matched by real assets. If this fact were better understood, perhaps the false notion that federal debt is bad and private debt is good would be less widely held.

Messrs. LUBIN and RUTTENBERG wish to be associated with Mr. NATHAN'S comment.

** FRED LAZARUS, JR.—Experience with federal grant and loan programs makes it doubtful that these could ever be decreased or terminated.

Mr. SHUMAN wishes to be associated with Mr. LAZARUS' comment.

1. There should be more adequate planning for postponable projects; suitable expenditure programs should be enacted for a number of years so as to permit greater executive flexibility in timing.

2. For countercyclical expenditures, projects and programs should be initiated or expanded only if these expenditures are essential and useful and if the length of the project as well as its time pattern are appropriate. To combat a recession a high ratio of spending in the early period relative to subsequent periods would be favorable.

3. Changes in planning and budgeting techniques would help to make expenditure policy more flexible. The possibility of advance appropriations for public works programs should be considered.

4. Efforts should be made to provide incentives for state and local governments to modify their public expenditure programs in a countercyclical direction.*

The Budget Statement

The feasibility of undertaking a wise discretionary fiscal policy depends largely on having the necessary background information assembled and made available to Congress and the public in the most meaningful and understandable form. The conventional or administrative budget, as presently formulated, inhibits proper fiscal stabilization decisions. The concepts of revenue and expense in the conventional budget are legal concepts and do not show the full economic impact of the budget. Trust-fund operations such as those of the social security and highway funds are excluded, and accruals not matched by current cash disbursements such as interest on savings bonds are included.

The cash-consolidated budget, which measures cash transactions with the public but consolidates all the trust-account transactions, provides a more useful measure of the impact of the government on economic activity. Nevertheless, in public discussion the major focus still remains on the administrative budget. In addition, although the cash budget is an

---

* CHARLES B. SHUMAN—The enactment of advance expenditure programs to be activated by the executive is subject to dangers and possible abuse. Once a program has been approved by Congress there would be constant political pressure for the President to activate it. Advance authorization would tend to give authorized projects a priority over unauthorized projects that actually might be more desirable in the light of changing conditions.

Fluctuating interest rates now create an incentive for some variation in state and local expenditures. The use of federal grants to encourage countercyclical variations is likely to lead to waste and a further transfer of state and local responsibilities to the federal government.

improvement on the conventional budget, its main function is to estimate the Treasury's debt management requirements, and it has various defects as an indicator of the economic impact of the budget. To cite only one example, it treats the purchase of goods and services, such as the payment of wages and salaries, in the same fashion as the lending of funds by government agencies. There is no reason to believe that the economic effects of such diverse expenditures, one of which involves income earned and one of which involves borrowing, will be at all similar.

For this and other reasons, economists find the income and product budget developed by the Department of Commerce more helpful in determining the total impact of the government on the economy. Among its other advantages this budget excludes transactions that do not give rise to current income, distinguishes between government purchases of goods and services and transfer payments, and places the corporate income tax on an accrual rather than a cash basis.

It should also be noted that for many purposes public expenditures, which are treated in the national income accounts on a cash basis, need to be considered on a basis of the time when orders are placed. For instance, the economic impact of public expenditures frequently coincides more nearly with the placement of the order or contract than with the eventual payment on the contract.

At a more subtle level, it should be observed that the present way of looking at changes in budget deficit or surplus does not provide a clear picture of the economic effects of budget policy. As the budget surplus or deficit is now estimated for subsequent fiscal years, the estimate depends not only on proposed changes in tax and expenditure policies but also on projected changes in the level of national income. Yet the economic significance of changes in the budget surplus or deficit differs depending upon whether the change is due to positively designed variations in tax rates or public expenditures or whether it is the consequence of changing levels of economic activity. In order to separate these two effects, a comparison should be made between the budget surplus or deficit which would come about if the old and the new budget policies were applied to the *same level* of national income. This comparison should also be made against a high-employment income level at reasonably stable prices. Then it would be possible to see how, and to what extent, changes in the tax and expenditure structure would affect the balance of receipts and expenditures under different economic conditions. The purpose of the high-employment, stable-price-level budget would be to reduce the probability of erroneous fiscal decisions; it does not follow, of course, that the *correct* action would necessarily be the one which would balance this budget.

A proper appraisal of the role of budget policy in economic stabilization requires that the federal budget be presented in several different ways:

1. The present conventional or administrative budget and the cash consolidated budget need to be supplemented by a budget as it will be reflected in the national economic accounts.

2. The significance of changes in tax and expenditure policy should be presented in the budget under the assumption of a high-employment level of income and reasonable stability of the price level.

3. Information should be given which will show the impact of public expenditures on an order basis.

All this information is needed to make a proper assessment of the impact of government fiscal policies. Moreover, a presentation of this full range of relevant information will tend to prevent undue emphasis from being placed on the administrative budget, which now dominates public discussion even though it often presents a misleading guide for proper fiscal stabilization decisions.

Fiscal Policy and Economic Growth

Up to this point the discussion has been concerned mainly with the relationship of fiscal policy to short-run problems of economic stabilization. The remainder of the chapter deals rather with the long-run problems of growth.

The long-run rate of economic growth under conditions of high employment depends importantly on the level of private capital formation. Consequently, this section begins with the effects of fiscal policy on the over-all level of private capital formation. The starting point is an outline of two extreme positions, with recognition in advance that the valid interpretation at any given time almost certainly lies somewhere between these extremes.

The first position views the problem of growth as turning essentially on the levels of private saving and capital formation. Assuming that resources are always fully utilized, they may then be devoted either to consumption or to capital formation. The larger the fraction of resources used for capital formation, the higher will be the rate of growth. As total output rises in the course of economic growth, both consumption and capital formation will surely increase. But the division of the increment of output between consumption and capital formation is not fixed. If a larger share goes to private capital formation, labor will be combined with more capital. The productivity of labor will then rise more rapidly, and total output will grow at a correspondingly faster rate. Following this argument, in order to accelerate growth, fiscal policy should seek to increase private capital formation by reducing consumption and so increasing saving. Underlying this position is the assumption that the resources thus freed from producing for consumption will be used instead for capital formation. Phrased differently, investment is always expected to adjust to the level of saving. Increased private saving may be secured by substituting taxes which fall on consumption for taxes which fall on saving. Or it may be obtained by raising the general level of taxation so as to generate public saving in the form of a budget surplus. This surplus (public saving) may then be channeled into investment by making it available to the capital market, through either debt retirement or government lending. In order to obtain the desired increase in private capital formation, financing in capital markets may be eased further by appropriate Federal Reserve policies. This is a prescription for growth through a combination of monetary ease and a tight budget policy.

The opposing position denies the two basic assumptions of the first one: that capital formation must be private rather than governmental, and that resources withdrawn from production of consumer goods will inevitably be transferred to the production of capital goods. Contenders for the second position note that public capital formation has played an important part in the past and may conceivably play an even more important part in the future. With regard to private capital formation, most of these critics grant that consumption and investment need not stand in a fixed ratio and agree that private investment may respond in some degree to an increased availability of saving. At the same time, they hold that investment will not be sustained at a high and rising level unless a high and rising level of consumer demand also exists to justify continuous increases in capacity. Although they concede that under certain conditions the capacity created by today's production of capital goods will be used tomorrow for an even greater production of capital goods, they think it unlikely that investment can create its own demand in the long run, even if credit is made available on easy terms. In their view a policy which aims at increasing private capital formation by reducing consumption may well lead to unemployment rather than to increased investment. This line of argument leads to the conclusion that if fiscal policy is to hasten growth through faster private capital formation, a high and rising rate of consumer demand is a necessary prerequisite.

Those who formulate fiscal policy must chart their course between these two positions, neither of which is universally valid. There is ample evidence that the saving has sometimes been abortive and led to reductions in income and employment rather than to investment. One needs only to cite the experience of the thirties, and more recently that of 1949,

1954, 1958, and the second half of 1960, to illustrate this point. Additional evidence is supplied by the tendency of the economy to develop excess capacity during the second half of the fifties. Unemployment has remained above 4 percent since the Korean War and has shown an upward trend. The economy has progressed in absolute terms but not by as much as it might have, considering the growth in labor force and capacity. Thus, clearly, the first position outlined above does not persistently conform to historical fact.

On the other hand, experience teaches that, over time, the capital stock has grown more rapidly than the labor force and that this has been one of the causes of rising productivity. Also, in the course of a business cycle, investment does vary independently of consumption, and it responds in varying degrees at different times to conditions in the capital market. Private business investment has remained at a generally high level since World War II; it has compared most favorably with the prewar years and has constituted the same proportion of the gross national product as in the twenties. Consequently, the second extreme position, like the first, is certainly not *universally* applicable to conditions in the real world.[*]

While few would disagree with the above discussion, there is great room for controversy on how the performance of the postwar years could have been improved by fiscal policy. Lower levels of tax rates and easier credit would have raised the level of aggregate demand and would have raised the level of employment. However, it is controversial whether this could have been accomplished without more inflation. A higher level of budget surplus combined with easier credit terms might have shifted resources from consumption to capital formation, but it is doubtful, especially in view of the growing excess capacity in the late fifties, whether such a policy could have sustained capital formation at a higher level. Instead unemployment might have risen even more than it did. In other words, because conditions fitted neither of the extremes described in the preceding pages, those responsible for executing monetary and fiscal policies were confronted with a complex problem not subject to solution by any simple formula. The same difficulties are likely to prevail in the future.

If it is difficult from this vantage point to redefine what policy should

---

[*] CHARLES B. SHUMAN—I see no similarity between the thirties and the more recent periods cited above. I can see no danger that overinvestment will lead to unemployment on anything more than a frictional basis. In a competitive, private enterprise system the market tends to correct mistakes before they become too serious. The depression of the thirties is too complex to discuss in a footnote. In recent recessions the economy has shown a remarkable recuperative power; however, unemployment has been increased by policies which forced wages to levels which have artificially accelerated efforts to reduce labor requirements.

have been in the fifties, prescription for the future is that much more troublesome. Experience suggests that it is necessary to maintain a proper balance between private consumption and investment if a vigorous and sustained rate of growth is to be achieved, but what constitutes a proper balance is subject to change at different phases of the business cycle and with changing secular forces underlying the operation of the economy. Although the effects of stabilization policy are cumulative and are felt in full force only over the long run, the design of policy at any one time must meet requirements of the immediate situation as well. Thus short-run and long-run aspects of policy for stabilization and growth are intertwined and cannot be separated arbitrarily. Nevertheless, economic conditions may, for sustained periods, be such as to approximate one or the other of the two positions described above.

If conditions are such that the objectives of increased growth and minimum unemployment can be met by raising the general *supply* of saving, this may be achieved by changing the composition of the tax structure to rely more heavily on taxes which fall on consumption and less heavily on taxes which fall on saving. It appears, however, that drastic shifts in the tax structure would be required to bring about a net change in saving of several billion dollars. Changes in the progression of the personal income tax or changes in the balance between sales and personal income taxes are not very potent in this respect. Substantive changes in saving and consumption could be obtained by varying reliance on the corporation profits tax or by introduction of a personal tax on spending. Such adjustments would be highly controversial and run counter to the principle that the long-run design of the tax structure should be such as to secure an equitable distribution of the costs of government.

If the supply of saving needs to be increased, it would appear desirable to increase the general level of tax rates so as to obtain a budget surplus and to make this surplus available to private investors through a policy of debt retirement. Since the purpose would be to encourage long-term capital formation, the debt to be retired should be long-term debt, because this competes most closely with long-term investment in private assets. While it may not be easy to achieve a surplus and to increase saving in this fashion, it would even be more difficult to achieve this objective through large-scale changes in the composition of the tax structure.*

The case against reliance on adjusting the composition of the tax structure is strengthened further because it is not a question of a permanent adjustment. Underlying economic conditions change, calling for

---

* CHARLES B. SHUMAN—A preferable way to achieve a surplus might be to reduce government spending.

revision in the emphasis to be placed on encouraging saving or encouraging consumption. Extensive changes in tax structure, repeated at more or less frequent intervals, are highly undesirable as a matter of basic tax policy. Adjustments in the level of surplus or deficit, relying on changes in the general level of tax rates, are much less objectionable.

The Commission recommends that when economic conditions are such that unemployment is at minimum levels and when growth may be accelerated merely by raising the supply of new investable funds through increased private saving or a larger government surplus used for debt retirement, primary reliance should be placed on increasing the government surplus rather than on the drastic change in the tax structure required to accomplish an equivalent result.

Similar reasoning applies when conditions are such that the objectives of increased growth and minimum unemployment demand a higher level of consumption. This may be accomplished either by changing the composition of the tax structure from taxes which fall on consumption to taxes which fall on saving, or by reducing the general level of tax rates, incurring a deficit, and thus releasing income, part of which will be used for additional consumption. For the same reasons, the latter approach is again to be preferred.

When economic conditions are such as to require a higher level of consumption, primary reliance should be placed on reducing the level of tax rates rather than on changes in the composition of the tax structure.

The preceding paragraphs have dealt with the effects of tax policy upon the general supply of saving. It needs to be added that tax policy also affects the *willingness of investors to engage in capital formation* by using the supply of funds available to them. A policy for economic growth demands that investment incentives should be attractive and remain attractive and that tax deterrents to capital formation should be minimized. In this context, the issue of tax structure cannot be avoided: while a policy of surplus provides an alternative means of increasing the supply of saving, it does not provide an alternative for raising incentives to engage in capital formation.

Taxation of profits may directly affect the willingness to invest through its effect on profitability. Such effects depend not only on the rates of tax. Depreciation rules and other aspects of defining taxable income—for instance, the treatment of capital gains—are also of great importance. Special incentives through accelerated depreciation on new investment, or an investment allowance, may make an important contribution. While it would go beyond the purview of this Commission to consider these problems in detail, there is a definite need for a review of our basic tax structure with the aim of minimizing tax deterrents to business capital formation. This concern is consistent with the previously expressed view that changes in tax structure are not a desirable means to control the general level of saving.

Moreover, the effects of tax policy on the willingness to invest cannot be separated entirely from its effects on the supply and types of saving. Business investment depends significantly on the availability of internal business saving, and it should be noted that accelerated depreciation and a tax credit on new investment serve to increase both investment incentives and gross business saving. Saving that originates in high personal incomes may be particularly relevant to financing investment in new industries and processes. The purposes of growth may be served by combining some degree of leveling off in high bracket rates with measures aimed at a broader and more uniform application of the revised rate structure. In any of these cases it is important, in adjusting the tax structure, to avoid damaging effects on the supply of specific types of saving.*

The size of the budgetary surplus that can be achieved in a full-employment economy will depend upon the strength of expansionary forces existing in the economy at the time. When private investment incentives are exceptionally strong and the rate of private saving is relatively low, a sizable budget surplus would be appropriate and can be achieved. But there are also times, and the present period may be

---

* GAYLORD A. FREEMAN, JR.—The Commission's recommendation for a reduction in the too steeply graduated rate of tax on personal income should receive the support of all those interested in stimulating the economy.

The present high rate structure is the product of confusion and error. Firstly, the Revenue Act of 1931, which raised the lowest bracket tax from 1½ to 4 percent, provided for an approximately proportionate increase in all other *rates*. This increased the previous top rate from 25 percent to 63 percent. The impact of this change on *net income* was punitively progressive.

The second major increase in progressivity was supported by the economic reasoning, since proven invalid, that (1) our economy had matured (that is, investment opportunities were disappearing) so that high consumption and low savings were to be encouraged; (2) high income recipients saved excessively, but their savings did not find their way into investment; and (3) lower income recipients consumed their income, and these expenditures created jobs.

These economic assumptions are no longer accepted as valid, but the steep progressivity remains and has been aggravated by subsequent increases.

Some degree of progressivity may be a desirable attribute, but such steeply graduated rates are not justified by the revenue produced. Rates over 50 percent produced only 2 percent of total individual income tax revenue. The present level (up to 91 percent) can be described only as punitive. Although there has in the past been some economic support for such a penalty, it is no longer valid and we can no longer afford it. It has encouraged deception and stifled risk taking and, by diverting attention from production to speculation, has acted as a depressant to national economic growth. This adoption of the Commission's recommendation to reduce the upper bracket rate would prove most helpful in achieving higher rates of economic growth and lower levels of unemployment.

one, when the tax structure that would generate a large surplus at some potential full-employment level of income would be self-defeating. The existing investment incentives and other private spending forces may not be strong enough to overcome the deterrent effects of the existing tax structure on both consumer expenditures and investment. Or we may get a mild recovery that would sooner or later give us a balanced budget while leaving unemployment too high. The result would be that neither the "potential" budgetary surplus nor high-level employment would be achieved.

To overcome these effects, a cut in tax rates or an increase in government spending (or some combination of the two) would be appropriate in order to achieve and maintain full employment. Another possibility is a rearrangement of the tax structure to increase investment incentives, so that saving released by the potential surplus can actually materialize and be transformed into a productive asset. To be consistent with the Commission's earlier position, however, such changes in the tax structure must be related to the necessity to maintain a longer-run sustainable balance between investment and consumption.

PUBLIC CAPITAL FORMATION

Capital formation occurs in the public as well as in the private sector of the economy. Just as certain types of consumption are provided for through the public budget, so are certain types of capital formation. Budget policy and growth are mutually related. Not only does public capital formation contribute to growth, but economic growth results in automatic gains in the yield obtained from present rates of tax. For instance, if the gross national product grows at the rate it has grown in the past, the yield of federal taxes can be expected to rise by a very large amount over the next decade and to take an increased proportion of income. It does not follow from this that revenues will be so ample as to erase the problem of priorities. The automatic gain may be absorbed to a considerable degree by increased requirements of defense and related functions. Alternatively, the government can reduce tax rates to offset the increase in revenues that will be forthcoming with an increased GNP. The allocation of the increment in tax yield between public expenditures and private uses must be decided on its merits.

As the economy grows, levels of consumption, both public and private, will rise. Just how much of the increase should be private and how much public need not be considered here; this is for the democratic process to decide. Similar increases will occur in capital formation as the economy grows. Here it is important to note that a rising level of public capital formation is an essential complement to private capital formation and will rank high in the needs of a growing economy.

Public capital formation as a source of economic growth may take the form of acquisition of durable goods owned by government, such as dams, school buildings, research institutions, or highways. Or it may take the form of public services such as those of school teachers or extension workers who increase the productivity of labor or of other private resources. It may also consist of public outlays for research and development. All these forms must be included when considering the scope of public capital formation to avoid overemphasis on capital formation of the construction type.

Our present procedures for the planning, enactment, and execution of public capital expenditures are not well adapted to provide for a sustained and farsighted program of public capital formation. Such a program should be planned on a continuous and long-term basis. This program should not be limited to outlays involving the acquisition of physical assets but should include growth-inducing services such as outlays on research and on certain types of education. As with the reform of the tax structure, the review of public capital formation must include the state and local level.*

The Commission recommends that, in order to establish priorities and to conduct an efficient program, Congress should explore which expenditure programs are of particular importance to growth and enact a program of such capital expenditures on a five-year basis. The review of public capital formation must include the state and local level. Indeed, a comprehensive program for public capital expenditures cannot be developed without a fresh look at the appropriate division of responsibilities between the various levels of government and the interrelation of the revenue sources.**

TECHNOLOGICAL PROGRESS

The discussion of the role of capital expenditures as an essential ingredient of today's high level of productivity needs to be broadened in still another direction. The emphasis until now has been on the quantity of capital formation, public or private, rather than on its quality. But the growth in productive capacity has been to an important degree the result of the improving technology of capital goods rather than of the increase in the mere quantity of these goods. Since most technological improvements require new capital investment, capital formation and

---

* CHARLES B. SHUMAN—Some public capital is necessary, but the substitution of public capital for private investment may reduce growth. I do not subscribe to the idea that an annual expansion factor for public investment would necessarily facilitate the achievement of an agreed-upon rate of growth.

** See Mr. THOMSON'S comment on page 125.

technological improvement generally cannot be separated. But deprecia-tion allowances of corporations, running over $20 billion a year, provide a broad base on which increased productivity can be achieved through replacement by more efficient equipment, quite apart from net additions to the capital stock.

Over the last two decades, public policy has made major contributions to growth through technical progress. Expenditures on research and development, which are of major importance in this connection, have shown rapid growth over the last decade, rising from about $3 billion in 1949 to nearly $12 billion in 1959. Of this total about $7 billion were financed directly by government, and tax policy had much to do with the growth in privately financed outlays to about $5 billion.

At the same time, the record is not as spectacular as it appears. The government-financed outlays have been devoted largely to defense. While there is a substantial spill-over into civilian use, the impact is by no means as direct as it would be if the main purpose were economic growth. The privately financed outlays similarly overstate the true contribution, because it is difficult to divide outlays for development into expenditures which make a genuine contribution to growth and into those designed merely to capture a larger market share. Of the total of $12 billion in 1959, less than $1 billion was classified as in support of basic research, while over $8 billion went into outlays of a development type.

Looking ahead, high priority should be given to budgetary provision for basic research and the training of research talent. Such aid should be placed on a sustained basis, and it should play a key role in the gov-ernment's contribution to higher education. The option of immediate write-offs for research and development expenditures of private firms for tax purposes has been helpful to technical advance and should be continued. Attention should be given, however, to the difficult task of defining research and development in such a way as to limit this privilege to outlays that genuinely contribute to economic growth.

There is much to be said in favor of growth through technical prog-ress. However, there are other problems. Efforts to speed up tech-nological progress will not come to fruition in terms of economic growth unless improvements in knowledge are applied in improved methods of production. To expedite the application of new techniques, public policy must take into account the costs of transition and the adjust-ments involved.

While the economics of growth requires that the best use be made of technical improvement, it does not require that the social costs involved should remain uncontrolled. The record of public policy in dealing with the social costs of technical change should be bettered. This in-volves advance planning for technical schools that will be needed, training, increased labor mobility, as well as special measures to deal with the specific problems of displaced persons and distressed areas and industries resulting from technological changes. Knowledge of the types of special measures that are likely to be effective is limited; efforts to overcome this lack should be speeded up. This is an important task of fiscal policy in a growth economy, which must be coordinated with the more general function of stabilization.

By way of summary, a restatement of the Commission's main conclusions and recommendations on growth through technological progress follow.

1. Technical progress has been a major source of economic growth in the past, and public policy has made a major contribution to the growth of research in the past decade. Vigorous policies to promote technical progress should be encouraged. At the same time programs need to be developed to share the costs of adjusting to technical change. *

2. Looking ahead, high priority should be given to budgetary provision for basic research and the training of research talent. Such aid should be placed on a sustained basis, and it should play a key role in the government's contribution to higher education.

---

* STANLEY H. RUTTENBERG—*Point No. 1*—The word "social" should be inserted in the last sentence in front of cost so that the sentence would read, "At the same time programs need to be developed to share the social cost of adjusting to technical change." I think this is implicit from the discussion which precedes this point.

Mr. LUBIN wishes to be associated with Mr. RUTTENBERG'S comment.

CHAPTER SIX

PRIVATE
FINANCIAL
INSTITUTIONS

Variety is the salient characteristic of our private financial institutions. Some of these institutions are chartered by the federal government, others by the states. Some are stock companies, others are mutuals. Some are taxed, others are exempt from federal taxation. Some are specialized in their source of funds, some in the use to which their funds are put.

Despite their many differences, nearly all perform one common function. They serve as intermediaries between savers and borrowers, providing the financial assets savers want and the funds borrowers want. By offering financial assets that differ in liquidity, in maturity, in yield, and in risk, they attract funds from a wide variety of savers. At the same time they make funds available to borrowers on a wider variety of terms than individual savers could if they dealt directly with borrowers.

Not every intermediary stands as the direct link between borrower and saver. Some, such as the small loan companies and sales finance companies, link ultimate borrowers and other intermediaries. The security exchanges and brokers and dealers provide the machinery for marketing and trading the debt and equity instruments of borrowers. And many financial institutions perform other economic functions in addition to that of intermediary.*

---

* IRWIN MILLER—The recommendations in this chapter are aimed at accommodating our private financial institutions to the needs of the present day only. But our economy is still evolving. Regional distinctions are disappearing. Distant areas are becoming increasingly interdependent. New kinds of financial needs are arising. By the time any significant portion of these present recommendations might be made effective, the conditions which they were designed to serve will in all probability have altered in major degree. The need, therefore, still remains for a study of our private financial institutions which will take a serious look at the future character of our economy as it may be expected to be a generation from now, and indicate the features any system of private financial institutions may have to possess in order not to impede our advance, and in order to serve appropriately the new needs of the new day.

The Private Financial System

Because capital is a scarce resource, the economic system must provide a mechanism for allocating it efficiently among competing uses. In a perfectly working market, the allocation would be done by interest rates, used in its broad sense to mean the price paid for funds. In a perfect market, differences in interest rates would persist only because of differences in the risk and cost of serving various classes of borrowers and savers and in the liquidity of loans. Intermediaries would allocate their funds among all potential borrowers willing to pay rates of interest at or above the going rate with appropriate allowances for risk, liquidity, and costs. The intermediary would pass on the return less its costs and profits to the savers as interest, as dividends, or in other ways. Savers would then decide the amounts and the forms in which they wish to hold financial assets.

Borrowers differ in risk of default and in other ways. Savers differ in their preferences among the types of financial assets. And there is one set of interest rates for ultimate borrowers and another set for the various instruments provided to savers by intermediaries. Changes in the structure of these rates depend on the changing composition of borrowers' demands and of savers' preferences; the level of the rate structure varies with changes in the total demand of borrowers and the total supply of funds by savers.

But we do not have so perfect a system. The unit character of U.S. banking, for example, has limited interregional flows of commercial bank credit. As a result some borrowers, generally in smaller communities and rural areas, have been handicapped in obtaining funds. Moreover, private financial institutions differ from other businesses in that they are important lenders of other people's money. This, along with their uncertainty that returns would justify the risks, has made them hesitate to extend credit to new or risky ventures. These characteristics also are responsible in part for the existence of financial regulation, which restricts the freedom of lenders to extend funds in accordance with their own judgment. In addition, inadequate information, fallible human judgment, and the exercise of market power, particularly within local areas, have tended to lessen the efficiency of the system. The actual allocation of credit has given rise to claims of discrimination, justified or unjustified, by unsatisfied borrowers.

EVOLUTION OF THE SYSTEM

During this century the private financial system has grown both in absolute terms and in relation to the economy. Since 1900 the financial assets held by private financial institutions have increased from nearly $20 billion to over $600 billion. Their share of the ownership of total assets, physical and financial, has increased from 12 to 15 percent. Today they are the dominant holders of corporate bonds and residential mortgages.

The financial system has adapted itself to changing conditions as it has grown. The demand deposit business of commercial banks comprises a smaller share of the total assets of private financial institutions than in 1900 (see Table 3). Commercial banks now obtain a larger proportion of their revenue from consumer and term loans and on security invest-

Table 3

DISTRIBUTION OF ASSETS OF PRIVATE FINANCIAL INSTITUTIONS,
1900, 1929, 1945, AND 1958

(percent)

	1900	1929	1945	1958
Commercial banks	52.9	41.8	56.5	39.5
Demand deposit business a	47.3	29.5	45.8	28.7
Savings and time deposit business a	5.6	12.3	10.7	10.8
Mutual savings banks	12.7	6.2	6.0	6.2
Savings and loan associations	2.6	4.7	3.1	9.1
Credit unions			0.1	0.7
Finance, mortgage, and loan companies	1.1	2.1	0.7	3.4
Life insurance companies	9.0	11.0	15.8	17.8
Other insurance companies	2.6	3.5	3.3	5.0
Private pension funds		0.3	.8	4.1
Investment companies b		4.7	1.3	3.3
Personal trust departments c	15.9	18.9	10.2	9.3
Security brokers and dealers	3.2	6.7	2.1	1.6
Total	100.0	100.0	100.0	100.0

Details may not add to totals because of rounding.

a Allocated in proportion of deposit liabilities.
b Includes investment holding companies.
c Includes common trust funds.

SOURCE: 1900 and 1929—Raymond W. Goldsmith, *Financial Intermediaries in the American Economy since 1900*, Princeton University Press for the National Bureau of Economic Research, 1958; 1945 and 1958—unpublished NBER figures.

ments than from short-term commercial loans. As a group, savings and loan associations, mutual savings banks, savings departments of commercial banks, and life insurance companies have increased their share in the assets of all private financial institutions from 30 percent to 44 percent. Some continue to specialize in mortgages, and the percentage of mortgages in their portfolios has increased; the group as a whole, however, holds a much larger share of outstanding nonmortgage debt than it held earlier. Private pension funds, investment companies, and credit unions, which were virtually nonexistent in 1900, accounted for 8 percent of the assets of all private financial institutions in 1958.

The twenties were one of the most expansive and inventive eras in the history of financial institutions in the United States. Several types of credit instruments and specialized financial institutions which later were to acquire increasing importance were created and developed. These include standardized installment consumer credit and the separate institutions specializing in this type of lending—a response to the large-scale use of consumer durables, particularly passenger cars. In the late twenties closed-end investment companies were introduced and grew rapidly in response to the popularity of common stock investment among people of small means. Moreover, this period witnessed the introduction on a significant scale of credit unions and private pension plans.

In the thirties and forties, financial innovations reflected the large-scale intervention of the federal government in the financial sphere. Government social security and pension plans, government lending organizations, government-guaranteed mortgages, and government deposit insurance had direct effects on the financial system. Large corporations and large financial institutions developed the direct placement of corporate bonds, partly in reaction to provisions of the Securities and Exchange Act of 1933. And the tremendous increase in government debt during the war was responsible for making short-term Treasury obligations the principal instrument for the investment of liquid funds.

In the fifties changes in practice in the financial system were reflected in greater use of lease-backs, new financing techniques in the oil and gas industry, foreign investment through international organizations, and, more recently, the creation of small business investment companies under the SBIC Act of 1958. The rapid growth of open-end investment companies was another feature of the fifties.

GROWTH OF REGULATION

Public regulation of private financial institutions in the United States predates the founding of the Republic. The federal government, on the basis of its powers over money, interstate commerce, and the general welfare obtained in the Constitution, has passed laws providing for chartering and regulation of commercial banks, savings and loan associations, and credit unions. The states also charter and regulate these financial institutions and others under their residual powers. A distrust of concentrated financial power throughout our history also has favored the development of this dual system of regulatory authorities. This distrust was partly responsible for the regional character of the Federal Reserve System; today, it hinders efforts to unify regulations under federal authority and to permit financial institutions to improve their services to the public by expanding their operations geographically.

Financial legislation has also been influenced by the desire to accomplish other objectives, such as the wide promotion of thrift, the encouragement of home ownership, the provision of small loans, and control of the money supply. For example, the reserves that commercial banks are required to maintain against their demand deposits are varied as the authorities seek to influence changes in the money supply. Savings and loan associations are restricted largely to mortgage lending to foster home ownership. Mutual savings banks, established to promote thrift among low and middle income groups, frequently are limited in the types and amounts of deposits they can accept.

Another impetus to financial regulation has been the breakdown of financial institutions and markets from time to time. Financial panics were recurrent throughout the nineteenth century. And in this century, during the thirties, the banking system again collapsed, despite the protection supposedly provided by public regulation and by the Federal Reserve System. Disorganization in the corporate security market, defaulted mortgages, and technically insolvent financial institutions were also features of the period. Such disasters have usually been followed by legislation attempting to protect both institutions, savers, and the economy from financial distress.

Financial abuses have also led to financial regulation. The excesses of "free banking" in the mid-nineteenth century led to the National Banking Act. "Loan shark" evils before World War I led to the Uniform Small Loan Law in 1916. The Armstrong Investigation in New York in 1906 set the pattern for the present regulation of life insurance companies. Abuses by corporate insiders, irresponsible sales of new security issues, and fraudulent transactions in the sales of existing securities resulted in legislation administered by the Securities and Exchange Commission in the early thirties. Regulations of investments of funds, terms of borrowing, and capital funds of financial institutions are all partly traceable to experience with financial abuse.

The pattern of financial regulation which has emerged from this complex of forces relies upon numerous state and federal regulatory authorities. It often subjects single financial institutions to multiple regulatory authorities and preserves the domain of specialized institutions. Above all, it emphasizes safeguarding the liquidity and solvency of the individual institution by restrictions on their investments, chartering, interest rates on deposits, and by other devices.

BASES AND SCOPE OF RECOMMENDATIONS

The regulation of financial institutions should safeguard both the money supply and the small saver. Safeguarding the money supply is necessary to insure a means of payment that is universally acceptable and protected against a sharp drop caused by widespread bank failures. The small saver must be protected because he is less able to practice effectively the market principle of *caveat emptor*. Protecting these elements of the system also contributes to greater economic stability by assuring that recessions do not degenerate into financial panics, loss of confidence, and economic stagnation.*

In normal times imprudent management of a financial institution may harm the small saver or reduce the money supply. To prevent this, financial regulation traditionally has attempted to assure the liquidity and solvency of *individual institutions*. It has sought these objectives through control by statute and examination of the quality and types of assets that could be acquired and of the adequacy of capital and reserve cushions.

Experience with financial panics in this country clearly has indicated that the illiquidity and insolvency of large numbers of institutions resulted from general economic distress rather than mismanagement. The hope that financial panics would be eliminated by the Federal Reserve System was dimmed by the experience of the early thirties. Commercial banks and thrift institutions became illiquid and insolvent despite the Federal Reserve and traditional financial regulations. In consequence, it gradually became evident that a strengthening of financial regulation, in the form of measures to protect the liquidity and solvency of the *system* was also necessary. The Federal Reserve was given more power to deal with liquidity crises. Federal deposit insurance was adopted to prevent runs on basically sound banks and to protect the small saver against bank failure. And nonfinancial legislation such as the Employment Act of 1946, by providing for a more stable economy, has helped to make traditional regulation more effective.

Both approaches for safeguarding the financial system should be retained and strengthened. Strengthening the protection now afforded the small saver and the money supply should enable the financial system to make a more effective contribution to the maintenance of low levels of unemployment. Therefore, the Commission proposes some revisions in the program of federal deposit insurance. The Federal Reserve should provide liquidity directly to the commercial banks in times of general or regional economic distress, and the Commission urges that the banking system should be assured that this will be done. Indirect access of nonbank financial institutions to sources of liquidity in periods of gen-

---

* FRED LAZARUS, JR.—The moderate and evolutionary tone of this chapter is not appropriate to the job ahead. What we need is action now to encourage a freer system of enterprise by stimulating competition among financial institutions, removing restraints on the flow of savings and investments, under proper safeguards, and thereby making possible a faster response to market conditions.

eral economic distress are also supported. And the inducements to financial management to make their own provisions against illiquidity and insolvency in the normal course of events should be supported.*

The Commission recommends the gradual reduction of restrictions on the investments various institutions can make. Measures which enable financial institutions to increase the mobility of funds, which increase their efficiency in facilitating payments and stimulating savings, and which encourage them to accept appropriate risks involved in financing the types of investment most essential to growth strengthen their potential contribution to growth. The geographical area in which deposit and lending institutions may operate should be extended, so that borrowers and savers will have more choices. The Commission supports greater equality of opportunity among the various thrift institutions in their competition for funds of savers. The contribution to growth from these measures would result primarily from the effective use of available funds rather than from increased saving.

These recommendations stress greater mobility for investment and greater equality of opportunity for financial institutions to offer services they now provide. They would enable the financial institutions to become less specialized in investment, if they so desired. The recommendations are not intended to alter the specialized powers of these institutions to offer the forms of financial assets and the services which they now provide. Demand deposits would continue to be provided only by commercial banks, and the claims offered to the public by these and other financial institutions would remain unchanged. The basic similarities in the time and savings claims which these institutions issue, in spite of many legal differences, do not warrant the extensive and diverse regulatory restriction on their investments which presently exist.

Some effects on the interest rate level and structure may result if the Commission's recommendations are implemented. To the extent that saving is increased or that competition among lenders reduces interest charges the tendency would be toward a lower interest rate level. To

---

* THEODORE O. YNTEMA—It is generally agreed that the central bank is responsible for maintaining the liquidity of the banking *system* and providing for any abnormal cash drain on the *system*. A similar responsibility is recognized toward the banks in a region. The responsibility of the Federal Reserve to an individual bank however is not clear in many minds. I suggest that this responsibility be clarified: that the Federal Reserve declare that it will discount for any bank experiencing an unusual cash drain and a contraction in its assets. There is every reason to require that each commercial bank maintain a total asset value sufficient to cover its deposit liabilities and to provide a margin of safety. There is no good reason why any bank should be forced to call or dispose of loans when it is subject to an abnormal deposit drain. A bank should hold sufficient liquid or quickly maturing assets to take care of normal deposit drains; but it should not be inhibited from making longer term commitments, such as term loans, when they are needed for economic development and growth.

the extent that previously unsatisfied borrowers are enabled to get loans which involve higher risks and higher investigation and administration costs, the tendency would be for a higher average rate level. The structure of interest rates also might be changed. With more flexibility in investment, lenders could allocate funds more rapidly to higher yield areas, thus meeting the pressing demands for funds more quickly.

The recommendations for greater freedom in the investment of funds are consistent with the direction in which the system has been moving. Some period of transition may be required in those instances where the changes are more novel. Where additional opportunities are offered to financial institutions, they should be allowed to take advantage of them only if they wish to do so, and then only when they have made thorough preparations. Evolution rather than revolution is required.

The Commission's recommendations seek to reconcile partially conflicting objectives. One strand seeks to preserve and increase the safety of the financial system. The other seeks to provide greater flexibility for portfolio investment, increased mobility of funds, and increased alternatives for both savers and borrowers as means to stimulate economic growth. The Commission strongly believes that both objectives must be fulfilled simultaneously and stresses that the recommendations are interrelated.

Thus enactment into legislation of parts of the Commission's recommendations, without recognition of this basic point, would be very undesirable and even hazardous.

The existence of multiple regulatory agencies—50 states and several different agencies of the federal government—complicates implementation of the Commission's objectives. The general approach to this problem should be one of persuasion and inducement. If the recommendations, such as those for liberalizing investment powers and branching, were adopted for federally chartered institutions, federal charters would be more attractive. More institutions would seek them, and the scope of state chartering would be reduced unless state regulations were modified similarly. The acceptance of the Commission's recommendations by key regulatory states might persuade other states to adopt them. Reliance upon the federal government and key regulatory states to set the pace and spirit of regulation is fully consistent with preservation of the dual system of regulation.

The recommendations are restricted to commercial banks, savings banks, savings and loan associations, credit unions, life insurance companies, and private pension funds. These institutions hold more than three-quarters of the assets of all private financial institutions and are the principal depositories of the country's financial savings. Since they all offer fixed dollar obligations, they are active competitors for funds of savers.

Moreover with the exception of the private pension funds, these financial institutions are subject to extensive regulation. The same basic types of regulation—regulations on entry, investments, and capital and reserves —apply to all. More specialized types of regulation are applied to fire and casualty insurance companies, investment companies, personal trusts, and personal loan companies. Various other financial institutions—sales finance companies, factors, and mortgage companies—are largely unregulated as financial institutions, although taxation and other general government measures affect their operations.

Although there are many similarities among these institutions selected for study, there are also differences, and these have prompted us to treat credit unions, pension funds, and life insurance companies separately, while grouping for purposes of recommendation commercial banks, savings banks, and savings and loan associations.

Commercial Banks and Thrift Institutions

CHANGES TO PROMOTE ECONOMIC GROWTH

A multitude of regulations promulgated by the states and the federal government now govern the kind and amounts of assets that commercial banks, savings banks, and savings and loan associations may hold. The restrictiveness of these regulations and their unequal application have handicapped these institutions in directing their lending into areas and uses where more profitable opportunities exist. The regulations also often discourage initiative and competition, which in turn reduce the contribution of the private financial institutions to economic growth. The financial system would be better able to adapt to the now unforeseen future credit needs of the economy if it were granted greater flexibility in investing. Safeguarding small depositors and the money supply, until now a main objective of investment regulation, may be better accomplished in other ways.

Debt investments

The Commission recommends that the regulatory authorities be authorized to permit greater flexibility to savings banks and savings and loan associations to acquire a wider range of suitable long-term debt instruments. Commercial banks should be allowed the same flexibility in investing their time and savings deposits. Financial institutions should be permitted to change their investment practices but they would not be obliged to do so.*

Implementation of this recommendation should be gradual. Changes in the attitudes and conventions of lenders and their examining authorities will take time. Furthermore, retraining of management and recruitment of new skills are required before institutions properly should enter into new fields of investment.

If liberalization of lending is to make an effective contribution to the mobility of credit, restrictions on financial institutions which narrow the area of lending geographically should be eased. State laws that, in effect, set up barriers against out-of-state lending, on sale and lease-backs as well as on mortgages, should be revised. Efforts should be made to lower the costs of mortgage foreclosure by reducing advertising costs, simplifying court procedures, and eliminating long redemption periods. Restrictions on the length of time a financial institution may hold property acquired through foreclosure should be liberalized. Mortgage investment by out-of-state financial institutions should not be construed as doing business in the state under the meaning of statutes relating to foreign corporations.

The Commission recommends that restrictions on financial institutions which prevent or impede lending over a wider geographical area

---

* See Mr. FREEMAN'S first comment on page 164.

FRED LAZARUS, JR.—The present proposal should provide more alternatives for borrowers and savers. However, it is too restrictive in that lenders would only be competing for long-term loans. The definition of suitable debt instruments should be broadened to include all debt instruments. The potential effect of this broad definition, if adopted, would be to reduce even further the administrative and legislative division of the loan market into short- and long-term markets. Reasonable men may differ about the wisdom of permitting commercial banks, which issue demand liabilities, to acquire long-term and thus less liquid assets. But there is no reason for not permitting thrift institutions and the time and savings deposit departments of commercial banks to acquire short-term debt because holding short-term debt would obviously not impair their liquidity.

Mr. YNTEMA wishes to be associated with Mr. LAZARUS' comment.

STANLEY H. RUTTENBERG—I believe that the time and savings departments of commercial banks should be operated separately from the other functions of the banks. If this were done, then time and savings departments of commercial banks and thrift institutions should be permitted to acquire not just "a wider range of suitable long-term debt instruments" but permitted to acquire all types of debt instruments.

In order to separate the money-creating function of commercial banks from their intermediary function it would be desirable to require complete separation of both assets and liabilities of these respective activities into separate departments. It should then be possible for the monetary authority to control the money supply and if desired, the quality of assets acceptable by commercial banks in their demand deposit creating activities. Moreover, if the time and savings deposit departments were separate it would then be possible to provide for equality of opportunity between all institutions competing for savings.

than at present should be liberalized and that state laws restricting interstate lending, on sale and lease-backs and mortgages be eased to encourage the free flow of funds.*

Equity investments

There are at present a variety of restrictions on investments in equities by financial institutions. Mutual savings bank regulations vary by states, but, in general, they are somewhat more liberal than those governing national banks and savings and loan associations, which are usually prohibited from acquiring equity investments.

The Commission believes that heavy reliance on equity investments is inappropriate for institutions whose liabilities are in fixed dollar terms. However, some of these institutions have long had a limited power to invest in equities and have handled the privilege wisely to their own and their customers' benefit. Commercial banks in the normal course of business sometimes come into possession of equities, usually ones put up as collateral against loans that later defaulted. Even though it might be in an institution's interests to hold these equities at their discretion, it must dispose of them under present restrictions. Moreover, if institutional lenders, commercial banks in particular, were permitted to acquire a limited amount of equity in firms to which they were extending loans, the lenders might adopt more liberal loan policies toward risky, but promising, and often small, ventures, for they would then share in the success of such firms. Now they are entitled only to the interest on the loans no matter how large and prosperous a firm becomes, and they lose even that interest if it fails.**

The Commission recommends that investment in equities continue to be restricted. However, commercial banks, in the investment of their savings and time deposits, savings banks, and savings and loan associa-

---

* ROBERT R. NATHAN—The most effective steps to overcome geographic impediments to the free flow of funds lie in the direction of more federal government chartering and regulating of financial institutions. Excessive concentration of power is to be deplored, but our national economic life is too strongly influenced by monetary and credit policies and institutions to warrant resigning ourselves to half-way measures under the banner of "states' rights." Federal chartering of all financial institutions which accumulate savings across state lines or which lend across state lines should be required.

Messrs. LUBIN and RUTTENBERG wish to be associated with Mr. NATHAN'S comment.

** CHARLES B. SHUMAN—There may be justification for some relaxation of existing regulations to permit commercial banks to hold equities acquired in the normal course of business. In my opinion, however, it would be highly undesirable to permit commercial banks to acquire equities in firms to which they are extending loans.

tions should all enjoy the least burdensome restriction which is commonly available to any one of them.*

Federal charters for savings banks

At present commercial banks and savings and loan associations may obtain federal charters. Since only 17 states now provide for the establishment of savings banks, it is not possible to establish savings banks in two-thirds of our states. Federal charters for savings banks would permit operation in any state, and this would stimulate competition and enterprise among financial institutions, improve the banking facilities in some communities, and perhaps encourage greater conventional mortgage lending activity in all areas.**

The Commission recommends that federal charters be made available for mutual savings banks.

Branches for national banks

Since World War II, and especially since 1952, branch banking has spread rapidly. Only 22 percent of bank offices were branches in 1945; 43

---

* WILLARD L. THORP—This sets no limit on permitted investment in equities except the outside case. This logic leads one to taking off all restrictions since no objection would appear if some institution were allowed 100 per cent freedom. There ought to be a limit—perhaps to the outside limit now existing.

Mr. LUBIN wishes to associate himself with Mr. THORP'S comment.

GAYLORD A. FREEMAN, JR.—The recommendations in these two paragraphs are intended both
  (a) to encourage commercial banks to make loans of types which they do not now make in the volume which the Commission deems desirable, such as loans to small business, the farmers, and others, and
  (b) to enable such banks to acquire (both through the settlement of defaulted corporate loans and otherwise) some amount of equities moderate in relation to the size of the bank.
If these are desirable goals, it is unwise to limit the amount of these loans and investments to a portion of the time and savings deposits only, for
  (a) such assets are not allocated to any one category of deposit—and, indeed, to the extent that there is any implied allocation, such commercial, industrial and agricultural loans would more likely be linked to demand rather than time and savings deposits—and
  (b) the acquisition of stock (at least that acquired in lieu of defaulted loans through corporate reorganizations) would, if attributable to any type of deposit, more likely be linked to demand rather than time and savings deposits.

** GAYLORD A. FREEMAN, JR.—As the Commission has stated earlier, the recommendations in this chapter must be taken as a whole. With that in mind, and in the belief that through greater equality of chartering, investment, branching, supervision and taxation, competition, on a more equal basis, will be stimulated, I support this recommendation. Without simultaneous enactment of provisions for equality in such other respects, I could not support this suggestion.

percent were branches in 1960. While some of the branches resulted from
mergers with existing banks, about three-quarters of them were established as new offices. Most branch banking, however, is local, with
branches existing in the head-office city or county.

Federal legislation permits national banks to branch to the same extent as state banks are allowed by state law. As of 1958 state-wide branch
banking was permitted in 16 states, varying degrees of local branching
were allowed in 21, and branching was prohibited in 11.

Much of the postwar growth in branch offices has been in response
to the migration of people and industry from cities into the suburbs.
While the migration of people and industry has not been restricted by
city, county, or state boundaries, the migration of banks by branching
often has been restricted.

Even when branching is permitted, the regulatory authorities in acting
on applications sometimes use standards which unduly restrict competition. For example, in evaluating the "convenience and necessity" to the
community of a new branch some tendency exists to stress the "necessity"
by permitting new offices only when the market can provide a profitable
business for this office without reducing the business of existing offices.
In general, applications for unit banks take precedence over applications for branches. In some jurisdictions branches of local banks are
favored over branches of outside units. These policies on market entry
may unduly restrict competition among banks.

Although the evidence is not conclusive, it suggests that competition
among branches of several large institutions and with unit banks will
produce more adequate banking facilities in a community than competition among several small independent institutions. Liberalization of
branch banking which gives proper balance to the desirability of competition should diminish the concentration of banking power which now
exists in some communities served by one or perhaps two banks. The
economy needs, and will support, many small as well as large banks. The
evidence suggests that small unit banks can compete successfully with
large branch banks even in the long run.

The Commission opposes concentration of financial power that discourages financial innovation, minimizes economies in operation of
financial institutions, and prevents competitive sharing between borrowers, depositors, and shareholders of the benefits from innovation and
operating economies. The Commission expresses its concern about the
need for clarification of present legislation and diffusion of authority for
administrative action in relation to financial mergers. At the same time,
in its opinion, policy in regard to mergers should be discriminating.
Mergers that result in operating economies and which are forced by competition to pass on the benefits of operating economies clearly should be
encouraged by public policy. The Commission's judgment is that more

precise criteria than are now in use can and should be evolved for drawing the line between mergers that are and mergers that are not in the
public interest.

The Commission recommends:

1. The provisions of the National Banking Act should be revised so as
to enable national banks to establish branches within "trading areas"
irrespective of state laws, and state laws should be revised to provide
corresponding privileges to state-chartered banks.*

A "trading area" is defined as a geographical area that embraces the
natural flow of trade from an outlying geographical territory to and from
a metropolitan center. It may be state-wide, less than state-wide, or more
than state-wide. The task of drawing boundaries should be delegated to
an appropriate governmental agency as was done in establishing Federal
Reserve districts.

2. In exercising this power to grant branches, the chartering authority should adopt the following practices.

a. It should avoid undue concentration of the local market.

b. It should give new entrants a chance to compete even if their
business must be partially bid away from existing competitors, and
should place considerable reliance on the applicant's integrity, managerial competence, and his judgment in regard to the earning prospects of the new branch.

c. It should treat the applications for new branches on a par with
new unit bank applications.

d. It should treat applications for new branches of nonlocal banks on
a par with applications for new branches of local banks.

Branches for federal thrift institutions

Federal savings and loan associations can branch over wider areas
than can state-chartered associations, and they may branch in 11 states
in which branching by state-chartered associations is prohibited. Mutual
savings banks, now without federal charters, are subject to state regulations on branching.

---

* STANLEY H. RUTTENBERG—Point B (1). I would prefer to see spelled out a
little more affirmatively and in a little more detail, the necessity of avoiding "undue
concentration of the local market" as a result of permitting financial institutions to
establish branches. Otherwise, I fully concur in the recommendation that commercial
banks and thrift institutions be permitted to branch.

CHARLES B. SHUMAN—I agree that some relaxation of the existing regulations
prohibiting branch banking in certain areas would be desirable; however, I am not
prepared to recommend that such a relaxation be forced on unwilling states by permitting the national banks to establish branches without regard to state laws.

The Commission recommends that branching privileges recommended for national banks be made available to federally chartered mutual savings banks and savings and loan associations. State laws should be liberalized to conform.

Payment of interest on deposits

Since 1933 commercial banks have been prohibited from paying interest on demand deposits, and the Federal Reserve and the Federal Deposit Insurance Corporation have regulated the maximum rates payable on their savings and time deposits. This legislation was adopted to reduce competition for deposits among commercial banks and thereby to relieve pressure for increased earnings which led to imprudent loans and investments. By rendering special services and in other ways, some banks, in effect, now pay interest indirectly on demand deposits.

The Commission recommends continuation of the present prohibition of interest payments on demand deposits.

Additional considerations apply to the regulation of interest payments on savings and time deposits of commercial banks. During most of the period since 1933 maximum interest rates on deposits have exceeded the rates which the banks actually paid. But this has been less true recently, as other financial institutions, which were usually exempt from rate regulations, have competed for the funds in savings and time deposits of commercial banks. In addition, the Treasury has also been a Competitor.

Competition for savings accounts has come largely from thrift institutions. Mutual savings banks, not insured by the Federal Deposit Insurance Corporation, are not subject to federal regulation of interest rates on deposits, and in some states where a large volume of savings bank deposits are located, there is no legislative provision for regulating interest rates on deposits. Dividends on depositor shares in federal savings and loan associations are not regulated by statute, and regulations on dividends of state associations vary among the states.

Competition for time deposits also has been intensified. Maximum rates on time deposits of banks are regulated, but the yields on marketable short-term investment paper and Treasury securities are not regulated. Consequently, commercial banks, especially in periods of rising short-term yields, find it difficult to retain and compete for the funds of corporations, state and local governments, and foreigners.

The Commission recommends that the present statutes authorizing regulation of interest rates on savings and time deposits for commercial banks be revised (1) to convert the present power into a stand-by authority rather than continuous regulation, (2) to include under the

appropriate regulatory authorities savings and time deposits and similar liabilities of savings banks and savings and loan associations, and (3) to permit differentiation among types of deposits, including those of U. S. residents and those of foreign residents. The Commission further recommends that these institutions should be subjected to maximum rates only when in the opinion of the appropriate authorities further interest rate competition for these deposits is deemed not in the public interest, and that when applied, consideration be given to maintaining appropriate but not necessarily identical interest rate maxima for competing institutions.*

Prohibiting the payment of interest on demand deposits and permitting it on time and savings deposits requires a precise definition of each type of deposit if the difference in treatment is to be equitable. Regulation Q of the Federal Reserve Board defines demand deposits precisely. The definitions for time and savings deposits are less specific, and both are tending to become more and more like demand deposits.

Reserves against time and savings accounts

The principal reason for the required reserves against savings and time deposits or savings and loan shares for banks and some thrift institutions is to impress upon financial management the need for making provision for liquidity. However, the experience of some thrift institutions, particularly mutual savings banks, suggests that the prudence of management and alertness of the examining authority have long enabled these institutions to provide adequately for liquidity without a statutory requirement.

---

* STANLEY H. RUTTENBERG—I dissent from the recommendation that interest rate ceilings on savings and time deposits of commercial banks be revised in the way this paragraph suggests. I believe that the interest rate ceiling has served an exceedingly useful purpose in relieving the pressure for increased earnings which lead to imprudent loans and investments. However, I recognize that thrift institutions are permitted to pay a rate of interest that is higher than that which time-and-savings departments of commercial banks are permitted. This can and should be equalized.

I do not concur in the recommendation that a differential interest rate be paid to U. S. residents and foreign residents. As I have indicated in my footnote on page 235 in Chapter Eight this problem could be handled by the Treasury issuing special type securities for foreign governments and central banks.

CHARLES B. SHUMAN—I do not favor point (3) which recommends authority for institutions to differentiate "among types of deposits, including those of U. S. residents and those of foreign residents." It seems to me that any differentiation among types of deposits should be based on such things as (1) the amounts involved, (2) the regularity with which additional deposits are made and (3) the length of time money is left on deposit. The residence of depositors is not necessarily a sound basis for differentiating among types of deposits.

If, however, it is deemed wise to continue statutory reserves against savings and share accounts, two changes are desirable. The requirements should be designed to minimize any differential effect on the earning capacity of various institutions competing for savings. Both the form and the percentage amount of reserves required now vary according to type of institution and regulatory authority. Perhaps the greatest contribution to equalizing the effects of these differences on earnings would be to permit liquidity reserves to be held in cash or short-term government securities. The present requirement that member bank reserves against savings and time deposits be held in cash or in balances at the Federal Reserve prevents a bank from earning any income on these assets.

The Commission believes it is unnecessary to require statutory reserves against savings and time deposits in banks and competing institutions. Management and supervisory authorities are able to see to it that such liquidity as may be necessary with respect to such deposits is maintained.

The Commission recommends (1) that existing statutory reserve requirements on time and savings deposits be repealed, and (2) that, pending repeal of such requirements, those banks and competing institutions subject to these requirements be permitted to hold their required reserves in the form of either cash or Treasury securities with maturities up to five years. *

CHANGES TO PROMOTE ECONOMIC STABILITY

The Commission's recommendations in the previous section emphasize institutional flexibility and equality of competitive opportunity. Its recommendations below are designed to strengthen the liquidity and solvency of the financial system and to foster responsibility to match the greater flexibility.

Federal deposit insurance

Savers frequently believe that their deposits in all financial institutions are insured. However, not all banks and savings and loan associations carry deposit insurance. Deposit insurance available to commercial banks and mutual savings banks differs somewhat from that available to savings

---

* STANLEY H. RUTTENBERG—My comment in Chapter Three on the question of reserve requirements for savings and time deposits in commercial banks as well as in competing institutions, is applicable here.

I do think that the present regulations on reserve requirements for commercial banks' time-and-savings departments should continue, and I think that the Federal Reserve Board's authority should be extended to set reserve requirements on thrift institutions.

and loan associations. Deposit insurance should be brought in line with the savers' beliefs and practice.

The Commission recommends that federal deposit insurance for all savings banks and savings and loan associations be available from the Federal Savings and Loan Insurance Corporation, and that chartering authorities urge such participation. *

The last upward adjustment of the amount insured per depositor took place in 1950 and it was the first since 1933. In view of continuing increases in the average size of deposits, the maximum insurance on each account should be reconsidered in the next few years.**

Liquidity for the system

The basic source of liquidity for mutual savings banks and savings and loan associations normally should be the provision made in their own investment portfolios. It appears desirable to make provision for additional liquidity in the event of needs in abnormal circumstances. Assistance in meeting temporary or seasonal liquidity needs would be provided by the federal home loan banks, which now serve in this capacity for many savings and loan associations and a few mutual savings banks. To serve this function more fully, efforts should be made to ease the initial stock purchase requirement for membership in the Federal Home Loan Bank System to assure that more eligible institutions join.

The Commission recommends that membership be made more attractive for all eligible thrift institutions. †

If these recommendations were implemented, the liquidity for thrift institutions would pose a problem only if the normal resources of the home loan banks became inadequate in a period of widespread economic difficulties. The Commission considers that the powers for dealing with this contingency now exist in these statutes, which provide limited access to the Treasury by the home loan banks and authorization to the Federal Reserve, if it so desires, to purchase certain home loan bank securities.

These recommendations involve substantial changes in the concept and operations of the Federal Home Loan Bank System, and they should

---

* STANLEY H. RUTTENBERG—All savings banks and savings and loan associations should be required to be federally insured.

** STANLEY H. RUTTENBERG—I see no reason why the Commission should not now recommend that the maximum amount insured by the Federal Deposit Insurance Corporation and the Federal Savings and Loan Insurance Corporation (or a combination of these two into one organization) be raised to at least $15,000 and perhaps even $20,000.

† STANLEY H. RUTTENBERG—Membership should not only "be made more attractive," but should be made compulsory.

be considered with the specific recommendations concerning this system in the next chapter.

Incentives for capital adequacy

The capital, surplus, and reserves of financial institutions provide a cushion to absorb unusual losses that cannot be absorbed by current earnings. This cushion enables them to assume certain risks without endangering their solvency and thus promotes both the safety of depositors and the extension of risk credit.

Capital requirements for financial institutions should be based on the amount and riskiness of their assets. Banking standards are moving in this direction, and this approach should be developed further for all types of financial institutions so as to provide differential standards of capital adequacy which would be applicable in securing charters as well as in subsequent regulation.

Requiring an equity cushion based on portfolio riskiness would result in two incentives which work in opposite directions. One would be to accumulate reserve cushions to take on more risk assets. The other would be to minimize risk asset acquisition to avoid the need to increase the existing reserve cushion. Further efforts should be devoted to devise incentives which might increase simultaneously both risk taking and reserve cushions.

One possibility is to design federal deposit insurance to increase incentives for financial institutions to build up higher reserve cushions relative to their risk assets.* For example, at present the insurance premium paid by the insured banks is a flat rate assessed against average total deposits. This arrangement could be modified to take into account the capital adequacy of the insured institution. The average rate might be the flat rate paid at present, and the rate applicable to each institution might be set below or above this average depending on whether its ratio of capital and reserves to risk assets is high or low.

Another possibility is to use tax incentives to promote the retention of earnings. Under the federal corporation income tax, the tax provision for bad debt reserves is a type of tax incentive which encourages retention of earnings for commercial banks, mutual savings banks, and savings and loan associations. This provision, however, is not the same for

---

* FRED LAZARUS, JR.—The present methods of deposit insurance, supervision, and examination should be changed. Depositors should be protected as they are now, but insurance rates should vary depending on the risks involved [especially (1) category of loan, (2) length of loan, and (3) capital, surplus, and reserves]. The examiner would be carrying out an audit, listing assets by type, rather than inquiring into the safety or quality of particular loans. Thus, the management would be free to take on riskier loans but might have to pay higher insurance premiums to reflect the risks involved. Premiums would be based on actuarial experience for specific categories of loans.

commercial banks as for mutual savings banks and savings and loan associations and does not apply to credit unions.

Under present tax provisions, commercial banks may deduct specific losses as they occur or accrue a tax free reserve for bad debts based on their past loss experience. A bank electing the reserve method chooses any 20 consecutive years since 1927 as its base period. The annual average ratio of bad debt losses over the period selected applied against current eligible outstanding loans determines the amount allowable as a tax deduction from current income, and the reserve may accumulate up to three times the average loss ratio (of current eligible loans) for the 20-year period.

Of the banks holding over four-fifths of all deposits, about half choose the reserve method. Their permissible reserve averages 2.4 percent of eligible loans or about 1 percent of deposits, with wide variations among individual banks. The accumulated reserve at the end of 1959 was about $2.2 billion, an increase of $215 million during the year.

Since 1951 mutual savings banks and all savings and loan associations have been permitted for tax purposes to deduct from taxable income as bad debt reserves any amount they determine as reasonable, provided that the resulting total of surplus, undivided profits, and the bad debt reserve does not exceed 12 percent of total deposits.

Although, nominally, these are bad debt reserves to cover losses on worthless debts, they are conceived by the institutions concerned more broadly as "general protective reserves" to protect depositors and account holders not only against worthless debts but also against other contingencies such as losses on the sale of securities and losses which may result from an economic disaster. Since the actual tax-free accumulations under the law have generally exceeded reserves required for worthless debts, the tax provisions may be considered as a tax incentive to build up reserve cushions.

These present tax provisions do not provide a satisfactory method of assuring capital adequacy for the financial system. They do not apply equally to competing institutions. The application of present tax provisions to mutual savings banks and to savings and loan associations results in virtually no tax payments by them as compared with commercial banks. Stock and mutual savings banks and associations are treated alike for the federal tax, although stock savings and loan associations should not be included in a tax formula specifically designed for mutual institutions. Moreover, while the tax formulas for both mutual and stock institutions provide limits for the accumulation of bad debt reserves, for commercial banks this limit is not related to the over-all capital and surplus cushion.

It is easier to state the need for capital adequacy and for equality of treatment among competing financial institutions than to design a tax formula which accomplishes these objectives. The principal difficulty is determining how to achieve equitable tax treatment for mutual and for stock institutions.

The basic differences between mutual and stock institutions can be stated simply. First, mutual institutions can secure additional reserves only from retained earnings. Stock institutions can secure additional capital-reserve cushions from the sale of additional stock as well as by retaining earnings. This difference is significant, even though in practice existing bank capital-reserve cushions were largely built up from retained earnings. Second, earnings retained in mutual institutions belong to owners who under the laws and court decisions of some states are the depositors or share owners at the time of liquidation. Investment of retained earnings may increase the return to existing depositors or share holders, but they do not receive the capitalized value of this enhanced earning power if they withdraw their funds. Earnings retained in stock institutions belong to the owners who are the stockholders. To the extent that the increased earning power from retained earnings is reflected in the market value of the institutions' stock, the existing shareholders may realize the capitalized value of this enhanced earning power from a sale of the stock.

The distinctions between mutual and stock financial institutions account for the different tax treatment in the past and for the considerable debate at present as to the kind of tax provisions that will provide equal treatment. The Commission does not recommend a specific tax provision but is confident that the responsible authorities can work out a satisfactory practical tax formula to secure better the objectives of capital adequacy and equitable treatment of competing institutions.

The Commission recommends that commercial banks, mutual savings banks, and savings and loan associations be subjected to the federal corporate income tax in such fashion as to contribute to capital and reserve adequacy and to ensure competitive equality (to the extent that the federal tax is a competitive factor). The Commission also recommends that when reserves accumulated through special tax provisions are used for purposes not intended by this special treatment, they should be subjected, as now, to the full corporation tax rate.*

---

* FRED LAZARUS, JR.—Another basic principle which should be followed in revising the tax treatment of financial institutions is this: financial institutions should not be taxed more favorably than nonfinancial businesses. This principle has not always been followed in the past.

Messrs. LUBIN, NATHAN, and RUTTENBERG wish to be associated with Mr. LAZARUS' comment.

ROBERT R. NATHAN—I believe that this paragraph should in no sense be interpreted to mean that stock institutions should be permitted the tax advantages now afforded mutual savings banks and all savings and loan associations as spelled

In addition to promoting capital adequacy by insurance premium and tax incentives, financial institutions also should be encouraged to build a reserve cushion by means other than capital, surplus, and reserves. Two suggestions which should be explored are the authorization to issue debentures subordinated to the claims of the depositors and to issue preferred stock.

Management and examinations

The Commission's approach to regulation requires administrative as well as legislative changes. Its recommendations emphasize the similarities and diminish the differences between commercial banks and thrift institutions, and, at the same time, they suggest a reorientation of supervision and examination.

The Federal Reserve, the Comptroller of the Currency, the Federal Deposit Insurance Corporation, and state banking authorities are the examining authorities for commercial banks. The FDIC also examines federally insured mutual savings banks. Federal savings and loan associations are examined by the staff of the Federal Home Loan Bank Board.

The Commission recommends increased coordination of examining and supervisory authorities. At the federal level there should be only one examining authority for commercial banks. The Comptroller of the Currency and his functions and the FDIC should be transferred to the Federal Reserve System* The Commission also recommends that there

out on page 172. I support the statement on page 172 that "stock savings and loan associations should not be included in a tax formula specifically designed for mutual institutions." Whether deductions from taxable income of excessively liberal bad debt reserves for mutual institutions should or should not be continued is a matter of basic policy. Because of the differences spelled out on page 173 between mutual and stock institutions, I favor a continued difference in tax treatment, though the present provisions for bad debt reserves for mutual institutions might well be somewhat reduced.

Mr. RUTTENBERG wishes to be associated with Mr. NATHAN'S comment.

* JAMES B. BLACK—While, no doubt, a consolidation of regulatory functions of institutions outside the Federal Reserve System is desirable, I am reluctant to concur that they should be transferred to the Federal Reserve. It seems to me that the imposition of additional responsibilities on the Board cannot but interfere with its principal objective, the formulation and execution of monetary policy.

JESSE W. TAPP—I do not believe that it is desirable to transfer the regulatory functions of the Comptroller of the Currency and of the FDIC to the Federal Reserve System. The primary concern of the Federal Reserve should be with the formulation and execution of monetary policy.

A consolidation of the chartering, branching, insuring, examining, and other regulatory functions with respect to banks outside of the Federal Reserve System, might be desirable.

Messrs. FLEMING and THOMSON wish to be associated with Mr. TAPP'S comment.

be a unified authority at the federal level for the examination of all federally insured savings and loan associations and mutual savings banks. The activities and standards of these two federal authorities should be coordinated with each other and with the respective state examining and supervisory authorities.*

The management of financial institutions in making loans, and examiners in reviewing them, frequently deal with loans to new, promising ventures which are important to encourage economic growth. Clearly some lenders and examining authorities are fully aware of the significant role which financial institutions can play in encouraging these enterprises. Yet new ventures, untried products, and novel financing techniques present difficult problems for lender and examiner, requiring experience, insight, and technical competence and also an understanding of how the regulation of financial institutions can further the aims of the whole economy. Since the Commission believes that safety and growth are consistent it feels that both managers and examiners of financial institutions should always bear in mind the role of our financial institutions in promoting economic growth. Unless this is understood, the mere alteration of the statutes will accomplish very little.

The Commission has been impressed with the importance of the quality of management in the efficient operation of the private financial system in the public interest. But lacking investigatory powers, it has not dealt with the possibility of abuses under present regulations.

In view of the rapid postwar growth of financial institutions, however, the Commission recommends that Congress review the adequacy of existing legislation and that supervisory authorities review their existing regulations and examination procedures to ensure against any unwarranted personal benefits accruing to individuals responsible for handling institutional funds, which might be associated with or derived from the use or investment of the funds.

Other Private Financial Institutions

PRIVATE PENSION FUNDS

The largest, most rapidly growing, private pension funds are the non-insured corporate pension funds handled largely by banks as trustees.

---

* STANLEY H. RUTTENBERG—If we have a FDIC that receives all commercial banks and a FSLIC that receives savings intermediaries then it would be consistent to have all commercial banks examined and supervised by FDIC and all savings intermediaries examined and supervised by the FSLIC. Obviously then "the activities and standards of these two federal authorities should be coordinated . . ."

There are three major plans. The level-of-benefit plans provide that eligible employees will receive a specified pension benefit. Money-purchase plans generally have a fixed contribution determined by the terms of a collective bargaining agreement or contract creating the retirement plan; the pension benefits vary and depend on the reserve fund resulting from the contributions and the income earned by the fund. Profit-sharing retirement plans are like money-purchase plans except that the contribution varies with the level of company profits. While data are not available, there is general agreement among specialists that the largest part of the assets of corporate pension funds are held against level-of-benefit plans and that the funds held against profit-sharing plans are relatively small.

The investment latitude permitted pension trusts—the law allows the investment provisions of the trust agreement to prevail—now provides adequately for flexibility in the use of their funds geographically and among various types of financial investments. The investment powers of the pension trusts are broader than those for commercial banks, thrift institutions, or even life insurance companies.

However, pension trusts have concentrated 80 percent of their investments in the bonds and stocks of corporate business, while Treasury securities and other investments account for the remainder. They have moved only slowly into mortgage lending, although progress is being made in this direction.

The Commission believes that as a general principle the trustees who invest pension funds, whether banks, the companies themselves, or others, should be guided by appropriate investment rules. The evidence examined, although not definitive, suggest that this is now not always the case. The pressures of bargaining arrangements, the desire of employers to minimize contributions by attempting to maximize the earning of the fund, and the freedom of investment permitted under trust agreements have upon occasion resulted in investment practices which are not "prudent."

It would be helpful if certain guides were available specifying the relation of the investment of the funds to the affairs of the company and to the employee beneficiaries. The investment of the funds should be separate and distinct from the other affairs of the company and of the beneficiaries. In this operation the test of success is an appropriate balance of safety and income maximization. With certain exceptions, such as profit-sharing incentive funds, investment in the debt, property, or equities of a sponsoring company, or in projects directly related to the beneficiaries, does not necessarily meet this test.

A clear and concise summary of the investments of every pension fund should periodically be made readily available to the beneficiaries. It would stimulate discussion, clarify misunderstandings, and focus attention on the importance of sound investment practices.

More effective safeguards also should be provided for the protection of beneficiaries of pension funds against mismanagement and maladministration. Pension funds generally have been free of mismanagement and maladministration which would serve as the basis for legal action, although some abuses have been found in the welfare funds which provide life and health insurance benefits. Recent studies suggest that present remedies are not adequate to deal with infractions that might occur. For example, the underlying premise of the Federal Welfare and Pension Plans Disclosure Act of 1958 is that the individual participant in the pension plan is expected to detect maladministration and invoke legal remedies to protect his own interest, whereas experience has shown that employee suits alone are inadequate as enforcement remedies.

The Commission recommends that an appropriate regulatory body should be given added responsibilities over private corporate pension funds. These responsibilities should include the power: (1) to study and develop appropriate standards of prudence in investment of the funds; (2) to enforce such standards; (3) to assure periodic disclosure to beneficiaries of the financial statements of the fund; and (4) to bring suit against malfeasors on behalf of the plan participants and their beneficiaries.

LIFE INSURANCE COMPANIES

The investment flexibility permitted life insurance companies by statute has been gradually increased since 1906, and it is now greater than that available to commercial banks, mutual savings banks, and savings and loan associations although still less than that available to private pension funds. Life insurance companies are now allowed to invest in a variety of credit and equity instruments, but limits are set on their holdings of particular assets, and each type of asset must meet specified minimum standards before it can be acquired.

The regulatory device of "leeway" or "basket" clauses, which have come into use in some states during the last decade, has provided added flexibility for life insurance investments. These clauses generally enable life companies to invest up to some proportion of assets or of capital and surplus in types of assets not otherwise permitted, and not specifically prohibited. Such arrangements, for example, make possible direct lending by life companies to small businesses and indirect lending by enabling life companies to invest in state development credit corporations. These clauses afford life companies an opportunity to experiment and innovate in their lending while at the same time assuring protection to their policyholders.

The Commission recommends that other states follow the practice of permitting "leeway" or "basket" clauses.

The latitude permitted life companies in lending and in establishing branches and agencies to service policyholders nationwide is much broader than that for mutual savings banks, savings and loan associations, and even commercial banks. However, to some extent the geographic flow of investment funds has been influenced by state laws which apply lower tax rates to companies whose investments in the state meet certain standards; other laws prohibit writing insurance for residents of a state unless a percentage of the company's reserves on such policies are invested in that state. The Commission does not favor regulatory restrictions of this sort because they tend to divert investment from normal channels and to insulate local markets against outside competition.

Life companies are chartered and regulated by the several states and federal charters are not available. Thus life companies are confronted with a variety of state laws and regulatory practices which sometimes favor domestic over out-of-state companies. Competition among the states to attract and favor domestic companies can and has led to lower standards. Investment laws, for example, differ among states, and it is not always apparent whether those of the state of domicile or of another state apply in any instance. These difficulties have not prevented many large companies from doing business in most states, although they have led to complications. The maintenance of satisfactory regulatory standards, particularly in investment, has been preserved by conditions which have created a handful of key regulatory states, the most important of which is New York.

Life companies domiciled in New York have a sizable share of the industry's assets. The price of admission to the large New York market has been observance of New York's insurance laws and regulatory standards. While this arrangement has worked reasonably well over the last half-century, the economic growth of the rest of the country has gradually eroded the importance of New York as a key regulatory state.

In order to avoid increasing complications of multiple state jurisdictions the Commission recommends that overriding federal charters and regulation to encourage uniformity of high standards should be available to insurance companies.*

---

* ROBERT R. NATHAN—Consistent with my views expressed in my comment on page 163 of this Chapter, I would favor compulsory federal chartering of all insurance companies doing business in more than one state.

Mr. RUTTENBERG wishes to be associated with Mr. NATHAN'S comment.

CREDIT UNIONS

Credit unions are cooperative financial associations, corporate in structure, which are chartered by both state and federal authority. Their main functions originally and at present are to extend credit to their members and to promote thrift among them. Rates of interest on loans are limited by statute or supervising authority. The working funds of the credit union are furnished chiefly by sale of shares to members; dividends are declared out of earnings. When necessary, additional funds can be obtained by borrowing from outside sources, normally banks or other credit unions.

There are two types of credit unions—"open" in which membership is formed among the residents of a well-defined community, and "closed" in which members have a common employer or belong to the same fraternal, religious, or other social organization. The bulk of them are of the closed type.

Credit unions have been among the fastest growing financial institutions in the postwar period. Although originally organized to extend short-term cash credit at nominal rates of interest to their members, over the years their operations have changed to include credit extensions against real estate and consumer durable goods. In this respect, an increasing number have acquired characteristics of commercial operations rather than voluntary mutual aid organizations. But the typical credit union today is still a small, voluntary organization with no trained personnel in the finance field and subsidized by employers. However, there are some large credit unions which employ full-time trained staff and are characterized by operating practices that correspond to other commercial lenders.

Because of their specialized characteristics and the basic voluntary self-help feature of credit unions, the Commission has not made specific recommendations with regard to them. If credit union shares are made eligible for deposit insurance, the appropriate insurance body would be the Federal Savings and Loan Insurance Corporation. Membership in this insurance scheme would necessitate supervision of their operations by the insuring body. The conditions of membership in the insurance scheme would have to relate to other than mortgage loans, thereby requiring further change in the FSLIC. Presumably the insurance premium would be based on the loss experiences of credit unions rather than thrift institutions as a class.

Credit unions still account for only a small share of financial savings: they are of increasing importance in some localities as competitors with other thrift institutions. The Commission makes no recommendation concerning the present tax exemption of credit unions but believes that as credit unions grow in size and gradually change their characteristics to those resembling commercial institutions, their tax exemption should be reconsidered.

CHAPTER SEVEN

FEDERAL
CREDIT
PROGRAMS

In the last chapter the federal and state regulations governing private financial institutions and the effects of these regulations on the flows of credit were discussed. This chapter deals with federal credit programs, whose influence on credit flows has been increasingly important.*

---

* STANLEY H. RUTTENBERG—These comments relate to the entire chapter, but are followed by a few specifics.

I cannot subscribe to the conclusions and recommendations set forth in this "Federal Credit Programs" chapter. There needs to be a balanced appraisal of direct loans versus loan insurance. For home building, FHA and VA loan insurance proved to be quite successful in accomplishing its intended purpose. For other purposes loan insurance may sometimes be useful and sometimes direct federal loans may be necessary. In some instances the real alternatives are direct federal loans or federal grants. In those cases loan insurance will not be helpful.

I find the alternatives presented in the first paragraph of the section on "Types of Credit Programs" (page 185), which sets the tone for the entire chapter, give an unrealistic appraisal of the alternative forms of federal financial assistance that may be used to achieve a national purpose. If the government wishes to stimulate or assist a particular segment of the economy through the provision of financial aid, it can furnish such aid in the form of tax abatement grants, direct loans or loan insurance.

If the aid is in the form of repayable federal loans, the loans may carry an interest rate below the cost of money to the Treasury; that is, the 2 percent rate on rural electrification loans or an interest rate that covers the cost of money to the Treasury plus a margin for administrative expenses such as college housing loans or an interest rate comparable to market rates such as small business loans, VA direct loans, or public facility loans. The loans may be handled through a federal agency or through a federally sponsored agency. Insurance of private loans, except for the VA loan guaranty program, invariably involves the payment of an annual insurance premium or fee by the borrower as well as the interest payable on the private loan.

These are the real alternatives facing Congress when it considers federal assistance for a particular purpose.

On June 30, 1960, direct federal loans outstanding amounted to about $23 billion, over four times the $5 billion outstanding in 1945. Private loans partly or wholly guaranteed or insured by federal agencies had increased to eleven times their 1945 level and stood at $67 billion on June 30, 1960—12 percent of total private debt outstanding. Taken together, new credits of over $20 billion a year are being extended in direct and guaranteed loans.

Federal direct loans and federally guaranteed or insured loans outstanding for housing mortgages, low-income housing, urban renewal, and local public works amounted to about $72 billion in 1960. In agriculture about a fifth of all production and mortgage credit has been furnished by federally sponsored programs. Loans for the price support of farm products have averaged over $2 billion yearly from 1950 to 1960. The rural electrification program takes the form of a credit program. Since World War II, U.S. government agencies have extended credits of over $20 billion for economic development, exchange stabilization, financing of U.S. exports, and subscriptions to the capital of international lending agencies. Finally, federal credit assistance has been used to finance transportation—ocean transport, airlines, railroads—and is becoming of some importance in the financing of small business.

What purposes have these federal credit programs served? Have they competed with private institutions or have they been complementary to them? How have they affected the operations of private credit institutions and financial markets? Under what circumstances is one type of program more appropriate than another? Has their existence and the fluctuations in the amount of credit extended or underwritten hindered or helped

---

Determination of the form of federal financial assistance to be provided depends upon the circumstances confronting the segment of the economy to be aided. Where private credit is available, but somewhat hesitant in making a particular type of loan, federal loan insurance or guaranty will serve to provide the necessary additional security to attract private capital at market interest rates, as evidenced by the fact that the yields on FHA or VA-aided mortgages are close to those on conventional mortgages, as compared to the yields on Treasury bonds. Where private credit is not readily accessible owing to a lack of private institutions (termed "market imperfection" on page 184), rather than the borrowers being poor credit risks, direct federal loans at "market" interest rates (if the market were available) is employed, such as direct VA loans or public facility loans.

However, where Congress, in terms of national purpose, decides to stimulate a particular activity, but at no cost to the Treasury, it has, and can be expected to continue to, establish direct loan programs with an interest rate set not at market rates, but at a level sufficient to cover the cost of money to the Treasury plus administrative expenses. In the case of housing for the elderly, Congress enacted such a direct loan program in 1959 to achieve rentals below those obtainable under FHA insured mortgages, but higher than those available in subsidized public housing.

These are matters that tended to be ignored by the Commission in this chapter, despite its assurance that it has "examined all active federal credit programs and also those established during the great depression but since terminated."

the implementation of monetary and fiscal policies? How can they be used as instruments of economic control? How can they contribute to economic growth? Questions such as these provided the focus for the Commission's investigation.*

Scope of Inquiry

The Commission examined all active federal credit programs and also those established during the great depression but since terminated. The scope of the study, however, was soon limited, and specific recommendations are made only for programs that have a pervasive influence on major sectors of the economy and on the money and capital markets. In general, recommendations pertain to the relationships of the programs to the private credit market, their role in improving the effectiveness of the financial system, and their impact on and potential contribution to federal stabilization activities. Only domestic programs are covered in this chapter; some aspects of international credit programs are discussed in Chapter Eight.

The basic purpose of federal credit programs is to redirect the flow of loan funds, private and public, so that particular types of credit use are stimulated. Our economic system relies largely on the market mechanism for the allocation of credit among would-be users. But the market system does not work perfectly, especially in the face of an uncertain future, and in some instances the government has deemed it appropriate to intervene in the credit allocation process to affect the allocation of resources and the composition of output.

Continuing federal credit programs have been established to meet two kinds of situations apart from those programs developed to help persons or businesses temporarily in trouble because of a natural catastrophe or other emergency. In the first, the government intervenes to remedy what appear to be imperfections in the functioning of the private

---

* ROBERT R. NATHAN—The questions posed in this paragraph have been given study and attention in this chapter but I believe that the principal focus has been on the past and the present and not on the future. As our productive capabilities expand and permit greater fulfillment of our needs and wants it may become more rather than less necessary to influence the flow of credit so as to achieve policy objectives which the private market mechanism may not fulfill. The eradication of slums, the rebuilding of city centers, the provision of rapid transit, expansion of water supplies, techniques to solve the low-income family problem and other objectives may well require new federal credit programs. Such programs have made significant contributions in the past without any real interference with our free enterprise economy and can make even greater contributions in the future to help assure increasingly broad participation in the benefits of the abundance made possible by our expanding productive potential.

Mr. RUTTENBERG wishes to be associated with Mr. NATHAN'S comment.

credit system. Some borrowers believe that they have to pay too much for credit and receive too little and that they are unfairly penalized because of their size, their location, or the intended use of the funds. Institutional factors, such as unit banking, traditional loan policies, imperfections in competitive practices, or governmental regulations may be responsible for the apparent discrimination. Or borrowers may have too little information on sources of credit, and lenders may have too little information to be able to assess accurately the risks involved in particular classes of loans. These conditions when valid give rise to "credit gaps." Credit programs designed to close these gaps aim to achieve more nearly the credit allocation that would result if the private competitive market system operated more perfectly.

The second type of situation is one in which the government seeks to achieve social, economic, military, and other policy objectives which even a perfectly functioning market system would not achieve. At best a private market mechanism is able to assure the allocation of credit to those uses in which the credit recipient believes the benefits to him are greater than the costs of using the credit. Government intervention in credit allocation diverts resources to specific activities in which the public plus private benefits from the particular credit use are believed to justify the costs involved. For example, the national defense value of a large U.S. merchant marine is the justification usually presented for especially favorable credit terms, among other subsidies granted to private ship owners for the purchase and construction of merchant ships. Direct government expenditures, direct grants, or favored tax treatment are alternative means to achieve the desired resource use. If credit programs are used, however, a subsidy in the form of below-market credit terms or interest rates is required to ensure the desired credit allocation.

Often it is hard to tell whether market imperfections or the desire to achieve particular objectives led to the development of a given federal credit program. For example, an inefficiency in the private credit market may limit unduly the supply of mortgage credit. Correcting this inefficiency will stimulate housing construction and also help achieve a social goal. Not all borrowers who claim that they are discriminated against by private lenders and plead for government credit assistance have a justified claim. They may be able to use credit profitably only if it is made available on a subsidized basis. But there appear to be no precise guides to ensure an accurate identification of valid credit gaps. One can look only for signs of systematic and chronic discrimination, insufficient credit despite a favorable comparison of returns and costs, discontinuities of credit terms, and unexplained differentials in interest rates in the private credit markets.

The Commission gave particular attention to programs apparently designed to remedy the imperfections of the private credit system, and it examined the effectiveness of the various types of credit program in this role. Consideration was also given to whether market imperfections might be more effectively remedied by measures other than credit programs, such as changes in existing government regulations affecting the organization and operations of private lending institutions.

Congress often enacts an interrelated complex of measures when it seeks to achieve a given public objective. A credit program may be simply a convenient method for extending part or all of the needed assistance. Because such matters as agricultural, housing, and transportation policies extend beyond the purview of the Commission, an appraisal of the appropriateness of the objectives of the programs was not made. Congress, in enacting these programs, has expressed its judgment as to the national interest of the objectives which the programs seek to attain. The Commission did examine, however, the effectiveness of the types of credit activities established to accomplish the purposes sought and the methods by which they are financed in relation to our major national economic objectives. In a few instances new types of programs have been suggested to accomplish more fully the objective of established programs.

Types of Federal Credit Programs

There are four major types of federal credit programs. They involve (1) direct government loans, such as loans to small business firms by the Small Business Administration, (2) loans by federally sponsored credit institutions, such as the mortgage loans of the Federal Land Bank System, (3) guarantees of private loans, such as the residential mortgage loans to veterans by the Veterans Administration, and (4) insurance of private loans, such as the residential mortgage loans of the Federal Housing Administration. The four types differ in organization, in their sources of finance, in their potency to reallocate resources, in the extent to which they supplement or compete with private credit institutions, and in their elements of subsidy.

Under a direct lending program a government agency obtains funds generally from the Treasury and extends loans directly to private parties.

Federally sponsored credit institutions generally are designed to be self-supporting after an initial contribution of government capital. They sell securities in national capital markets to obtain funds which are loaned to private financial intermediaries. These institutions, in turn, extend credit to private borrowers.

Under loan guarantee and loan insurance programs, the government underwrites the credit of private borrowers, either partially or in full. The loan funds are provided by private lenders. Normally under insurance programs the loan recipient pays a premium for the insurance which is intended to cover its cost. Under guarantee programs the government bears this cost through its willingness to assume the losses on bad loans. These definitions of "insurance" and "guarantee" are used in the ensuing discussion, even though in practice some guarantee programs charge the borrower a fee.

A credit program reallocates resources only insofar as it increases the credit available to specified borrowers, reduces his costs through lower interest rates and easier terms, or both. In a direct loan program the interest rate and terms are under the complete control of the government. Credit terms can be much more liberal than those available in the private market, and interest rates can be set at any level. The terms and interest rates on the loan may be so close to those available in the private market as to involve little or no subsidy; they may be so liberal that the loan constitutes almost an outright gift. Thus, a direct loan program is most readily adaptable to achieving a desired resource allocation.

In the other types of programs, credit terms and interest rates must be kept more nearly in line with those prevailing in the private market simply because it is necessary to attract private funds. Consequently, their power to reallocate resources is weaker. In a guarantee program the credit terms can be more liberal than the borrower could obtain otherwise because the credit of the government is substituted for that of the private borrower. But the interest rates that will induce private lenders to extend guaranteed loans will depend on general money market conditions and on their appraisal of the relative credit worthiness and costs of handling competing loan opportunities. The *cash* subsidy is the cost to the government of losses from bad loans and administration expenses. The *total* subsidy to borrowers, however, includes the value of the guarantee, which enables them to borrow on more liberal terms and at lower interest rates than would otherwise be possible.*

A loan insurance program is similar except that an insurance fee is charged at a level designed to cover the costs to the government of the program, and hence no cash subsidy is intended. Thus, the cost to borrowers under loan insurance is slightly higher than under a guarantee type of program, and, as a result, there may be less inducement to bor-

---

* STANLEY H. RUTTENBERG—The Commission chapter defines "total" subsidy to borrowers under federal loan programs as the difference between the federal interest rate and market interest rates for such loans. This leads to the questionable proposition that if the government interposes its credit between the market and particular borrowers (by issuing Treasury bonds and lending the proceeds at a slightly higher interest rate), so that loans are made at interest rates lower than those otherwise obtainable by such borrowers, the loans are subsidized. If, however, a bank interposes credit between the market and particular borrowers (by issuing bankers acceptances to an importer whose credit is not established in the exporter's country), such loans are not subsidized.

row. From the lender's point of view, however, the two types are similar.

Federally sponsored credit institutions must be self-supporting as soon as the capital contributions of the government have been repaid and replaced by private capital. Both credit terms and interest rates will be closely in line with those of private credit. If, however, the government sponsorship enables them to obtain funds at lower cost than private institutions can, and if they gain advantages of scale of operations or freedom from regulatory constraints, they may offer slightly better terms and lower rates than private lenders. On the basis of lower interest rates and easier credit terms this type of program may have the least power to reallocate resources.

The types of credit program also differ in the manner and extent to which they compete with private lenders and affect competition among private lenders. Direct lending programs compete with private lenders only to the extent that they stand ready and do extend credit to borrowers who could obtain funds from private lenders. Guarantee and insurance programs have tended to increase competition within the private financial system inasmuch as the government underwritten loan is not subject to the same geographic and other investment restrictions as nonguaranteed loans. More private lenders can compete for them. In fact, insured and guaranteed loans also constitute a new form of competition with Treasury securities. Most federally sponsored agencies stimulate competition in financial markets by introducing a new set of institutions to compete with private financial intermediaries. All these forms of increased competition affect the credit terms and interest rates not only of the supported loans but of all comparable loans in the sector of the economy involved.

General Guides and Recommendations

Based on its study of federal credit programs, the Commission developed seven broad guides for federal credit programs. These guides relate to the selection of particular types of credit programs for various purposes, sources of finance for credit programs, and their use as countercyclical measures. Each is stated and explained in general terms and then illustrated by examples drawn from existing credit programs. Specific recommendations are made for some of the programs used as illustrations.*

The Commission has not surveyed new opportunities to utilize federal credit programs to reallocate resources. Others have stressed urgent national needs which will require government assistance if they are to be

---
* See Mr. RUTTENBERG'S second comment on page 199.

met. If Congress determines that reallocations of resources are desirable in the national interest, federal credit programs may well be the form of government assistance used to achieve them. In this event the general guides developed by the Commission should be useful in the establishment of such programs.

Others have argued that some existing programs have accomplished their original objectives and are no longer needed. There is also a need within the government for periodic reappraisals of the importance of the needs being met by existing programs and the extent and type of assistance necessary to meet continuing needs. The general guides established by the Commission may also be useful in such reappraisals.

SELF-SUPPORTING CREDIT PROGRAMS

Federal credit programs designed to improve the allocative functioning of private credit markets and to stimulate greater enterprise and competition therein should be self-supporting. In general, loan insurance programs are preferable to programs that establish federally sponsored lending agencies. (First Guide)*

The Commission believes that government intervention to improve the effectiveness of credit markets should be designed to influence existing private financial institutions or to stimulate new private institutions rather than to establish governmental direct lending agencies. If a true credit gap exists, there should be no need for subsidized credit; federal intervention should aim at increasing competition and enterprise in financial markets. Loan insurance programs and federally sponsored credit institutions are appropriate forms of federal credit activities for this purpose.**

---

* STANLEY H. RUTTENBERG—I am also disturbed by the continued reference to loan insurance programs or loan guaranty programs being preferable to federally sponsored lending agencies. I concur in this recommendation generally, but loan insurance or guaranty programs are not always preferable to direct loan programs since at times they are not capable of providing the needed innovation and stimulus to development of the types of financial instruments which can effectively cope with the particular national problem for which Federal financial aid is sought.

Mr. LUBIN wishes to be associated with Mr. RUTTENBERG'S comment and adds the following comment: "A case in point is our early experience with government guaranteed FHA mortgages. Due to the novelty of these mortgages during the formative period of this program both insurance companies and banks hesitated to purchase them."

** STANLEY H. RUTTENBERG—A central hypothesis runs through this chapter, that government intervention to improve the effectiveness of credit markets should be designed to influence existing private financial institutions or to stimulate new private institutions rather than to establish governmental direct lending agencies. If a true credit gap exists, there should be no need for subsidized credit; federal intervention should aim at increasing competition and enterprise in financial markets. Loan

A self-supporting loan insurance program, through creating a new financial instrument, stimulates greater competition in each local financial market and enables private lenders to compete in more distant markets. By virtue of its size and its unique capacities for assessing and bearing risks, government may be able to reduce the private costs of lending.

The Commission suggests that new federally sponsored credit institutions be established only if credit gaps cannot be closed effectively by stimulating increased competition among private credit institutions. Most federally sponsored credit institutions are quasi-governmental institutions which compete with existing private institutions. Interest-free government capital may be required to get them going, which generates a claim of unfair competition with private institutions. Even when the government capital has been repaid and replaced with private capital, they appear to have an advantage because government sponsorship enables them to raise loan funds through their own security issues at a slightly lower cost than they could otherwise. Finally, because new institutions are generally slow and halting in their development, this form of credit assistance may be slower in becoming effective than a program of loan insurance.

Residential housing provides an outstanding example of the use of loan insurance. The Federal Housing Administration mortgage insurance program was established in 1934 to generate a demand for housing and thereby to stimulate employment and to bring order out of the chaos then existing in the mortgage market. Currently the stated objectives of the program are the promotion of sound financing of residential property, stability in the mortgage market, and improvement of housing standards. The Veterans Administration mortgage guarantee program, though not self-supporting, is so similar in major principles to the FHA program that they are discussed together.

In each year since the war these two underwriting programs have helped finance between a quarter and a half of the nonfarm residential

---

insurance programs and federally sponsored credit institutions are appropriate forms of federal credit activities for this purpose.

Where a true credit gap exists, it is often due to the timidity or hesitancy of private institutions to try financial innovations or to explore new risk situations. During the thirties, the Public Works Administration adopted and further developed the financial instrument known as revenue bonds to stimulate the financing of state and local public works. Only after these bonds were proved to be financially sound (most of these bonds were later sold at a profit), were private institutions willing to handle this type of financing at reasonable interest rates.

Another example of the stimulating effects of government lending is the successful direct federal loan program for college housing. This $1.7 billion program (slated to be increased by another $1.4 billion during the next five years) has never experienced a default during its 10 years of operation. This federal program has stimulated private financing, as evidenced by the increasing number of college housing bond issues now being privately underwritten.

housing starts. In no year during the fifties has government underwritten residential mortgage debt been less than 40 percent of total residential mortgage debt outstanding. At the end of 1960 it amounted to about $63 billion, an amount larger than the net debt of all state and local governments combined.

The genius of the underwriting programs is that they operate on both the borrowing and lending sides of the mortgage market at the same time. By enabling borrowers to acquire loans for longer periods at lower down payments and at lower interest rates than private lenders offer on conventional loans, the programs stimulate housing demand. On the lending side, the government's underwriting of default risk, its development of greater homogeneity in the security behind mortgage loans through the establishment of appraisal and construction standards, its insistence on amortization, and the development of experience records on low-down-payment loans have induced institutional lenders to supply more mortgage credit. By creating a more homogeneous and more marketable debt instrument the programs have reduced geographical differentials in rates through stimulating competition for mortgage loans among, as well as within, local markets.

Commercial banks, mutual savings banks, and life insurance companies have become more active in local as well as distant mortgage markets because underwritten loans are generally exempt from restrictions on their mortgage investment powers. Each has a larger proportion of its assets in residential mortgages than it had in the twenties, and the proportions have grown markedly since the war. Although savings and loan associations do not have large holdings of government underwritten mortgages, nevertheless the competition of the underwritten mortgage and the experience records on insured and guaranteed mortgages have been factors leading them to liberalize terms on their conventional mortgage loans.

The underwriting programs have required little Treasury support during the postwar period. The FHA program has consistently taken in more funds from insurance operations, fees, and default proceedings than it has expended for administration and losses, with the result that a substantial reserve has been accumulated. Because the VA levies no guarantee fees, it has always required some funds from the federal budget.

The need for a federal underwriting program in the future is apparent. The demand for new residential construction during the sixties, especially the latter half, will probably be greater than in the fifties. The projected increases in the number of new families, and the prospective rise in family income affecting both new and replacement requirements will stimulate private housing demand. And programs for improving our cities will require more rapid replacement of dilapidated dwellings. Unless federal underwriting programs are continued, and unless some of the impediments and restrictions on the mortgage lending of private financial institutions are eased along the lines discussed in the preceding chapter, obtaining the necessary flow of funds at reasonable rates would be difficult.

The Commission recommends the continuation of the Federal Housing Administration loan insurance programs to facilitate the flow of private funds into residential construction. *

The recommendation is limited to the FHA program because the VA program is scheduled to lapse in the near future. Two separate agencies to underwrite residential loans entail unnecessary duplication. Even if Congress should desire to continue the veterans' special preference, this could be done through FHA machinery, for example, by having the VA pay the FHA insurance premium for veterans.

The FHA program was established in a period of severe unemployment when the increase in housing demands stimulated by the program could be expected to generate increased construction and employment with little or no effect on construction costs. At times in the past decade, however, the stimuli from the FHA and VA programs have contributed to rising prices of new and old houses and to higher construction costs as well as to an increased volume of residential construction. The programs should be operated to minimize inflationary pressures, a problem discussed in a later section of this chapter. In addition, every effort should be made by FHA to simplify its operating procedures and regulations. The multiplicity of current subprograms adds to the complexity of the FHA insurance system.

One major weakness of the underwriting programs has been the limited availability of FHA and VA housing loans in areas at a distance from large cities. The voluntary home mortgage credit program was initiated in 1954 as a joint industry–government venture to channel FHA and VA loan requests from applicants in rural areas to participating

---

* STANLEY H. RUTTENBERG—I am also disturbed by the insistence upon the need for continuing FHA loan insurance programs as recommended in this paragraph, while at the same time making reference to the fact that the impediments and restrictions on the mortgage lending of private financial institutions must be eased along the lines discussed in the preceding chapter. I think this attitude is basically wrong. If the federal government is going to have loan insurance and guaranteed programs, there are certain kinds of socially desirable policies which the private financial lending institutions should follow. References to the removal of impediments and restrictions in effect implies, let the government insure or guarantee all the programs, take all the risk out of lending, but permit the private financial institutions to continue to benefit without undue interference. This, in my judgment, is indefensible.

lenders in financial centers to overcome this imperfection. And in October 1957 the certified agency program was set up on an experimental basis to make FHA insurance available to all qualified home buyers in areas remote from FHA offices. Approved lenders in communities located 30 miles or more from an FHA insurance office were empowered to process mortgage applications, to use the services of local appraisers and inspectors approved by FHA, and to issue mortgage insurance commitments on behalf of FHA. The VA has had a direct lending program to make home loans to veterans in areas where guaranteed mortgages could not be obtained from private lenders. These experiments are important innovations in expanding the scope of underwriting activity or its equivalent to smaller communities.

In order to ensure the continued availability of insured loans in all areas of the country, the Commission recommends that the voluntary home mortgage credit program and the certified agency program of the Federal Housing Administration be encouraged.

When the VA housing programs terminate, the voluntary home mortgage credit program and the certified agency program of the FHA are expected to meet most of the demands for insured mortgage loans of borrowers, veterans and nonveterans, in areas remote from FHA offices. If, however, important needs are not met, an FHA direct lending program similar to the terminating VA program may be necessary. A direct loan should be made, however, only if evidence indicates that efforts to obtain an insured loan through other programs have failed. And the same credit standards and terms should be used for direct loans as those applicable under the FHA insured loan programs.

Federally sponsored credit agencies in agriculture

The federally sponsored credit programs for agriculture, the first of which was established in 1917, have been revised and expanded and today are coordinated and supervised by the Farm Credit Administration, an independent government agency. This cooperative credit system for agriculture provides mortgage credit through federal land banks and land bank cooperatives; production credit through federal intermediate credit banks and production credit associations; and marketing and purchasing credit through banks for cooperatives and through agricultural marketing, purchasing, and business service cooperatives. Financed originally with government funds, the system will soon be wholly privately financed. The system is self-supporting, and covers the Farm Credit Administration's administrative and supervisory costs. Total loans outstanding are now about $4 billion, and represent about 15 percent of all credit extended to farmers.

When the land bank system was established in 1917, maturities of farm mortgages were short, usually five years; credit was limited continuously in sparsely settled areas and generally limited during recessions; and equity requirements and interest rates were high. Because of this system owned and operated by farmers and its competitive impact on other lenders, maturities have been lengthened, up to 40 years; amortization has been introduced; interest rates are lower and interest rate differentials among regions and among loan sizes have been reduced; and funds are more readily available at all times and places. Similarly, the intermediate credit system has resulted in a more stable supply of loan funds, longer terms for loans, and lower interest rates on production credit for farmers. Finally, the banks for cooperatives have provided increased marketing credit at lower costs.

In this instance a new set of institutions was probably necessary to provide a source of funds as an alternative to local unit banks in many rural communities. Yet this cooperative credit system took a long time to reach its present stage of effectiveness, and government capital is not yet completely retired from all the programs, although they have not constituted a current charge on the budget for many years.

Loan insurance for agricultural credit

Despite the success of the federally sponsored credit system in agriculture, important credit problems remain. Rapid technological advance in agriculture has enabled a farm family to handle a much larger farm than previously and has increased greatly the capital requirements for an efficient family-sized farm. When the total capital for real estate and other productive assets for such a farm ranges from $50,000 to $100,000 or more, few farm operators, especially young farmers, find it easy to acquire the necessary equity to become owner-operators.

Technological advances have also contributed to the surplus problem. Productivity in agriculture has increased more rapidly than the demand for basic farm products, and if greater advantage were taken of known technology without a reduction in total resources devoted to agriculture, the surplus problem would increase. Yet for economic growth, agricultural as well as other products must be produced efficiently, and entry for potentially more productive farmers must be kept open.

This problem is far broader than credit policy, but credit might be used for the likely reallocation of agricultural resources. Its major function would be to make possible the orderly transfer of capital and land resources in agriculture to larger and more efficient operating units.

Conceivably, credit could also speed the transfer of resources out of agriculture. Federal credit programs might provide nonrecourse loans to farmers who are leaving agriculture based on their farm assets and perhaps their household equipment.* Such loans would assure farmers a minimum sale value of their assets and would make funds available to cover the costs of moving, of maintaining the family for a few months, and even of making a down payment on a house. Loans might also be made to attract nonfarm business to rural communities. Almost certainly such credit would take the form of direct loans on a subsidized basis.

However, measures to maintain high levels of nonfarm employment, to provide facilities for retraining and finding jobs, or to increase the supply of housing in nonfarm communities may be more effective than relocation credit programs. And the greatest contribution to economic growth will result when workers drawn from the farms are re-employed in nonagricultural pursuits; it will not help if they are simply added to the unemployment rolls in cities.

The two major credit needs involved in making the transition to fewer but larger and more efficient farms are credit for the transfer of farm real estate among farm operators and intermediate-term credit for acquiring other capital assets. Specific recommendations on these two credit needs are made with full awareness that the surplus problem may be aggravated. They are made on the assumption that appropriate steps can be devised and will be taken to deal with the surplus problem.

About two-thirds of all farm transfers involve the use of credit. The major institutional lenders, including the land bank system, finance less than a third of all farm transfers. Institutional lenders, either for legal or other reasons, generally do not provide a loan for more than 65 percent of the appraised value of the property involved. This still leaves more to be financed than many farmers can manage from their own resources.

The Commission recommends that a limited self-supporting federal insurance program be developed and administered by an established farm credit agency for mortgage loans featuring low down payments, long maturities, and not necessarily complete amortization. Such insurance should be available only under stringent conditions, perhaps such as (1) the farm unit should be large enough to take advantage of existing technology and provide a satisfactory level of family income under

---

* CHARLES B. SHUMAN—I would delete from the second sentence the phrase "based on their farm assets and perhaps their household equipment." I think it would be sounder if the CMC were to recommend that the proposed loans be made on the basis of the borrower's ability and character, on a recourse basis, but without security.

reasonably good management, and (2) adequate farm plans should be developed by the borrower.*

Professional services for developing the plans and management consulting would be supplied for a specified period or until the mortgage has been reduced to a level appropriate for a conventional farm mortgage.

The Commission acknowledges the risks attached to this program, but believes that they are outweighed by its potential value. Insuring loans based on business assets is quite a different matter from insuring residential mortgages. The risks involved are far less predictable because the earning power of the business asset depends so much on the managerial skill of the farm operator. In addition, it depends on the behavior of the price of his product. Under these circumstances, loss experience is less predictable, hence establishing an appropriate insurance fee may be difficult.

Another difficulty is that to the extent that the programs increase the total supply of farm real estate credit, they may tend to increase the price of land and further reduce the generally low net return on farm real estate. If, however, the annual repayments on the mortgages are large, the price effect of land values will be minimal. Lastly, farm operators who finance with little equity may lose what little capital they have if land prices decline moderately or if their incomes fall abruptly for reasons beyond their control.

The Commission recommends also a federal loan insurance program for intermediate-term credit of three to ten years to help farmers finance the acquisition of the capital assets, other than real estate, required for an efficient farm unit.*

Professional services for the development of an efficient farm plan and management consulting might also be supplied in connection with these loans.

At present most of the funds required for such investment are supplied by farm operators themselves, partly aided by installment credit from farm equipment dealers. But if the adjustment in farm size is to be speeded, more adequate *external* credit is needed. At present commercial banks are the largest external source of intermediate-term credit for farmers. Their loanable funds depend largely upon bank deposits

---

* FRED LAZARUS, JR.—I am opposed to these recommendations since I do not believe that the need for these programs has been proved. In fact it appears to me that these new programs would make it even more difficult to solve our national farm problems.

made locally, and under the unit banking system, the local supply of agricultural credit has sometimes been limited, particularly if an area has suffered a decline in income. Because many agricultural loans in a single area may default at the same time as the result of some natural disaster, banks have hesitated to become overly committed to loans in one locality or crop. Consequently rural banks cannot adequately diversify their assets within their local areas, and they have not used for local lending even the limited funds available to them. Instead country banks as a class have acquired a sizable volume of Treasury securities and have had excess reserves throughout the postwar years. A loan insurance program would increase the flow of funds to farmers from local banks and other local institutions and might also attract funds from outside the local area.

Credit for small business

Two federal credit programs already aid small business firms. The direct loan program of the Small Business Administration makes direct loans to small businesses that are unable to obtain credit from commercial sources, and the SBA also participates in loans with private lending institutions. Second, the SBA was authorized in 1958 to license and regulate private small business investment corporations whose purpose is to provide intermediate and long-term loans and equity capital to small business firms. The SBA can assist SBIC's by purchasing their subordinate debentures and by making loans to them in limited amounts.

In addition, several states have established business development or development credit corporations. As one of their activities, they have participated in small and new business financing. These organizations merit encouragement for their contribution to the distressed area problem as well as to small business financing.

These programs were designed to aid small business on the grounds that small business is unable to obtain medium- and long-term credit on as favorable terms as larger firms, and that the growth and health of small business is essential to a free enterprise system and a potent force through innovations in promoting economic growth. Small businesses must rely primarily on local or personal sources of funds, and thus they are at a disadvantage compared with firms that have access to regional or national capital markets.

It is extremely difficult to evaluate the empirical data on the adequacy of small business financing. Opinions differ on whether the problem is quantitatively significant and on whether it is becoming more or less acute. The share of small business in all business has not declined; instead small business has grown rapidly in the postwar period. But how much more rapidly small firms would have grown if more credit had been available cannot be ascertained.

The evidence is also inconclusive on whether a significant gap still exists in credit facilities for new and small business firms which have a realistic prospect of successful operation since the establishment of the SBIC program. As yet the life of the SBIC's has been too short to show how far they will contribute to small business financing. However, the program appears to be promising.

If, however, later evidence suggests that the SBIC program is not adequate for its task, consideration might be given to the development of a loan insurance program available to all lenders, including posssibly SBIC's.* Such a program should be designed with enough risk shifted to the insurance program so that private lenders would adopt more liberal lending practices. But the risk shifted should not be so great that lenders would use the program as a dumping ground for all undesirable loans. For example, if the insurance covered only the first 10 percent of the loss, such a program would likely have no effect; alternatively if it covered 100 per cent of the loss, private lenders would find it profitable to make irresponsible and imprudent loans. A proper balance could be achieved by adjusting the insurance charge and the sharing of risk between the private lender and the insurance organization so that additional credit to small business would be provided.

SUBSIDIZED CREDIT PROGRAMS

*Federal credit programs designed to alter the allocation of resources to achieve a public purpose which even a perfectly functioning private market system would not attain require a subsidy in the form of below-market interest rates or credit terms. The choice among types of credit programs should be made on the basis of which will be effective at the least cost and which will interfere least with the private financial system. Where it can be effective, a loan guarantee type of program should take preference over the direct lending type of program. (Second Guide)***

The Commission recognizes that simply improving competition in credit markets will not necessarily secure that reallocation of resources

---

* FRED LAZARUS, JR.—I am not persuaded that such loan program is needed, and fear that it would encourage unsound lending practices.

** STANLEY H. RUTTENBERG—The Commission notes that "The choice among types of credit programs should be made on the basis of which will be effective at the least costs and which will interfere least with the private financial system." Since both direct loan programs and loan insurance programs are generally self-supporting, this least cost criteria might have been pursued further. While it is generally recognized that direct loan programs will result in an increase in the Federal debt, with a consequent effect upon Treasury interest rates, the Commission should have considered the extent to which the large volume of government insured obligations compete with Treasury bonds for long-term funds and whether such competition led to an increase in Treasury long-term interest rates. (See also my footnote on page 191.)

and production in the private economy required to secure specific national objectives—social, economic, military, or other—without further government intervention. A financial subsidy or incentive will be necessary to induce private firms to produce the desired item or service. The subsidy or incentive can consist of direct payments or grants, the remission or reduction of taxes, access to credit on especially favorable terms, technical assistance, or a combination thereof. Each form involves a net financial cost to the government.

If Congress desires to provide the subsidy through a credit program, a loan guarantee type of program with no fee charged to the borrower is preferable, if effective, to a direct loan program. Loan guarantees operate through private credit institutions, while direct loan programs may involve the time-consuming process of establishing a new government agency. The amount of subsidy which the government can extend to the ultimate borrower by assuming the costs of the guarantee, however, is limited by the lender's alternative opportunities among non-guaranteed loans and securities with higher net yields.

If a greater reallocation of resources is required than results from the diversion of funds induced by the government guarantee, then a direct loan program is the only type of government credit program which will work. It can be more effective because the government can control completely the terms of the loan and the rate of interest charged. In such a program, however, eligibility standards for borrowers should aim at excluding those who, without the program, could have used private institutions to finance the same undertakings.

Illustrations of subsidized credit assistance are many. A few are cited below. The Commission has made no recommendations, however, as to the appropriateness of the objectives of these programs.*

Public housing and urban renewal

The Public Housing Administration was established during the depression to develop and administer a program of low-rent public housing for low-income families. PHA provides financial aid, technical assistance, and development and management services to participating local housing authorities. In the early stages of a project, the PHA makes direct loans to local authorities which are repaid when the projects are permanently financed. The permanent financing is provided through the sale of long-term, tax-exempt, serial bonds by the local authorities, which are secured by a pledge of continuing contributions by the PHA equal to debt service costs.

After some twenty-five years of operation, there are less than half a

---

* See Mr. RUTTENBERG'S second comment on page 199.

million public housing units in the nation to meet the needs of low-income families. The technique of federal loans and subsidies to local housing authorities for the construction and operation of public housing projects apparently has not solved the problem of low-income housing.* If Congress desires to make a greater contribution to housing low-income families, an alternative approach seems desirable. Because, however, this program involves so many factors other than credit, the Commission has made no specific recommendation.

The urban renewal program is designed to assist municipalities in removing slums and blight and in redeveloping land so that it may be used most advantageously. The program encompasses planning advances, direct loans, and grants to localities for projects involving the rehabilitation of blighted areas. The part played by credit is quite limited and is likely to remain so as long as the present structure of the program remains unchanged. The urgency and likely future growth of urban redevelopment, however, may call for changes in the forms of financial assistance employed, and this may become one of the major credit programs in the years ahead.**

Special assistance programs of FNMA

The special assistance function of the Federal National Mortgage Association was established to support special housing programs, such as

---

* STANLEY H. RUTTENBERG—It is inappropriate to ascribe the less than half a million public housing units to "the technique of federal loans and subsidies to local housing authorities." In the early stages of a project, public housing financing is invariably handled through the sale of temporary loan notes to private investors, which notes are secured by PHA requisition agreements. Since 1949 the permanent financing has been provided by the sale of long-term tax exempt bonds, secured by a pledge by PHA to pay annual contributions equal to debt service costs. In effect, both the short-term and long-term public housing financing are based on what amounts to a government guaranty of private credit.

Mr. NATHAN wishes to be associated with Mr. RUTTENBERG'S comment.

** STANLEY H. RUTTENBERG—The Commission says, "The urgency and likely future growth of urban redevelopment, however, may call for changes in the forms of financial assistance employed, and this may become one of the major credit programs in the years ahead."

The special assistance programs of FNMA (see the next section) for housing for the elderly, minorities, etc. are dismissed with, "The complexity of the present method discourages rational consideration of the appropriate subsidy for any given program." Despite the social necessity for these types of programs, no recommendations are made.

On the other hand, "Specific recommendations are made for some of the programs used as illustrations," (page 187) while in other instances (page 198), "The Commission has made no recommendations . . . as to the appropriateness of the objectives of these programs." In the agriculture and housing areas, there are specific affirmative recommendations. In other areas such as urban renewal, slum clearance, low-income housing, mass transportation systems, college housing, and the like, no recommendations are made. All of these areas should be treated alike, either recommendations should be made on all or on none.

Alaskan housing, defense housing, and housing for the elderly. This activity is financed entirely by the Treasury. It was originally intended that FNMA would support these special housing programs by commitments to purchase mortgages insured by FHA, and that the mortgages would then be sold to private investors, if necessary at a discount, rather than held to maturity. Since FNMA has tried to operate without loss, it has been unwilling to sell these acquisitions below their purchase prices, which generally were above market prices. The agency has thus become a substantial holder of these special types of mortgages, and, in effect, a direct lender.

Although needed houses have been built under these special assistance programs, a question arises as to whether the special assistance procedure is preferable to a direct loan procedure. The complexity of the present method discourages rational consideration of the appropriate subsidy for any given program.*

Agricultural programs

The Farmers Home Administration, a division of the Department of Agriculture, operates direct loan programs designed to aid farmers unable to obtain adequate credit elsewhere to establish efficient farming units. These credit programs, in contrast to those of the federally sponsored agencies, involve loans at below-market rates and usually involve technical assistance.

The Rural Electrification Authority was established as a depression measure to help finance rural electric cooperatives at a time when only 10 percent of U.S. farms were electrified. Today, over 96 percent of U.S. farms are electrified as a result both of the REA and of the increased emphasis by private utilities on extending electric facilities to farms. Farm electrification in turn has made possible the use of many of the advances of technology in agriculture.

The rural electric cooperatives obtain external funds from the REA which in turn borrows from the Treasury. The amount of new borrowing is limited by annual congressional authorizations. The *cash* subsidy in this program is only implicit; it arises from the difference between the 2 percent interest rate charged the REA by the Treasury and the actual cost of the money to the Treasury. In the last ten years this implicit cash subsidy has amounted to over $300 million. Because the Treasury can borrow at a lower cost than any private borrower, the value of the *total* credit subsidy to the rural cooperatives exceeds the cash subsidy. Before 1945, provisions in the legislation related the interest rates paid by the REA to the interest costs of the Treasury, instead

---

* See Mr. RUTTENBERG'S second comment on page 199.

of the 2 percent rate today. While the appropriateness of the cash subsidy or its amount is not a matter for its consideration, the Commission does believe that the amount of the cash subsidy should be made an explicit charge in the budget.

Other domestic credit programs

In transportation, direct loan and guarantee programs have been used extensively either by themselves or in combination with direct subsidies and tax exemptions. The purchase and construction of ships of the U.S. merchant marine have been financed since World War I through government credit assistance and other aids. The short-haul airlines have had government credit assistance for the purchase of new equipment. The Interstate Commerce Commission is authorized to guarantee private lenders against loss of principal and interest on refinancing, improvement, and property maintenance loans of railroads.

Credit aids for education and for personal development and training may well grow into major proportions. The wartime loan program for students enrolled in accelerated courses, and loans under the National Defense Education Act of 1958 may be the forerunners of larger scale credit programs designed to promote economic growth.

CREDIT PROGRAMS AND ECONOMIC STABILIZATION

Since direct lending programs to achieve a particular allocation of resources resemble government expenditure programs, the amount of credit extended should be determined as a part of the budgetary process. However, merely because direct lending programs are credit rather than expenditure programs, the amount of credit extended should not be singled out as being either uniquely appropriate for countercyclical variation or uniquely insulated from such variation. (Third Guide)

A flexible fiscal policy requires the integration of credit activities involving Treasury outlays with other government expenditures. If the intent of Congress in establishing a program can be achieved only by a steady level of outlays year by year, such a program is not susceptible to countercyclical variation. But if the objective sought is longer run and can be reached with equal effectiveness with some variations of annual outlays, then such a lending program should be considered for countercyclical variation in furtherance of stabilization policy. In any case the same criteria for countercyclical variation should be used for direct government lending programs as for government expenditure programs.

Examples of possible countercyclical direct loan programs are those of the Community Facilities Administration and the Urban Renewal

Administration. Variable grants and credit terms to local communities could be employed to stimulate local public works and slum clearance in recession and to slow down the initiation of new projects during booms. The time lags may be so great, however, that this device might have only limited usefulness in short cycles.

An example of countercyclical variation of a program similar to a direct loan program is the support which the Federal National Mortgage Association from time to time has given to the mortgage market. On at least two occasions, in 1949-50 and 1958, Congress directed FNMA to undertake large market-support purchases of underwritten mortgages with funds obtained from the Treasury. These purchases were made in an attempt to stabilize the mortgage market and to provide additional mortgage funds for residential construction.

In 1949-50, FNMA issued advance commitments to purchase Veterans Administration mortgages at par at a time when the mortgages were selling only at discounts. As a result FNMA purchases increased sharply; it acquired more than half of all VA home loans on new construction. These purchases contributed not only to an increase in home construction but also to a rise in the prices of houses.

In 1958 a special $1 billion anti-recession program was authorized by Congress under which FNMA was to issue advance commitments to purchase at par Federal Housing Administration and VA mortgages of $13,500 or less. This program was authorized in April 1958, the month the recession reached bottom, and most of the actual purchases under the program were made in 1959, when housing construction was booming.

The inevitable consequences of trying to support such a broad segment of the market when contract interest rates on VA or FHA mortgages are below market rates are either massive purchases, if a serious attempt is made to make the below-market rates effective, or *ad hoc* rationing and windfall profits to some mortgage originators, if funds are not adequate to lower the market rates. Both consequences were realized in 1949-50 when FNMA was buying VA mortgages freely but not without limit. Windfall profits occurred under the special $1 billion anti-recession program of 1958. This type of assistance is particularly impractical, because when FNMA pays an above-market price, the originating intermediary who sells to FNMA rather than the home buyer gets most of the benefit.

The key issue with respect to short-run stabilization objectives is whether FNMA should be used to help stabilize the economy, the residential construction sector, or prices and interest rates in the mortgage market. In the postwar years residential construction has moved in a direction counter to general business and has tended to provide a stabilizing influence on the economy. This tendency arises because of the great sensitivity of residential construction to changes in the supply and prices of mortgage credit. Any attempt by FNMA to support prices and yields in the mortgage market will not only require a huge volume of government funds but will counter the forces of general monetary policy. Similarly attempts to stabilize residential construction by off-setting somewhat the variations in the flow of mortgage credit would tend to counter the effects of general monetary policy.

Self-supporting credit programs

Credit programs established to increase the effectiveness of the private credit system should be designed to be sensitive to general monetary policy. Some programs, especially loan insurance programs, should at times be used to supplement and reinforce general monetary policy by variations in lending terms. (Fourth Guide)*

Federal credit programs established to make credit markets more effective in serving a particular demand should not intentionally insulate that sector of the economy from the effects of monetary policies. Such programs presumably aim at making the price mechanism more effective in the allocation of loan funds and thereby at closing credit gaps. They clearly should not nullify the workings of the price system; they should instead allow the price of credit to fluctuate with general market conditions. In this way the effects of general monetary policy will be transmitted to the sector concerned.

Sometimes it may also be desirable to use the programs to supplement and reinforce general monetary policy. In housing, especially, variations in down-payment requirements, loan maturities, interest rates, and eligibility requirements affect the demand for mortgage loans. When the underlying long-run demand for housing is strong, the short-run demand fluctuates with the terms and conditions under which credit is available to finance acquisitions. Changes in down-payment requirements and in maturities alter the amount of monthly payments needed to carry a mortgage and significantly affect the ability of individuals to purchase houses. Thus, changes in the terms can influence the demand for housing and volume of home construction as well as the price of both new and existing housing.*

---

* CHARLES B. SHUMAN—I do not have a great deal of enthusiasm for the idea of varying down-payment requirements, loan maturities, interest rates, and eligibility requirements to affect the demand for mortgages. In conventional financing provisions of this type are varied in response to market conditions. In the case of government programs, most of the variation has been to liberalize terms. It would seem to me that it would be better to move in the direction of letting market conditions have more influence on the determination of mortgage terms under government guarantee and insurance programs.

Credit terms in government underwriting programs are generally more liberal than those prevalent for conventional mortgage loans. Since borrowers under the FHA and VA programs receive a special privilege, it seems appropriate that this privilege should be partially withdrawn when prices of houses and construction costs rise excessively or when general inflationary pressures are a threat to economic stability. It can then be restored when a greater stimulus to home buying and new construction is desired.

At the present time the statutory ceiling interest rate on VA mortgages and the administration of the contract rate on new FHA mortgages have the undesigned effect of inducing strong countercyclical variations in the flow of mortgage credit from private lenders and hence in residential construction. In a later section the Commission recommends the elimination of all such statutory ceiling rates, and specifically the ceiling rates on underwritten mortgages. The Commission believes that the level of residential construction appropriate for stabilization policy can be achieved with greater sensitivity by allowing contract interest rates to fluctuate with conditions in the mortgage market and by varying other credit terms as a selective control device. Discretionary changes of credit terms, however, should be made with caution, and consideration must be given to the time lag between changes in terms and in expenditures generated by underwriting programs.

The Commission recommends that the FHA and VA underwriting programs be used to aid in implementing the countercyclical and price-stabilizing policies of the government by variations in the terms of the underwritten loans and by allowing contractual interest rates to rise and fall with conditions in the mortgage market.

Home Loan Bank System

The Commission recommends that the Federal Home Loan Bank System operate its programs in close harmony with the general stabilization policies of the government.

Although the eleven district banks in the Federal Home Loan Bank System no longer have any government capital, the System is quasi-governmental. Its prime function is to provide liquidity for its member institutions which are being subject to unusual cash drains. In a severe emergency, its functioning in such a capacity is buttressed by the Treasury's authorization to purchase FHLB obligations.

Currently the members of the FHLB System consist almost exclusively of savings and loan associations. The assets of savings and loan associations are predominantly conventional residential mortgages with limited marketability. The associations, unlike other types of thrift institutions, do not hold a large volume of easily marketable assets which can be sold if funds are needed in excess of inflows from new savings, amortization, and interest payments to meet unexpectedly large net withdrawals of share accounts or to honor commitments to purchase mortgages made many months earlier. Associations rely on their ability to borrow from the home loan banks to meet their liquidity needs. The banks use funds available from both capital subscriptions and deposits of member institutions for such lending, and if additional resources are needed, they issue consolidated securities in the capital markets. In the absence of a ready market for conventional mortgages, the banks have in effect provided a source of liquidity for the savings and loan associations.

It has been suggested by others that the banks supply additional funds to the mortgage market by issuing more securities in the capital markets and lending the proceeds on a long-term basis to member institutions. The security issues might be attractive to savers who otherwise would not invest in mortgages directly or who would not make deposits in member institutions. The Commission doubts the wisdom of using the facilities of the FHLB System to attract new long-term funds into mortgage lending by enabling its members to be continuously in debt to the home loan banks. It is better not to combine in one institution the function of providing a source of liquidity for its members to use in abnormal circumstances and that of a continuous long-term lender to them.

The System clearly has exercised restraint in its lending to members thus far. However, the volume of advances and related borrowing have shown significant cyclical variation, which has offset somewhat the restrictive effect of general monetary policy on mortgage lending.

In 1955, the actions of the FHLB Board to control increases in mortgage lending by member associations by means of a direct limitation of the amount of borrowing from the banks upset the housing market. Commitments to lend for the purchase of a new house are made many months in advance of the final mortgage loan to the home buyer. If limitations are imposed by the Home Loan Bank Board which squeeze loan disbursements regardless of advance commitments, the result is likely to be very disruptive. Because a source of liquidity is useful only if it is available, the control should be placed at the inception of the commitment-lending process rather than at is end.

Control of the rate of issue of new commitments by members, however, is difficult. A more flexible interest rate policy on advances is suggested as one approach. There appears to be a fairly constant relationship between the interest rates charged by the banks on advances and their cost of borrowing in the market. A change in policy to relate the interest rates charged to mortgage rates prevailing or expected to prevail in each bank district might more effectively curb over-commitments by some members and hence future bank advances. The Commission urges experimentation in rate controls.

Sources of funds

Where the funds for direct lending programs come partly from the Treasury and partly from private financial institutions participating in direct loans on a guaranteed basis, the interest rates on the private participations should be varied in response to the needs of general monetary policy. If the financing of direct lending programs requires the issue of securities in national capital markets, Treasury issues rather than fully guaranteed issues of government corporations should be employed. (Fifth Guide)

The price support programs of the Commodity Credit Corporation represent a use of a credit program to implement a policy that in itself is not concerned with credit. In order to support the prices of farm products, the CCC purchases commodities directly from farmers, or it lends to farmers on a nonrecourse basis at 100 percent of the price support level with the crops as collateral, or it guarantees similar loans by private lenders. A farmer may discharge his obligation in full with no interest charge by turning over to CCC the pledged commodities within the year, or he may repay the loan and accumulated interest to acquire clear title to the crop. Handling a part of the crop support activities as a credit program is administratively easier than as a direct purchase program if farmers withdraw their mortgaged crop to use or sell, because the crop is generally stored initially on the farm rather than in a government facility. From the financial point of view, however, there is no difference.

The CCC finances its loans primarily by borrowing from the Treasury. The loan may also be made initially not by the CCC but by a commercial bank, with the CCC issuing to the private lender a "certificate of interest," a short-term, interest-bearing security payable on demand. The bank may deposit these certificates with the CCC at any time for cash, and at that time the CCC increases its borrowing from the Treasury to obtain the funds to redeem the certificates. Issuing certificates of interest postpones temporarily the drain on the Treasury for financing the price support program; there will be no drain on the Treasury if farmers repay their loans while still held by banks.

Because the certificates constitute a demand obligation, private lenders frequently transfer them back to the CCC whenever the yield on competing investments increases. At times this enables the private institutions to avoid the effects of restrictive monetary policy. If certificates of interest are to be used in the future, the interest rates on new loans should be varied to induce the holding or redemption of certificates in accordance with the prevailing monetary policy, or maturities on the participations should be lengthened so they are no longer demand obligations, or a penalty should be attached to the transfer to CCC of the guaranteed loan.

In the past, fully guaranteed securities of government credit corporations were sometimes issued to raise funds for direct lending. The government has wisely stopped this practice. If borrowing is necessary to finance the program, the issuance of such securities is likely to prove to be more costly and more cumbersome than direct Treasury issues and may conflict with appropriate debt management policies.

INTEREST RATE CEILINGS

Statutory or rigidly administered interest rate ceilings should not be employed in federal credit programs which rely on the private financial system for loan funds. (Sixth Guide)

It is fundamental to the operation of loan insurance or guarantee programs that private lending institutions be willing to make such loans. Since lenders have alternative investment opportunities, the rates on the underwritten loans must be attractive in relation to these alternatives if private funds are to be forthcoming.

Interest rate ceilings usually are intended to protect the borrower against an excessive interest cost and thus represent a form of price control. If lenders are unwilling to extend credit at rates at or below the ceiling rate, access to funds by the borrower privileged to use the federal credit program is denied, and he must shift to a higher priced alternative if he wants accommodation. The ceilings are not effective in protecting the borrower, and they interfere with and distort the adjustment mechanisms which would be set in motion by price changes. The Commission believes that there is no place for such arbitrary price controls in a market system regulated largely by flexible prices.

The outstanding examples of interest rate ceilings are those on VA and FHA underwritten mortgages. When the economy is prosperous and the demand for credit is strong, interest rates rise. At those times the ceiling rates on FHA insured and VA guaranteed loans make them eventually noncompetitive as outlets for the investment funds of lending institutions. Consequently residential lending under these programs drops appreciably whenever market rates are above the statutory rates. While some lenders still purchase underwritten mortgages at a discount, other institutional lenders hesitate to do so. They invest their funds elsewhere. Thus, when credit is tight generally, VA and FHA mortgage borrowers have difficulty in obtaining loans because of the ceiling rate.

To the extent that VA and FHA borrowers can still obtain underwritten loans, they are not protected fully by the ceiling rate. The originator of the mortgage, usually the home builder, arranges the mortgage with the home buyer at the ceiling rate. Since the builder can sell it only at a discount he appears to suffer the initial loss. Yet there is widespread evidence that at least part and sometimes most of this expected loss is passed on to the home buyer in less house for his money than he had anticipated. Also when underwritten loans are difficult to arrange, borrowers shift to conventional mortgages where the interest rate is more flexible. Because credit terms on conventional mortgages are more stringent, they do not represent a close substitute for the lower-down-payment, longer-maturity, underwritten mortgage. Home buyers with little equity for the larger down payment on a conventional mortgage are either rationed out of the housing market or are forced to resort to the very high-rate second mortgage market. The ceiling rate does not protect home buyers against a higher price for their credit when market rates are above the ceiling rate.

The instability in the flow of funds to underwritten mortgages caused by the ceiling rates has marked destabilizing effects on the residential construction industry but a countercyclical effect on the economy. Some have advocated retention of the ceiling rates to ensure this latter effect. Even without the ceilings, however, institutional lenders probably would still shift away from mortgage lending to some extent during periods of tight money because mortgage rates move more sluggishly than interest rates on some other investments. Borrowers would also be curbed somewhat by the effect of higher rates of interest in increasing the monthly payments on the mortgage. Residential construction would thus continue to be sensitive to monetary policy and behave in a countercyclical fashion, though perhaps to a lesser degree. And if greater fluctuations were desirable, they could be achieved on a more sensitive basis by variations in the lending terms of the mortgage contract being underwritten.

The Commission believes that the harmful effects of the ceiling rates on underwritten mortgages outweigh their automatic contribution to economic stabilization and recommends that they be abolished.*

---

* STANLEY H. RUTTENBERG—Instead of proposing the removal of the interest rate ceiling on FHA and VA insured mortgages, the Commission should have considered the contributory effects the insured mortgage interest rates had on Treasury interest rates and what could be done to prevent a recurrence of the record level of interest rates in 1959 when the Treasury bond rate was bumping at the statutory ceiling and other long-term rates were prevented from rising further by the laws governing usury. Accordingly, I am opposed to any removal of the interest rate ceilings on FHA or VA mortgage insurance or on any of the farm credit programs.

It is argued that FHA ceiling rates prevent borrowers from securing mortgages, or on the other hand, force borrowers to pay a discount. It might be wise for the Federal government to engage in direct lending as a means of preventing the use of discounting and as a means of holding down the interest rate charges that are made by private lending agencies.

The various interest rate ceilings or limitations that affect agricultural credit should also be removed.

The federal land banks cannot charge more than 6 percent on their farm mortgage loans. Many states have limits on the interest rate charged on agricultural loans. Under conditions of strong credit demand and high interest rate levels when ceilings have not been evaded by lender's fees, premiums, and other charges, their main impact has been to reduce the supply of credit available to farmers from that which would have been available in the absence of ceiling rates. If ceilings are effective and are enforced on the major institutional lenders, the ability of the farmer to obtain credit is reduced. Alternatively farmers turn to individuals and unregulated institutions, which often extend credit at substantially higher interest rates, so that the ceiling provides little protection to farmers.

Another type of price control relates to the margin between the interest rates lenders may charge to farmers and the rates at which they can borrow from the federal intermediate credit banks. The FICB system was designed originally to assist both commercial banks and other lenders in extending credit to farmers. The use of the system by commercial banks has been limited by the small margin they are permitted between the FICB lending rates and the rate which commercial banks may charge the farmer. Thus one of the original objectives of the system has been negated. Even though most country commercial banks have access to funds from their correspondent banks, a cordial relationship between the FICB's and commercial banks might better stabilize the credit available in some farm communities.

SECONDARY MARKET PROGRAMS

*Federal agencies to create and maintain secondary markets for financial instruments, such as mortgages, should buy and sell the instruments at market prices and should not attempt to control their prices. (Seventh Guide)**

The function of a secondary market institution is to provide a facility through which investors can purchase a particular type of financial instrument to increase their holdings and where they can sell to reduce

---

* STANLEY H. RUTTENBERG—When the government engages in secondary market operations, it does so not as a private dealer, but as a government. If credit policy calls for raising or lowering market interest rates, the government agency concerned should be free to employ whatever credit tools it has available to effect such policy, including buying and selling mortgages at, below or above market prices. If the government cannot carry out its policies in this manner it is not clear, to me, why the government should be operating in the secondary market.

their holdings. The institution's role is to make a market for the instrument and to reflect the forces in the market in the prices at which it deals. A government secondary market institution should act essentially like a dealer in other financial markets and both buy and sell at market prices. It should not attempt to control the market or to fix prices.

Since 1954, it has been the function of the FNMA secondary market operations to make a market in FHA and VA mortgages by dealing in them at market prices, thereby improving the liquidity of the mortgage instrument and facilitating the free flow of private funds into mortgage investment. The secondary market program was expected to operate eventually without expense to the government with funds obtained largely from its own security issues to the public. Procedures were also established so that FNMA could be transferred to private ownership.

It appears that as a result of the policies it has pursued, FNMA has not been successful in establishing an effective secondary market for underwritten mortgages. Unlike a dealer it has added most of the mortgages it has purchased to its mortgage portfolio. Sales have been only about a quarter of total purchases. The prices at which FNMA will sell and the limitations on types of mortgages it will purchase have precluded it from performing as an effective secondary market institution. Instead of being kept in close alignment with either current purchase prices or with market trends, sales prices appear to have been tied to the prices at which individual mortgages were purchased. Offers to buy similarly have been hedged by various restrictions and eligibility requirements.

There is a great need for a secondary mortgage market. The Commission prefers to see the development of private institutions to serve this function. If a number of private institutions were operating, a national market for government underwritten mortgages could come into being. Such institutions might also form the basis for initiating a secondary market for conventional mortgages, especially if greater standardization of state laws affecting mortgage lending is achieved.

The National Housing Act of 1934 provided for privately financed national mortgage associations to make a market for FHA insured loans. Under the conditions of the thirties, no associations were formed, and the RFC Mortgage Company and its successor FNMA undertook this secondary market function. The authority for national mortgage associations was deleted from the statutes in 1949. Current and prospective conditions are more conducive to the success of such institutions than the prewar situation was, and the reinstitution of authority for national mortgage associations might help stimulate the desired private secondary market facilities.

Pending the development of more effective private secondary mortgage institutions, the Commission recommends that the secondary market operations of FNMA be continued and made more effective. The special assistance and market support programs of FNMA which are inconsistent with the dealer function should be operated in an entirely distinct and separate manner from the secondary market operations, preferably by a separate agency.

CHAPTER EIGHT

INTERNATIONAL
MONETARY
RELATIONS

The United States is the world's largest trader, with exports and imports of goods and services much greater than those of any other country. As the largest holder of official exchange reserves of foreign nations and of privately owned foreign balances it has also become the leading world banker. These roles are closely interrelated and impose a responsibility to maintain a satisfactory balance of payments and a healthy economy to retain confidence in the dollar as a reserve currency. Achievement of our foreign policy objectives requires that these conditions be met by measures consistent with the freedom of trade and payments which we have taken the lead in promoting.

Speculation against the dollar in late 1960 and the continued large payments deficits serve as vivid reminders of how rapidly the international situation has changed from a few years ago when a chronic dollar shortage was feared. The speculation demonstrated again that a reserve currency country is subject to a special set of requirements in the management of its international financial affairs. The run against the dollar forced the United States to realize the importance of greatly reducing its payments deficit, even though its gold holdings were very large and exceeded foreign-owned liquid dollar assets, and of joining with other countries in the development of more effective arrangements to protect the world payments system from exchange crises.

The system of stable exchange rates of countries that are members of the International Monetary Fund is based on the fixed dollar price of gold and the interconvertibility of gold and dollars. The U.S. Treasury maintains the gold value of the dollar internationally by its unlimited willingness to buy gold from anyone and to sell gold to foreign official institutions, both at $35 an ounce. If, because of a U.S. payments deficit, official foreign institutions acquire more dollars than they wish to hold, the Treasury stands ready to sell gold to them to prevent the dollar from depreciating in terms of their currencies. Whenever foreigners need more dollars to make payments here, perhaps because of a U.S. payments surplus, the Treasury stands ready to buy gold to prevent the dollar from appreciating in terms of their currencies. Other IMF countries generally maintain the value of their currencies by buying and selling dollars or other currencies.

The principal assets with which authorities in other countries support their currencies are holdings of gold and of liquid assets in reserve currency countries, primarily the United States and the United Kingdom. In the postwar period these have been supplemented by deposits of various currencies with the IMF, which are available for the use of its members. The growth of foreign-owned liquid dollar assets in such reserve holdings has been a significant feature of the last decade, and has resulted from the large, continuing U.S. payments deficit, discussed in the balance of payments section.

The recent U.S. payments deficits have been much too large to be continued for long. Attainment of a satisfactory balance is a necessity, and deliberate policy measures must be adopted to secure this result. The problem of international adjustment is that of developing mechanisms to ensure the restoration of a satisfactory payments balance whenever severe imbalance occurs. It is more than a problem of money and credit, and other measures are also necessary for its solution.

The international liquidity problem is that of providing a supply of international reserves adequate for the needs of all countries in a framework relatively secure against exchange crises. When the U.S. payments position is satisfactory, its obligations to foreigners are not likely to prove troublesome. But in the normal course of events, cyclical changes in income in the United States and abroad are likely to result in payments deficits at some times and payments surpluses at other times. When deficits are large and appear to be continuing and gold is sold to help finance the deficit, concern may develop over the adequacy of U.S. reserves in relation to short-term U.S. liabilities to foreigners, both current and prospective.

A confidence or exchange crisis may develop if private parties shift from dollars into foreign currencies and if foreign official institutions convert a large part of their dollar balances to gold. These large demands for gold, which may lead to doubts about the continued ability of the United States to maintain its standing offer to sell gold, would represent an early stage of an exchange crisis. If no measures were taken to forestall further conversions of dollars into gold, further depletions of our gold stock might lead to the suspension of the convertibility of dollars into gold at a fixed price, to disruptive movements in exchange rates, and perhaps even to the adoption of trade and exchange controls.

Measures which succeed in correcting payments imbalance will obviously affect other countries. Consequently the United States must consider the effects of its actions on them; policies frequently must be negotiated. Because the nature of the problems and their solutions are multilateral, actions by the United States alone are often not feasible.

This chapter is addressed to the key problems of international adjustment and international liquidity. The aspects of the problem involving money and credit are discussed in some detail, and the nature of some other measures is also considered. These basic problems are discussed in the third and fourth sections; recent developments in the U.S. balance of payments are briefly reviewed in the next section.

The Postwar Developments

The United States has had a deficit in its balance of payments of $17.8 billion in the ten years 1951-60 (Table 4). This cumulative deficit was settled by sales of gold of $4.7 billion,[1] by the acquisition of liquid dollar assets by foreign official institutions, including central banks, of $8.8 billion, by foreign commercial banks of $2.7 billion, and by other foreign private parties of $1.7 billion.

Since 1950, the United States has had a payments deficit in every year except 1957. During the period from 1951-57 the average annual deficit was nearly $1 billion. Beginning in 1958, however, the situation changed markedly, and the annual deficits for the past three years have ranged from $3.5 billion in 1958 to $3.8 billion in 1960. Moreover, a much larger proportion of the deficits of the last three years was settled by the sale of gold, with total sales of $4.7 billion.

The U.S. balance of payments accounts have been arranged in Table 4 to focus attention on the major components and subtotals. The first ten items cover what might be called the "hard-core" accounts; the current account—the merchandise balance, the difference between exports and imports, plus net transactions in investment income and services such as ocean freight charges, interest and dividend payments, private remittances, and tourist expenditures; the government account—expenditures in support of U.S. military establishments abroad and economic aid in the form of grants and loans; and the private long-term capital account—net long-term investments, including equities by Americans

---

[1] In addition, $344 million of gold was subscribed to the IMF capital in 1959.

Table 4

U.S. BALANCE OF PAYMENTS, 1951-1960

(millions of dollars)

Line		1951-60 Average	1951-55 Average	1956	1957	1958	1959	1960
	Current account:							
1	Merchandise exports	+15,547	+13,360	+17,379	+19,390	+16,263	+16,225	+19,411
2	Merchandise imports	−12,399	−10,982	−12,804	−13,291	−12,951	−15,315	−14,717
3	Trade balance (1+2)	+3,148	+2,378	+4,575	+6,099	+3,312	+910	+4,694
4	Services and income, net [a]	+1,499	+1,382	+1,591	+2,174	+1,650	+1,305	+1,361
5	Current account balance (3+4)	+4,647	+3,760	+6,166	+8,273	+4,962	+2,215	+6,055
	U.S. government payments abroad:							
6	Military expenditures [b]	−2,685	−2,238	−2,955	−3,165	−3,412	−3,090	−3,034
7	Grants	−1,862	−2,076	−1,733	−1,616	−1,616	−1,623	−1,651
8	Loans, net [c]	−503	−202	−629	−958	−971	−358	−1,106
9	Total	−5,050	−4,516	−5,317	−5,739	−5,999	−5,071	−5,791
10	Private long-term capital, net	−1,408	−690	−1,932	−2,556	−2,514	−1,664	−1,967
11	Private short-term U.S. capital	−326	−171	−528	−258	−306	+89	−1,228
12	Errors and omissions	+353	+377	+643	+748	+380	+783	+905
13	U.S. payments balance (5+9+10+11+12)	−1,784	−1,241	−968	+468	−3,477	−3,826	−3,836
	Settlement of the U.S. payments balance:							
14	With foreign official institutions (15+16)	+1,348	+985	+234	−916	+3,086	+2,433	+3,716
15	Gold; sales or purchases	+467	+214	+306	−798	+2,275	+731	+1,702
16	Dollar assets, sales or purchases	+880	+771	+540	+118	+811	+1,702	+2,014
17	With foreign banks	+268	+179	+420	+50	+47	+1,145	+115
18	With foreign private parties	+167	+77	+314	+398	+344	+248	+15
19	Hard-core balance (5+9+10)	−1,811	−1,446	−1,083	+22	−3,551	−4,520	−1,703
20	Short-term capital flows (11+12+17+18)	+462	+462	+849	+938	+465	+2,087	−2,033

In this table a plus sign indicates a flow of funds toward the United States, a minus sign a flow away from the United States. The addition is algebraic. Details may not add to totals because of rounding.

[a] Includes pensions and private remittances and excludes military expenditures.

[b] Excludes military transfers under grants and associated exports of goods and services.

[c] Excludes subscription to International Monetary Fund of $1,375 million in 1959, of which $344 million was paid in gold and $1,031 million in non-interest-bearing short-term government securities.

SOURCE: *Survey of Current Business and Federal Reserve Bulletin.*

abroad, and by foreigners in the United States.* The difference between total receipts and payments on these items is the hard-core surplus or deficit, shown at the bottom of the table.

The next item (line 11) includes net short-term investments abroad by U.S. private parties and commercial banks. The "errors and omissions" entry covers unrecorded transactions and is calculated as a residual. Major changes in the level of this item are believed to result from short-term capital movements.

The conventional payments balance is the algebraic sum of the above items. A deficit—an excess of payments over receipts—is settled by the sale of gold to foreign official institutions and by the acquisition of liquid dollar assets by foreign official institutions, foreign commercial banks, and other private parties. The willingness of foreign commercial banks and other private parties to accumulate dollar assets reduces the amount of the deficit to be settled by transactions with foreign official institutions.

Private short-term capital transactions of Americans and foreigners and the errors and omissions item are grouped at the bottom of the table. This subtotal includes the volatile funds shifted between the United States and other countries in search of higher short-term interest returns as well as in expectation of changes in the structure of exchange rates.

Care must be used in inferring causal relationships from the balance of payments accounts. All U.S. exports do not represent purchases of U.S. goods by foreigners on a commercial basis. Some U.S. government grants to foreign countries are in goods, not funds, and the goods are included in U.S. exports. Some government loans stipulate that the proceeds must be spent in the United States, and the goods purchased are also included in U.S. exports. Some direct long-term investments by U.S. companies take the form of shipments of capital goods purchased in the United States to equip a plant in a foreign country. At least $2.2 billion of U.S. exports resulted from government loans and grants in each of the last five years (Table 6, line 23). Unfortunately, data are not available on the amount of U.S. exports that resulted from U.S. direct foreign private investment.

These data indicate that the U.S. payments deficit has not resulted from a deficit in the merchandise balance or from a deficit in the current account. Instead, U.S. exports have not grown fast enough in relation to the growth in U.S. imports to offset the change in net payments on government account and on the private capital account.

Moreover, the capital outflow on private account and on government account (Table 5, line 1) has exceeded the U.S. payments deficit in most

---

* CHARLES B. SHUMAN—I do not agree with the inclusion of all foreign programs in what the CMC calls the "hard-core" accounts. I do not accept the implication that nothing could be done about foreign aid. I believe it can and should be substantially reduced.

Table 5
CHANGES IN U.S. FOREIGN INVESTMENT, 1951-1960
(millions of dollars)

Line	1951-60 Average	1951-55 Average	1956	1957	1958	1959	1960
1 U.S. capital flows abroad	−2,529	−1,287	−3,619	−4,133	−3,815	−2,659	−4,628
2 Private long-term and short-term	−2,026	−1,085	−2,990	−3,175	−2,844	−2,301	−3,522
3 U.S. government loans a	− 503	− 202	− 629	− 958	− 971	− 358	−1,106
4 Repayable in dollars	− 112	− 91	− 11	− 232	− 561	+ 271	− 136
5 Repayable in foreign currencies	− 391	− 111	− 618	− 726	− 410	− 629	− 970
6 Foreign private long-term capital flows to the United States	+ 291	+ 224	+ 530	+ 361	+ 24	+ 548	+ 327
Net capital flows:							
7 Including government loans repayable in foreign currencies (2+4+5+6)	−2,238	−1,063	−3,089	−3,772	−3,791	−2,111	−4,301
8 Excluding government loans repayable in foreign currencies (2+4+6)	−1,847	− 952	−2,471	−3,046	−3,381	−1,482	−3,331
Related items:							
9 U.S. payments balance b	−1,784	−1,241	− 968	+ 468	−3,477	−3,826	−3,836
10 Earnings on U.S. private foreign investment	+3,194	+2,607	+3,417	+4,039	+3,560	+3,783	+4,112
11 Income distributed as profits and dividends	+2,241	+1,818	+2,417	+2,676	+2,615	+2,702	+2,912

In this table a plus sign indicates a flow of funds toward the United States, a minus sign a flow away from the United States. The addition is algebraic. Details may not add to totals because of rounding.

a Estimated.
b Line 13 of Table 4.

SOURCE: Survey of Current Business and Foreign Grants and Credits by the United States Government.

postwar years. In this sense, the United States has not been living beyond its income; rather it' has sold gold and liquid dollar assets to help finance an even larger amount of investment abroad. In addition, when earnings of U.S. firms retained abroad (the difference between earnings on U.S. private foreign investment, and the return flow of income as interest, profits, and dividends) are considered, the increase in the net U.S. international investment is even greater than the amount of the capital flows.

CURRENT ACCOUNT

In every postwar year the United States has had a surplus in its trade account and in its current account. Changes in the current account have been the main reason for year-to-year changes in the payments balance, and changes in exports have been the most important element of year-to-year changes in the current account. The variation in commodity imports has been smaller. Net receipts on services and investment income have fluctuated considerably, but their impact on changes in the payments balance has been small.

Changes in the relative prices of competing goods produced here and abroad, in consumer tastes, and in government quotas and exchange controls have also affected the U.S. merchandise account in the last decade. The most dramatic instance of a change in consumer tastes was the increased American demand for small automobiles not produced in the United States, although this change in demand also may reflect an increase in U.S. prices relative to foreign prices. The U.S. prices for some goods important in world trade apparently rose in relation to corresponding foreign prices, even though the indexes of the U.S. general price level did not rise more rapidly than those for most other industrial nations. Average labor costs per unit of output for all manufactures in the United States did not increase faster than corresponding costs in most other industrial countries.*

THE GOVERNMENT ACCOUNT

Payments of the U.S. government for military establishments abroad and for economic aid have averaged about $5 billion annually over the

---

* CHARLES B. SHUMAN—These paragraphs dodge the effect of wage rates on the competitive position of the United States in the international markets. Wages are not the only factor in determining competitive position. A country may have a competitive advantage on certain products even though its wage rates are far beyond those paid in competing countries, but when countries become more equal in technical productivity and other factors, differences in wage rates become of increasing importance. This is the present situation in many of our competitor nations.

last decade (Table 4, line 9), or about 20 percent of U.S. international payments. Government payments of this size and their proportion of the total payments are a new development of the postwar period. But the total government payments remained fairly stable after 1955, and did not cause the recent large increase in the U.S. deficit.*

The dollar outflow or loss of U.S. reserves resulting from these government programs is considerably smaller than total government payments. Procurement under some programs has resulted directly in U.S. exports. Some payments were financed from U.S.-owned currencies acquired from the sale of surplus agricultural commodities to foreigners (Table 6). It is estimated that the annual dollar outflow arising from the government economic programs of loans and grants, without allowance for repayments and interest income, ranged between $400 and $800 million in the last five years. Receipts of interest income and repayments of earlier government loans converted the gross outflow into a net inflow. The annual net dollar outflow for the military expenditure programs has ranged between $2.7 billion and $3.1 billion in the last five years. This net outflow on the military programs accounts for almost all of the outflow on all government programs.

PRIVATE LONG-TERM INVESTMENT

Net long-term capital outflows averaged about $1.4 billion during the past decade and were substantially larger in the last five years (Table 4). The decline in foreign exchange controls abroad, the granting of investment guarantees by the U.S. government for private foreign investments, and the profitable opportunities to acquire production facilities inside foreign tariff barriers induced U.S. firms and private investors to go abroad. The prospect of large common markets resulting from treaty developments abroad has also attracted U.S. investors.

Evaluating the impact of the capital outflows on U.S. reserves is complicated, because in some cases these outflows directly promote U.S. exports. Also the interest and dividend receipts from existing private foreign investments exceeded the net U.S. capital outflow by about $2 billion over the decade, though on an annual basis only once in the last five years.

---

* CHARLES B. SHUMAN—This paragraph and elsewhere indicates a strong bias toward liberal foreign aid payments. Increased trade and foreign travel is a more desirable way to help foreign nations than continual subsidies through soft loans and grants. To correct the unfavorable balance of payments situation, I would favor reduction in foreign aid rather than increased import or travel restrictions.

Table 6

U.S. Government Programs and the U.S. Balance of Payments, 1951-1960
(millions of dollars)

	1951-60 Average	1951-55 Average	1956	1957	1958	1959	1960
1 U.S. military expenditures abroad	−2,685	−2,238	−2,955	−3,165	−3,412	−3,090	−3,034
2 Financed from U.S.-owned foreign currencies a	+ 20	+ 5	+ 15	+ 55	+ 37	+ 33	+ 36
3 Sales of U.S. military equipment abroad	+ 203	+ 115	+ 158	+ 372	+ 296	+ 302	+ 326
4 Net dollar outflow (1+2+3)	−2,462	−2,118	−2,782	−2,738	−3,079	−2,755	−2,672
5 U.S. government grants abroad	−1,862	−2,076	−1,783	−1,616	−1,616	−1,623	−1,651
6 Financed from U.S.-owned foreign currencies a	+ 157	+ 27	+ 328	+ 288	+ 316	+ 283	+ 220
7 Spent in the United States	+1,138	+1,422	+1,076	+ 952	+ 831	+ 731	+ 675b
8 Net dollar outflow (5+6+7)	− 567	− 627	− 329	− 376	− 469	− 609	− 756
9 U.S. government loans abroad	− 740	− 555	− 489	− 997	−1,118	− 998	−1,022
10 Financed from U.S.-owned foreign currencies a	+ 129	+ 17	+ 130	+ 192	+ 305	+ 262	+ 318
11 Spent in the United States	+ 460	+ 363	+ 233	+ 663	+ 783	+ 576	+ 535
12 Interest income and repayments	+ 872	+ 809	+ 700	+ 827	+ 927	+1,321	+ 903
Net dollar outflow:							
13 Excluding interest income and repayments (9+10+11)	− 151	− 175	− 126	− 145	− 30	− 160	− 169
14 Including interest income and repayments (9+10+11+12)	+ 721	+ 634	+ 574	+ 682	+ 897	+1,161	+ 734
15 U.S. government export sales of surplus farm products for foreign currencies	+ 625	+ 162	+1,078	+1,233	+1,023	+ 925	+1,184
16 Disbursed for military expenditures abroad, grants, and loans (2+6+10)	− 305	− 50	− 473	− 535	− 658	− 578	− 558
17 Increase in U.S. holdings of foreign currencies	− 258	− 110	− 532	− 596	− 226	− 204	− 468
18 Adjustments c	− 18	+ 3	− 26	− 19	− 44	− 53	− 53
19 Payments in lieu of dollar payments d (Net dollar flow) (15+16+17+18)	+ 44	+ 5	+ 47	+ 83	+ 95	+ 91	+ 105
20 Total net dollar outflow (4+8+14+19)	−2,264	−2,106	−2,490	−2,349	−2,556	−2,112	−2,589

220

Table 6 (Continued)

	1951-60 Average	1951-55 Average	1956	1957	1958	1959	1960
Total dollar outflow on nonmilitary programs:							
21 Excluding interest income and repayments (8+13+19)	− 674	− 797	− 408	− 438	− 404	− 678	− 820
22 Including interest income and repayments (8+14+19)	+ 198	+ 12	+ 292	+ 389	+ 523	+ 643	+ 83
23 Total spent in the United States (7+11+15)	+2,223	+1,947	+2,387	+2,848	+2,637	+2,232	+2,394

In this table a plus sign indicates a flow of funds toward the United States, a minus sign a flow away from the United States. The addition is algebraic. Details may not add to totals because of rounding.

---

a Acquired from sales of U.S. farm products (line 15).
b Estimated.
c Result of changes in exchange rates, and advance payments from foreign governments.
d Other dollar-saving uses for various U.S. government programs.

SOURCE: *Survey of Current Business, Foreign Grants and Credits by the United States Government, Statistical Abstract of the United States,* and *International Cooperation Administration Operations Reports.*

PRIVATE SHORT-TERM INVESTMENT

Except in 1960, there was a net short-term capital flow to the United States in each year of the past decade (Table 4, line 20). Foreign banks and other foreign private parties were building up liquid balances depleted during the war and early postwar years. In 1960, U.S. and foreign-owned funds were shifted from dollars to foreign currencies in response to higher interest rates abroad than those in the United States, and to speculation against the dollar. The adverse change in the short-term capital account between 1959 and 1960 was about $4 billion.

CHANGES IN THE INTERNATIONAL ECONOMY

There have been several basic changes in the international economy with implications for our balance of payments problem in the future. Immediately after the war the United States was almost the sole source of many manufactured products. But now the world supply of industrial products has caught up with the backlog of world demand, so that international competition covers a much wider range of goods and is geared to price, quality, service, and financing.*

Now that the European market is larger and less fragmented, and production is on a larger scale, other countries have begun to engage in a scale of production which for so long greatly favored the United States. The rapid growth of incomes in the European countries and the reduction of trade barriers among them have enabled foreign producers to achieve the lower unit costs of large-scale production and thus to compete more effectively against U.S. producers both in the United States and abroad.

The apparent reduction in the time lag between the adoption of new techniques and new processes in the United States and their imitation abroad has also strengthened the competitive position of foreigners. For many years the United States has been a technological innovator and an exporter of technology. Prices of U.S. manufactured products remained competitive despite higher U.S. wages because of advanced technology and large-scale production. The more rapid adoption of advanced technology abroad weakens our competitive position in relation to countries with lower-paid labor.*

The decline in the export prices and receipts of countries producing primary products, a result of overproduction and competition with synthetics, has reduced their ability to purchase capital goods. These coun-

---

* See Mr. SHUMAN'S comment on page 218.

tries have customarily financed a large part of their purchases of capital goods from the United States with their earnings from exports to Western European countries, which were much larger than their earnings from the United States. Western European countries have thus benefited more than the United States from the decline in the export prices of primary goods. The gain to the United States from the decline in import prices has been less than the loss from the reduced volume of exports of capital goods.

As long as exchange controls were retained in Europe, the United States was protected against large outflows of private funds because U.S. investors were cautious about subjecting their capital to exchange controls abroad. With the return to currency convertibility, investment opportunities abroad have become more attractive to U.S. investors who now have fewer fears about blocked currencies. As investors become more knowledgeable about the opportunities for investing funds abroad at short term, increasingly large shifts of short-term funds are likely to occur whenever significant differences in interest rates develop.

There also have been institutional changes in the postwar period. The importance of New York as a principal international capital market has increased. Several multilateral financial institutions have been developed in response to various needs. The International Bank for Reconstruction and Development, together with its subsidiary institutions, has furnished technical assistance and financial assistance to low-income countries. Most of its funds available for loans have come from the sale of its securities in the United States, which have been attractive to investors because they are guaranteed by the U.S. government. The International Monetary Fund established a framework for changes in exchange rates and exchange controls, and provided financial assistance to its member countries to help meet temporary payments deficits. Most of its financial assistance has been in U.S. dollars acquired from the U.S. capital subscription.

As foreign countries developed surpluses in their international accounts during the postwar period, they reduced their trade and payment restrictions. Each reduction of exchange controls enlarged the market for U.S. exports and tended to keep the United States deficit from increasing even more than it did. With these controls now largely eliminated, other means must be found to adjust to payments imbalance.

Balance of Payments Adjustment

The continuing imbalance in international payments over the past three years, reflected in the persistent, large deficits of the United States and the persistent, large surpluses of some other countries, raises the question of the adequacy of the adjustment mechanism. Changes in consumer tastes, technology, productivity, resource availability, individual prices and price levels, government programs, national incomes, and interest rate levels affect the volume of international payments and receipts of each country. The maintenance of a satisfactory balance requires that the impact of these forces be offsetting over a period of time. If instead such changes generate an imbalance between payments and receipts, an adjustment mechanism is necessary to rectify matters.

Adjustments are necessary in national incomes, in price levels, in government programs, and in other factors affecting international transactions to restore a satisfactory balance in hard-core accounts when departures occur.[2] The availability and use of international reserves make it possible to finance temporary imbalances and provide the time necessary for the operation of the adjustment mechanisms.

Payments imbalance sets in motion some corrective forces under fixed exchange rates. An excess of payments over receipts in a deficit country normally leads to a decline in income, and thus to a decline in imports. The loss of reserves, through its restrictive effect on banks, tends to have a further contractionary impact on incomes and prices. Price declines resulting from reduced demand tend to stimulate exports. Higher interest rates tend to reduce the net capital outflow or to stimulate a capital inflow. In addition, if the deficit stemmed from increased imports or reduced exports, individual producers of import-competing goods might be expected to compete harder, engaging   t and price reductions and more effective selling to counter encr   on their markets. Producers of export goods would try to offs   cline in foreign sales. The excess of the receipts in a surpl   would have the reverse effects.

However, these corrective forces may be weakened in both de   and surplus countries if government measures are undertaken to m   ain high-level employment and stable price levels. Central banks ma re-vent the loss or gain of reserves resulting from the payments defic or surplus from contracting or expanding the reserves of the domestic bank-ing system. They may try to offset the changes in income resulting from the increased imports or reduced exports.

The corrective forces may also work slowly and be weak even without offsetting government actions. Because their strength depends partly on the proportion of foreign trade to national income, they are apt to be less effective if foreign trade is a small percentage of national income. And because large governmental payments are not likely to respond

---

[2] Since short-term private capital flows are temporary and quickly reversed, they are discussed in the section on international liquidity.

automatically to income and price changes, the corrective forces are correspondingly less effective.

If the self-correcting forces are rendered largely ineffective, the burden of adjustment falls on discretionary measures, such as monetary and fiscal moves, selective steps to increase receipts and reduce payments, trade and exchange controls, and changes in the structure of exchange rates. The measures best suited to one country may not be suitable for others because of differences in the importance of foreign trade in their economies, the composition of their trade, or other differences.

ADJUSTMENTS AFTER WORLD WAR II

After the war, the major industrial countries in Europe had strong demands for foreign products to rebuild and restock their economies. Their prices had risen more rapidly than U.S. prices so that extensive trade and exchange controls were necessary to maintain their scarce reserves. Many currencies were devalued in relation to the dollar in 1949, most by 30 percent, which brought the prices of foreign goods more nearly in line with U.S. prices. Since then, most industrial nations have reacted to improvements in their payments balance by gradually reducing controls over imports and payments. Enough controls were retained, however, to result in a payments surplus to permit the continued rebuilding of their gold and foreign exchange reserves. Monetary and fiscal measures were also used to keep their price levels from once again moving out of line. By the end of the fifties the improvement in the payments and reserve position of the major industrial countries had enabled them to eliminate most payments restrictions and restore external convertibility for their currencies.

The United States, with a large payments surplus immediately after the war, also contributed to the restoration of international payments balance. It gave help by offering foreign economic assistance, by carrying the major share of mutual defense, by tariff reductions, and by guarantees of U.S. private foreign investment. The United States accepted discriminatory controls on payments to the dollar area by other countries. These policies contributed to the elimination of the U.S. payments surplus of the early postwar period and to the development of the payments deficit in the fifties.

The international payments situation in 1960 has changed markedly from the dollar shortage period. Recent U.S. deficits have been too large to be sustained, raising the possibility that there may have been an overadjustment to the dollar shortage. The devaluations of 1949 now appear excessive. A number of the measures which the United States can use to restore a more balanced situation in our hard-core accounts and the measures appropriate for surplus countries are discussed below.

POLICIES FOR ADJUSTMENT

Restrictive monetary and fiscal measures in the United States may be too costly in terms of the level of domestic unemployment and the rate of economic growth. Controls on dollar payments may make it more difficult to get other countries to reduce their remaining restrictions and may breed retaliatory restrictions. An increase in restrictions would lessen the salutary impact of foreign competition on the price, wage, and productivity developments in the U.S. economy and elsewhere. Most measures have their shortcomings, yet choices, often uncomfortable ones, must be made to achieve a satisfactory payments balance.*

The classical policy prescription for reducing a payments deficit is a restrictive monetary policy. Such a policy results in higher interest rates, less credit, lower incomes and imports, and a smaller net capital outflow. It might also lower prices and stimulate exports. If the U.S. payments deficit could be attributed to more rapidly rising price levels here than in most other industrial countries these measures might be appropriate. But this is not the case, and they are likely to be expensive in terms of domestic objectives.

A substantial decline in U.S. incomes would be necessary to secure a significant decline in the dollar volume of commodity imports, for U.S. imports are only about 3 to 4 percent of our national income. Because of the reduced employment and the deterrent effect on growth, this solution would almost surely be too costly to be acceptable. And even if such measures resulted in a fall in prices, they would probably have little effect on exports unless they were long continued.

If restrictive monetary measures could effectively reduce the outflow of long-term U.S. capital, there would be less need to rely on an improvement in the trade balance. However, any improvement from a decline of U.S. capital outflows for direct investment abroad would be partially offset by lower U.S. exports associated with the outflow and by a smaller future return flow of receipts of profits and dividends from abroad. If the restrictive monetary measures affected primarily the purchase of for-

---

* STANLEY H. RUTTENBERG—Rather than point out the importance of the United States continuing as world banker, the Commission should direct its recommendation toward reducing and eventually eliminating the United States as a reserve currency country and world banker. We could then devote our major attention to strengthening the American economy at home, as well as improving our position as a world trader.

A move toward having an international monetary organization assume some of the international world banker responsibilities is a move in the right direction. The Commission only reluctantly refers to this problem in its recommendation on page 239.

eign securities, they would improve the payments balance more because U.S. exports would be less directly affected.

The adoption of such restrictive monetary and credit measures solely to secure an improvement in the balance of payments in the near future would lessen our ability to export in the longer run because it would lower the U.S. growth rate. With lagging incomes and demand the incentives to the development of new products and new processes, to new domestic investment, and to increases in productivity so essential to a healthy export trade would be chilled. And if foreign economies were growing faster, in comparison with the U.S. economy, they would be even more attractive as locations for U.S. direct investment.

The Commission believes that the costs in terms of unemployment and lower growth would be so great from trying to correct our balance of payments deficit by general monetary and fiscal policies that alternative means should be sought to achieve the necessary balance.

The use of monetary, credit, and fiscal measures to achieve adequate growth, high employment, and reasonably stable prices should contribute to an improvement in our payments balance. In the past, export industries have been among the leaders in increasing productivity. The international competitive position of the United States will improve if the economic climate contributes to continued productivity gains and if these gains are partially reflected in lower prices for goods important in international trade. Even though the year-to-year declines may be small, the compound effect over a few years may substantially affect international price relationships.

If restrictive monetary and fiscal measures are too costly in terms of domestic objectives, the burden for improving the payments balance in the context of the present structure of exchange rates must fall on selective measures to expand U.S. receipts, to reduce private payments, to reduce the drain from direct government payments, or a combination thereof.

Some measures to increase receipts are desirable in themselves, and the present situation is a compelling reason to adopt them. These include increased government efforts to induce other countries to lower still further, or to eliminate, their remaining restrictions on international payments, especially their discrimination against U.S. goods. Tariff reduction abroad is desirable.* Providing more information to U.S. exporters and to foreign importers through government assistance, and stimulating foreign tourism in the United States, also would help.

---

* CHARLES B. SHUMAN—Use of the word "desirable" indicates a weak position. I would contend that further reductions in tariffs and other barriers to trade between nations is imperative.

U.S. banks operating abroad assist U.S. producers of export goods by helping them finance their export sales and supplying them with information on foreign markets. These U.S. banks, however, are at a disadvantage in competing with the foreign branches of banks of other countries because U.S. regulations, resulting from emphasis on unit banking in this country, are superimposed upon the regulations of the host country. If U.S. banks were able to operate abroad on a less restricted basis, U.S. exports might be facilitated. These regulations should be eased where possible to permit competition on more equal terms.

An additional aid to exports would be the provision of more adequate sources for intermediate-term export credits in the United States. Liberal credit terms are an effective sales tool for capital goods, particularly in areas where financial institutions are not well developed. Many foreign governments provide extensive export credit facilities to their exporters, and their more liberal credit terms have given them a competitive advantage in the sale of medium-term capital goods. This competitive disadvantage to U.S. exporters should be eliminated.

The new export credit guarantee programs of the Export–Import Bank adopted in 1960 and 1961 may give U.S. exporters access to coverage against political, exchange, and credit risks equal to that available in other countries. But the financial institutions best able to evaluate foreign credit risks—commercial banks with international departments— have limited capacity to extend term loans, while the institutions that can provide term credit—the thrift institutions—do not now have the facilities for appraising foreign credit risks. If new private facilities develop to combine the credit-investigating facilities of the banks with the long-term credits available from the thrift institutions, the ExImBank guarantee programs may be sufficient to ensure the necessary credit. Otherwise, the ExImBank should increase the direct financing of U.S. exports.*

Reductions of government payments abroad may be difficult without sacrificing other important objectives. When the major government programs involving foreign payments were developed, it was ascertained that these programs would not then impair the strength of our payments balance. Other countries were eager for U.S. goods so that the dollars made available almost automatically resulted in an increased demand for U.S. goods. This condition no longer prevails. Our payments imbalance is a greater constraint than the federal budget on our ability to extend aid. The Commission does not undertake to pass on the validity of the size of our foreign aid programs, their success, whether they

---

* WILLARD L. THORP—No study was made of the Export-Import Bank, but the analysis in Chapter Seven supports the suggestion that such support should be given as is necessary to shift the lending activity relating to exports to private institutions. It might also be noted that at times the activity of the Export-Import Bank might contribute to the program for domestic stabilization.

should be increased or decreased. It does favor a considered and continuous effort to make these programs more economical and more effective.*

A large part of government grants and loans for economic aid gives rise to U.S. exports even though the recipients are not required to spend the proceeds here. Normally U.S. aid will be most beneficial to recipient countries if the dollars can be used to purchase goods from the least expensive source, even if this involves non-U.S. sources of supply. But tying the assistance to expenditures in the United States to lessen the U.S. payments problem would be clearly preferable to reducing the assistance, if these become alternatives.

The military expenditure programs are a more important cause of the dollar outflow than the economic loan and grant programs. Greater reliance on U.S. sources of supply would reduce the payments drain of the military programs and undoubtedly other adjustments could be made to ease this burden. The current negotiations for increasing the contribution of other free nations in financing mutual military expenditures and in providing economic aid to the underdeveloped countries should be pursued vigorously, especially for their assistance in reducing the U.S. payments deficit.

None of the above measures entails direct restrictions on imports of goods and services or on capital movements. The imposition of direct trade restrictions would result in a curtailment of world trade, the more so because of the probable retaliation. Restrictive trade measures might also develop vested interests domestically and thereby become difficult to eliminate when the payments situation improves. While measures can be devised whose direct impact will be borne by countries in persistent surplus rather than by countries whose payments positions are precarious, it is exceedingly difficult to apply them because of the political effects.

Many measures the United States might adopt to reduce a payments deficit are limited by the objectives of domestic and foreign economic policy. The commitment to domestic price stability and high levels of employment limits the extent to which monetary or fiscal policies can be used. Despite all the increased sharing and increased efficiency, it is likely that the dollar amount of foreign military programs and grant and loan programs cannot be radically reduced without a sacrifice of the objectives these programs are designed to secure. Tying foreign economic assistance to dollar procurement may reduce the benefits of foreign assistance. The tariff policy pursued by the United States over the last 25 years reflects a belief that international economic competition stimulates economic growth both here and abroad, and a departure

---

* CHARLES B. SHUMAN—The first sentence of this paragraph implies that the objectives of foreign aid programs are being achieved. This is not true in all cases.

from this policy would make it harder to induce other nations to reduce their restrictions against U.S. products. The adoption of exchange controls and capital export controls would also sacrifice the objective of payments freedom and efficient resource allocation.

The Commission acknowledges the validity of the objectives of all these policies. The firm commitment to seek them greatly reduces the number of measures that can be used to achieve a satisfactory payments balance, which must also be regarded as an objective of economic policy, even if it should prove to be a constraint on the achievement of other objectives. Because a specific program to reduce the U.S. payments deficit involves considerations beyond the scope of monetary, credit, and fiscal policies, recommendations for a comprehensive program are not presented here. The problem, however, requires the kind of comprehensive and coordinated consideration in the government recommended in Chapter Ten.

It is likely that there are enough specific measures other than restrictive payments controls and changes in the exchange rate structure available to the United States and to foreign countries to permit attainment of a satisfactory balance in our hard-core accounts without a sacrifice of domestic and international objectives.

MULTILATERAL POLICIES FOR ADJUSTMENT

A change in the structure of exchange rates is an alternative to deflation at home or inflation abroad as a way to change the relationship of the prices of goods and services among countries. For example, a devaluation of the dollar or an appreciation of the mark would tend to make German goods and services less attractive in relation to U.S. goods and services in all markets, and thus would tend to reduce the U.S. deficit and the German surplus simultaneously. But if the depreciating country is an important trader, the effects of the depreciation will be widespread and may set in motion forces for similar devaluations by many countries. If large U.S. payments deficits appear persistent, the need for a change in the exchange rate structure must be recognized, and the change can be either a U.S. devaluation or an appreciation of some other currencies.

Changes in the structure of exchange rates should not be looked upon as obviating the need for other measures needed to achieve payments balance, such as those promoting effective selling and more adequate credit to increase the competitiveness of U.S. goods abroad. Adjustment by countries in surplus is not advocated as a means of avoiding domestic measures in the United States or in other deficit countries. But surplus countries as well as deficit countries have a responsibility for the world payments system and should take appropriate steps, as the United States did during the early postwar period.

If a change in the structure of the exchange rates is necessary, it should be worked out through international negotiations with major industrial countries, perhaps through the IMF. Decisions to alter the value of a country's currency by more than 10 percent require approval by the IMF. The Commission believes that instead of maintaining only a passive attitude, the IMF should be encouraged to take more initiative in recommending and effecting changes in the exchange rate structure. Such changes, or discussions of them, will generally cause disturbances in exchange markets. Speculative capital flows will also certainly occur, and the IMF could take an aggressive role to minimize the impact of these shifts and their effects on reserves through supplying standby credits to countries subject to the speculative attack.

The Commission believes that the present dollar price of gold should be retained as a central pivot in the exchange rates structure among IMF member countries and that any needed realignment of the structure should be around this pivot.

A stable exchange rate structure policed aggressively by the IMF should prove workable, provided appropriate domestic policies are pursued. It is likely that the structure of exchange rates will require only occasional changes. But if changes in exchange rates are necessary, they are preferable to the development of a system of restrictive controls that would stifle world trade, or to the sacrifice of major domestic objectives to secure external balance.*

International Liquidity **

The problems of international adjustment and international liquidity are closely related. It is inevitable that temporary imbalances will

---

* MARRINER S. ECCLES—I think the report is weak in not dealing more realistically with our international balance of payments problem in the light of the phenomenal recovery and great increase in productivity of Western Europe and Japan.

I do not believe the United States can continue as the reserve currency country and world banker in the light of its present price structure. It should move as rapidly as possible to transfer this responsibility to an international monetary organization where currency values can be adjusted—upward or downward—over the longer period as the basic need is determined. Our alternatives are: greatly increased productivity and lower prices or tariffs, quotas, embargoes, exchange controls or the discontinuance of present foreign aid and defense policies.

** H. CHRISTIAN SONNE—I do not approve of the inclusion in the Report of the sections under the heading "International Liquidity."

My reason is that these sections deal with a subject that requires profound knowledge and lengthy study in cooperation with experts of foreign countries. Moreover, CMC is not and should not necessarily be equipped to handle this subject which, in my opinion, lies outside of CMC's field of inquiry.

develop between payments and receipts in a nation's international accounts. Consequently, to tide over the period until balance is restored,
a nation must maintain an adequate supply of assets acceptable for international settlements if it is not sure it will be able to borrow to finance its deficits. The more efficient the adjustments mechanism to
correct imbalances, the smaller will be the need for reserves.

Gold and liquid assets in reserve currency countries are the primary
assets acceptable as reserves. In addition, member countries have drawing
rights which enable them to obtain foreign currencies from the IMF.
At the end of 1960, official holdings of monetary gold by members
amounted to $35 billion, and the IMF owned about $3 billion of gold.
Official country holdings of foreign liquid assets were about $22 billion.
Of the latter about $10 billion were in dollar assets and $8 billion in
sterling assets. The IMF also owned about $12 billion of the currencies of
its members.[3] In addition to official holdings, private parties and financial institutions have substantial holdings of liquid assets in reserve
currency countries.

In the last ten years, world trade has been growing at an annual rate
of about 5 percent. Over the same period, monetary gold stocks have
been increasing at an annual rate of about 2 percent. Because the need
for reserves is related to the value of a country's trade and payments, a
continuation of these growth rates may lead to a shortfall of gold for
reserves. Meeting this deficiency will entail increased reliance on reserves
in the form of foreign exchange balances, probably through an increase
in the short-term foreign liabilities of reserve currency countries or increased reliance on the ability to borrow to finance a payments deficit.

Because reserves are needed to finance other payments as well as commodity trade, reserves may become inadequate even though they increase
at a rate appropriate for growth in trade. The international movement
of short-term funds in response to differences in interest rates presents a
special problem in this regard. These short-term capital flows are more
likely to be a problem for countries with well-developed financial markets and suggest the need for particularly large reserves or assured borrowing arrangements in these cases. And if the trend toward a higher
proportion of liquid assets in the total of the world's reserves continues
the protection of reserve currencies against exchange crises becomes increasingly important.

If international liquidity is to be adequate, both long-run and short-
run needs must be met. In the long run, as world trade and payments

---

[3] About 65 percent of these currencies are those of the United States, Japan, and the
industrial countries of Western Europe which are most likely to be in demand. And
because the currencies of the countries which are drawing on the IMF are not likely
to be in demand, its effective resources are less than its total currency holdings.

increase, the supply of assets acceptable in settlement of international payments must also increase. In the short run, arrangements must be made to safeguard the payments system against liquidity crises. Attaining these objectives requires decisions on measures the United States can take unilaterally to safeguard the dollar against exchange crises and on multilateral measures to provide an adequate supply of international reserves in a payments system secure against these crises.

STRENGTHENING THE U.S. BANKER POSITION *

The development of the dollar as a reserve currency was not planned. Our political and economic stability, military security, well-developed financial markets, and strong balance of payments position induced many foreigners to acquire dollars as an investment. Because of the standing offer of the U.S. Treasury to convert dollars held by foreign official institutions into gold at a fixed price, many foreign countries have felt that liquid dollar assets are as safe as gold.

Foreign countries benefited because reserves held as dollar assets yielded a small income. Their possible costs would be any losses they might suffer if the value of the dollar in terms of their own currency ever declined. This possible cost of holding liquid assets as reserves should be distinguished from the cost of holding reserves in any form, which is the cost of devoting a portion of national savings to investment in reserves rather than in productive goods.

As a reserve currency country the United States benefited in that it could acquire more foreign goods, services, and investments and extend more foreign aid than it would have been able to finance from its net receipts on hard-core accounts. The major cost to the United States is the greater exposure of the dollar to exchange crises, and a consequent possible need to formulate our domestic monetary, credit, and fiscal policies to minimize capital outflows. This dilemma between external and domestic objectives became acute in the second half of 1960, when the short-term capital outflow and the pressure on U.S. reserves limited the choice among measures which could be used by the monetary authorities.

The U.S. position as a world banker can be strengthened by a number of measures, some of which are unilateral in character, while others involve international agreements. The steps which can be taken unilaterally are discussed first.

The requirement that the Federal Reserve banks hold gold reserves equal to one quarter of their note and deposit liabilities tied up nearly

---

* STANLEY H. RUTTENBERG—I do not concur in this section. My remarks on page 226 are applicable to this whole section.

$12 billion U.S. gold at the end of 1960, leaving a "free gold" stock of less than $6 billion available for international settlements. This requirement was adopted originally to limit the ability of the Federal Reserve System to expand its notes and deposits. In fact, the gold holdings of the Federal Reserve System generally have been large enough so that the requirement has not imposed an effective constraint on the expansion of Federal Reserve notes and deposits. When it appeared in 1945 that it might prove to be a constraint, the requirement was reduced without any apparent adverse internal or international effects. The elimination of this requirement in the United States would not presage U.S. devaluation or U.S. inflation and would merely signify the abandonment of an archaic law.

The Commission believes that the threat of a confidence crisis would be greatly reduced if it were generally recognized, both here and abroad, that all of the U.S. gold is available to meet our international obligations. Any doubts about the U.S. policy should be removed by elimination of the gold reserve requirement at the earliest convenient moment so that all of the U.S. gold stock is available for international settlements.

The loss of gold to private hoards from monetary stocks diverts gold from its primary function as an international reserve asset. The free gold market in London where private parties of most countries, except those of the United States and the United Kingdom, may buy and sell gold permits a drain on the use of gold for international reserves. Although the London gold market presents a multilateral problem, the United States has a special stake in its management because that market is effectively a dollar gold market. When the private world demand for gold is strong, the burden of deciding whether to release gold to private hoards as a means of holding the free market price near the official gold parity falls upon the U.S. Treasury. The Treasury must decide whether in the long run it will be less disturbing to confidence in the dollar to let the price of gold fluctuate considerably above parity, or whether this should be prevented by feeding gold to the speculators from U.S. monetary stocks.

One solution might be for the United States to continue to supply gold indirectly to speculators at a price slightly above $35, as it did in late 1960. Or other countries might be persuaded to introduce legislation prohibiting private gold ownership at home and abroad, as the United States and the United Kingdom have done. Or speculation in gold might be made less attractive by allowing for greater fluctuation in its price, and thus greater possible losses. The somewhat larger possible losses might reduce the speculative demand for gold.

Sudden large shifts of liquid funds sensitive to international interest rate differentials and speculative expectations frequently serve little useful purpose. If a short-term capital outflow results from large interest rate differentials, a central bank might increase interest rates to eliminate the stimulus to the outflow and the drain on its reserves. If, however, the outflow occurred during a recession, such monetary policy would not be appropriate for domestic purposes.

Under these conditions the Federal Reserve should adopt those measures that provide monetary ease with the least depressing effects on short-term interest rates. Increasing the reserves of commercial banks by open market purchases of longer-term securities should reduce short-term rates less than if short-term securities are purchased. Greater reliance on fiscal measures would also reduce the amount of monetary ease needed to secure business recovery. The resulting larger deficit could be financed with short-term issues, which would keep short-term interest rates higher and would thereby discourage the outflow of short-term capital. Selling short-term issues during recessions is consistent with the proposals for debt management stabilization policy advocated in Chapter Four.*

In Chapter Six the Commission recommends that the present statutes authorizing the continuous regulation of interest rates on savings and time deposits of commercial banks should be revised. Greater freedom in setting interest rates on the bank deposits of foreigners would make it possible for large U.S. banks to offer interest rates competitive with those offered abroad, and enhance their ability to retain these deposits.**

Steps can also be taken to reduce the profitability and hence the volume of short-term capital flows. At present, many individuals shift funds abroad temporarily to take advantage of higher interest rates, though they plan to reverse the direction of this flow at some future date. To protect themselves against an adverse change in the exchange rate which would offset higher interest income, they cover themselves through purchases of dollars in the forward market. An official U.S. institution operating in this market could reduce the volume of flows by increasing the cost of purchasing dollars in the forward market, perhaps to the point where hedging would be too expensive to be worthwhile. The U.S.

---

* CHARLES B. SHUMAN—I am extremely dubious with respect to the argument presented in this paragraph. If the Federal Reserve buys long-term securities, the sellers are likely to invest some of their funds in short-term securities which would tend to raise prices and lower yields in the short-term market. This seems to have been the result of recent activity by the Federal Reserve System in the long-term market.

** STANLEY H. RUTTENBERG—I do not concur in the recommendation that the present statutory ceilings on interest rates paid on savings and time deposits by commercial banks be revised. In connection with the problem of holding short-term funds in the United States, I think the United States Treasury could issue special securities for foreign governments and central banks on which they could pay a higher interest rate than the regulations permit commercial banks to pay.

authorities could cover their technically short position by borrowing foreign currencies from the IMF or foreign central banks.

Some funds shifted abroad are not covered against the exchange risk because the current limits for exchange rate fluctuation are so narrow that the maximum possible loss from an adverse change in the exchange rate within these margins is quite limited. If, however, the limits were widened—from about $\frac{3}{4}$ of 1 percent to perhaps 2 or 3 percent—the maximum possible loss would increase correspondingly. As it increased, fewer individuals would be likely to shift short-term funds abroad for higher interest rates, particularly if they could not profitably hedge against the risk of adverse changes in the exchange rate. Thus wider exchange rate limits and active operations in the forward market supplement each other in reducing the shifts of interest-sensitive funds.

Widening the margins for exchange rate flexibility is a multilateral problem. An increase in the width of the U.S. gold points from $\frac{1}{4}$ of 1 percent to the maximum of 1 percent permissible under IMF regulations would probably induce other countries to widen the limits of the range in which their currencies can move in relation to the dollar. Further widening of the U.S. gold points and the support limits for foreign currencies might be desirable, but these changes would have to be undertaken under the sponsorship of IMF.

These steps should strengthen the U.S. banker position. Nevertheless, the longer-run problems of reserve adequacy and the vulnerability of reserve currency countries call for more fundamental changes in reserve arrangements. Such changes are primarily multilateral and are discussed in the next section.

MULTILATERAL ACTION

One way to increase international liquidity is to increase the quantity of reserves; another way is to make certain that a country will be able to borrow to finance a payments deficit. Accumulating reserves is a more expensive way than borrowing because it ties up national savings in assets with low yields. Countries have chosen to do so in the past because the ability to borrow has been uncertain.

Broadly speaking, an increase in the reserves available for all countries can come about in three ways. National treasuries or central banks can buy newly mined gold. This addition to their gold stocks is treated indistinguishably from gold acquired in the settlement of a payments surplus. In fact, the large gold producing countries sell most of their gold to other countries, to finance their own imports, and thereby gold becomes available for reserves of other countries.

Secondly, aggregate reserves are increased if some countries increase their holdings of liquid foreign assets in the reserve currency countries, which ordinarily result from the settlement of a payments surplus.

Thirdly, reserves can be increased through the IMF if countries increase their subscriptions to its capital. The increase in reserves from these subscriptions is in effect an increase in the amount of foreign currencies members can borrow from the IMF to finance a payments deficit. Aside from these increases in the IMF capital, therefore, the rate of increase of world reserves depends on the rate of gold production less the drain of gold into nonmonetary uses and on the degree to which other countries are willing to increase their holdings of liquid assets in the reserve currency countries.

World reserves could be increased by raising the price of gold in terms of all currencies. An increase in the gold price would stimulate gold production and all new gold output would have a higher monetary value. The gold-producing countries and the countries holding their reserves in gold would benefit most, particularly the reserve currency countries whose foreign liabilities would remain unchanged.

Aside from the doubtful wisdom of devoting additional resources to gold mining, the arguments against changing the gold price are based on the unequal sharing of benefits. The gold-producing nations, the Western industrial countries, and Russia would gain the major benefits. Most low-income countries hold little gold as reserves and would receive only a small share of the revaluation profits. Private speculators would also benefit greatly.

The Commission believes that the arguments against an increase in the world gold price counsel against such a step at this time. At some future date, if alternative methods of meeting the needs for increased reserves prove to be unsatisfactory, the revaluation of gold may be advisable, but it should be made under IMF sponsorship.

The IMF was established to assist its member countries in financing their temporary payments deficits by extending exchange stabilization credits to them. Its capital, now $15 billion, was obtained from subscriptions of member countries upon joining. The amount of each country's subscription was determined by its quota, which was roughly proportionate to its share in world trade. Twenty-five percent of these subscriptions was payable in gold and the remainder in the country's currency, usually in the form of a non-interest-bearing note. The maximum amount of assistance each country can expect to obtain from the IMF is based on its quota.

The IMF was set up as a multilaterally managed pool of currencies, in which each member country gave the IMF the right to lend its currency to other member countries which might need assistance in financing their payments deficits. Whenever a country wishes to obtain this assistance, it uses its own currency to purchase another currency already held by the IMF.

Under its present Articles of Agreement, the amount of assistance the IMF can extend is limited by its direct holdings of the currencies in demand, by the additional amounts of currencies which it can acquire by selling gold, and by the amount of foreign currencies that countries might lend it. Because only the currencies of members with payments surpluses are likely to be in demand, the maximum contribution that it may extend from its own funds at any one time is limited to about half its capital. The amount of assistance which the IMF can extend to supplement the gold and foreign exchange reserves of its members may have been adequate during the early postwar years when world trade was about $50 billion yearly and short-term capital flows were a lesser problem because of extensive exchange controls. By 1960 world trade had increased to nearly $120 billion yearly. But the capital of the IMF was only increased from $10 to $15 billion.

Because member countries have made only limited use of the IMF and have not tended to regard their Fund drawing rights as a part of their reserves, they have probably had a greater need for other reserves outside the IMF. Some countries, in particular the United States, have hesitated to use IMF assistance in financing their deficits. If all members were to count their drawing rights as an integral part of their reserves and use them accordingly, then the IMF's usefulness as a source of international liquidity would be increased.

If member countries make increased use of the IMF, two questions remain. Are maximum drawing rights based on country quotas adequate to meet a specific country's reserve needs? Are the present resources of the IMF adequate to perform effectively its function?

Maximum drawing rights could be increased by increasing the country quotas, as was done in 1959, or by lifting the limitation on drawing rights based on quotas. The IMF's total resources could be increased either by increasing quotas or by strengthening its ability to borrow the currencies of member countries.

Increasing country quotas to the extent necessary so that the United States and the United Kingdom could draw enough to finance the large short-term capital flows to which they are particularly subject might unbalance the IMF arrangements, in that it might be necessary to increase their quotas more than those of smaller countries. Some might object that this would increase the dominance of large countries in the IMF. This objection could be met simply by increasing the quotas of all countries by the same multiple. Any possible problem that some countries might not be able to subscribe the required amount of additional gold could be avoided by leaving the gold subscription unchanged and increasing only the currency subscription.

The advantage to the United States of increased quotas would be that it could draw a larger amount of foreign currencies than it now can.

The disadvantage would be that the IMF would have more dollars to extend to other members to help them to finance larger payments deficits with the United States. The United States might find its export surplus increased at a time when we wished to discourage a large export surplus because of its inflationary domestic impact.

A second proposal is for the establishment of lines of credit among the central banks of the industrial countries as a means to reduce the possibility of an exchange crisis arising from large shifts of short-term funds. Central banks participating in such an arrangement would agree to accumulate a limited amount of the currency of countries subject to such shifts rather than to convert it into gold. A country in deficit could temporarily incur a larger payments deficit than it might be able to finance comfortably with its own reserves. This would be particularly helpful for the United States and the United Kingdom, which are particularly subject to these shifts of funds. Central bank arrangements of this type were used by European countries in March 1961 to counter the large shifts of funds that followed the German revaluation.*

It has been proposed that the IMF issue debentures to central banks or treasuries of large industrial countries.[4] This would give the IMF standby power to borrow a limited amount of a country's currency if its holdings of this currency become inadequate in response to the demands of other countries. Purchasers of the debentures would only be required to make payments on them when the IMF needed their currency. Thus the IMF would request payment on debentures from the countries with payments surpluses and make this currency available to countries with payments deficits. For example, if the IMF's holdings of dollars became depleted while the United States had a payments surplus, the IMF would request payments on the debentures sold the U.S. Treasury.

In addition, the large industrial countries might undertake to join in the establishment of a Reserve Settlement Account as an IMF subsidiary to provide a means for financing the large shifts of short-term capital.[5] If there should be a large shift of short-term funds from the United States to England, the Bank of England would transfer its accumulations of dollars to the RSA rather than use these dollars to buy gold from the U.S. Treasury. Because the RSA would hold the dollars, the U.S. gold reserves would not be subject to a large sudden drain to finance the outflow of short-term funds. When the direction of this flow reversed, the British would draw down their claim on the RSA and

---

* See Mr. RUTTENBERG'S comment on page 226.

[4] Edward M. Bernstein, *International Effects of U.S. Economic Policy*, Joint Economic Committee Study Paper 16, 1960.

[5] Edward M. Bernstein, "The Adequacy of the United States Gold Reserves," *American Economic Review*, "Papers and Proceedings," May 1961.

supply the dollars to those who wished to shift funds to the United States.

It is implicit in these last four proposals that the problem of long-run reserve adequacy can be satisfactorily met from new gold production and from increased reliance on the IMF. This might be true if countries integrate their IMF quotas in their reserves so that a larger part of payments deficits are financed by drawing on the Fund. Reliance on an RSA rather than on owned reserves to finance the shifts of short-term funds would greatly reduce the possibility of an exchange crisis because the doubt about the ability of the country losing funds to finance the outflow would greatly diminish.

A different approach that has been offered is to transform the IMF into an international central bank ("Fund-Bank") which would eventually hold as deposits all the official foreign exchange reserves of its members.[6] International reserves would consist eventually of gold and deposits in the Fund-Bank. The Fund-Bank would thus replace the reserve currency countries as suppliers of international reserves.

In the transitional stage, countries would turn over a percentage of their total reserves of gold and liquid foreign assets to the Fund-Bank in exchange for deposits in the Fund-Bank. Initially the assets of the Fund-Bank would consist of gold and these short-term claims. The Fund-Bank would be empowered to create new deposits for the account of member countries with payments deficits. It would take their promissory notes and in exchange credit them with deposits of equal value. These deposits could then be transferred to other countries in settlement of payment deficits. Countries would be limited in the amount of gold they could withdraw from the Fund-Bank as their deposits increased, so that it would be protected against the exchange crises to which the reserve currency countries are now subject.

Because the rate of increase in reserves in the form of deposits in the Fund-Bank would depend upon the rate at which it would add to its assets, the nature of the assets the Fund-Bank might acquire after the transitional stage would be important. If it increased its claims on the underdeveloped countries, they could incur larger payments deficits. Its assets might then consist increasingly of promissory notes on these countries, while its deposits would probably be owned by the industrial countries. Alternatively the Fund-Bank might increase its claims on some industrial countries. If these countries then incurred a payments deficit, perhaps due to a large outflow of short-term funds, part of their deposit at the Fund-Bank would be transferred to countries in payments surplus, whose deposits would increase. Because of the possibility of being able

---

[6] Robert Triffin, *Gold and the Dollar Crisis, The Future of Convertibility,* Yale University Press, 1960.

to obtain large scale assistance from the Fund-Bank, countries would probably need to hold a smaller volume of reserves, on the general principle that the more a country can borrow in an assured way, the smaller the amount of transferable assets it has to own.

All these proposals are technically feasible. Provided that the resources available under each plan were sufficient and that members are willing to extend credit directly to other countries or indirectly through the IMF, the RSA, or the Fund-Bank, these proposals could successfully accomplish their objectives of assuring adequate liquidity in the long run and greater protection against exchange crises. The key issues are more political than economic. They involve the extent of the willingness of participating countries to place themselves in a position in which they may be committed to acquire a large volume of claims on other countries. If they had complete assurance that these claims could always be used freely in settlement of payments deficits and that they would never be subject to a loss because of a change in the structure of exchange rates, these claims would then meet the criteria which gold has met as a reserve asset—they would be as good as gold. Securing such assurances would necessarily involve a set of guarantees that debtor countries would have to extend to the creditor countries. Despite the good will and intention of the debtors, situations might arise in which it would be impossible for them to honor the guarantees.

The United States should seek now to strengthen existing multilateral arrangements and perhaps enter new ones to protect the world payments mechanism against exchange crises. This objective can be accomplished through greater cooperation with central banks of other industrial countries in handling short-term capital movements and through further evolutionary development of the International Monetary Fund. IMF resources should be increased so there is no doubt that they are adequate to meet the maximum foreseeable needs of its members consistent with their economic stability. This can be accomplished by further increases in member quotas and by formalizing the right of the IMF fund to borrow the currencies of countries in payments surplus.*

---

* See Mr. RUTTENBERG'S comment on page 226.

CHAPTER NINE

THE CHOICE
AND COMBINATION
OF POLICY INSTRUMENTS

In this chapter the kind of "mix" of monetary, debt management, fiscal, and credit policies appropriate to differing situations is outlined in a very general way in relation to the achievement of our goals of economic growth, low-level unemployment, and reasonable price-level stability. For each kind of policy instrument has a role to play in the achievement of those goals, but each has its limitations. Sole reliance cannot be placed on any one of them.

For economic prescription to be precise, economic diagnosis must be correct. Such diagnosis is likely to be laggard, imperfect, and sometimes wrong. In actual practice we shall usually be uncertain as to the character of our economic difficulties. This necessarily limits the effectiveness of the use of any single central instrument and of a combination of them. The improvement of diagnosis is vital to the full use of the refinements suggested in this chapter; nevertheless our policy measures can be combined more effectively than in the past even with the present state of the art of appraising current business conditions.*

In Chapter Two it was argued that the goals of low-level unemployment, reasonable price stability, and an adequate rate of growth cannot be achieved by policies directed only at controlling the level of demand. In this chapter attention is confined to the use of policy measures which influence the level of demand; it is assumed that appropriate measures other than those directed to altering demand will also be used.

It is inevitable that the operations of the federal government will exert a pervasive influence on the economy. The mere size of our defense

---

* THEODORE O. YNTEMA—This chapter suggests refinements in economic prescription that will often be impossible because of imperfect diagnosis.

program and the taxes necessary to finance it will influence every sector of the economy. Similarly, the large federal debt affects all kinds of financial transactions. A number of federal credit programs will continue in operation for the foreseeable future, and the conduct of those programs influences a wide variety of economic activities. Finally, the Federal Reserve's control of the money supply puts it inescapably in a position to influence economic activity.

The federal government must have a set of policies with respect to the level and composition of its expenditures, the structure of tax rates and composition of the debt, and terms on which it grants, insures, or guarantees loans, and the size of the money supply. And clearly it makes a difference what those policies are.

Because they influence our economy in so many important ways, it is essential that federal policies on expenditures, taxation, debt management, and credit terms should be explicitly chosen in such a way as to foster the achievement of sustained high employment, reasonable price stability, and an adequate rate of growth. Those goals cannot be achieved by the private enterprise system alone or by the federal government alone, but we are not likely to achieve them unless monetary, fiscal, debt management, and credit policies are chosen with reference to their effect on the achievement of those goals. It is not appropriate to blame the government for every defect in the performance of our economy. But when the economy's performance is not entirely satisfactory, it *is* appropriate to ask whether changes in government policies can be made to improve its performance.

The magnitude of the effect of the changes of all policy measures used and the varying weights to be assigned to different policy measures differ at different phases of the business cycle and with changing underlying forces affecting the behavior of the economy. Short-run and long-run stabilization policies necessarily overlap and interact, and ideally they should not be separated arbitrarily. If all policy measures could be varied quickly and easily without administrative problems and without disrupting private planning, and if they all produced their effects quickly, there would be no need to separate the problems of cyclical stabilization from those of the longer run. Yet such is not the case, and the problems are sufficiently different to justify separate treatment.

The discussion is in three parts. Because each policy measure has different characteristics, the criteria for determining how they should be combined are considered first. The implications of the constraints imposed by the balance of payments on the choice of policy measures needed to accomplish domestic objectives are also discussed in this section.

Second, the factors to be taken into account in choosing the longer-run levels or trends in taxes, government expenditures, interest rates, credit policy, and direct controls are discussed.

Finally, policy measures for economic stabilization are considered. These encompass short-run variations of tax, expenditure, monetary, debt management, and government credit policies which are directed to preventing or recovering from recessions due to deficient demand or from inflations stemming from excessive demand.

Characteristics of Policy Measures

The objective of stabilization policy is to keep the level of demand close to the output of the economy when it is using its physical and human resources at a high level, has reasonably stable prices, and is rising at an adequate rate. The most useful kind of stabilization measure is one which can be put into action quickly, which takes effect quickly, and whose effects can be quickly stopped or reversed. For it is desirable to be able to influence expenditures of businesses, households, and governments fairly quickly in either the upward or downward direction. Unfortunately, those policy measures which are judged most effective in terms of one of these criteria are not always best in terms of the others.

TIMING EFFECTS

The measures which can be put into action most quickly are those not requiring legislative action. They include changes in monetary policy and changes in both tax rates and government expenditures which can be made by executive decision.

Changes in tax rates or expenditures requiring legislation generally take longer to be adopted than changes in administratively controlled measures. The time required to activate them could be reduced somewhat, if the type of tax or expenditure change to be made in dealing with a recession or a boom could be planned in advance.

The lag between the adoption of a policy measure and the time when it begins to have much of an economic effect is probably shortest for a change in the first-bracket rate of the personal income tax. Because of the withholding procedure, some effects of such a tax cut would take place very quickly. A substantial effect would occur within three months of the effective date of the tax reduction, and a maximum effect in about six months. A similar timing pattern would occur in response to a tax rate increase.

The effect on expenditures of changes in general monetary policy seems to have a longer lag. Since the war, six to nine months have elapsed between the date of a definite shift toward an easy money policy and the first date at which a noticeable effect on housing starts occurred. An additional six months or so has elapsed before the maximum effect on residential construction expenditures. However, commitments on new mortgages may change earlier, thereby increasing new orders for housing and stimulating activity. The lags for other types of expenditures are at least as long. The same lags are observed in a shift from an easy to a restrictive monetary policy, though they may be undesirable on other grounds. But as noted in Chapter Three, measures can be adopted to shorten the interval elapsing between a change in monetary policy and its effect on economic activity.

If there are direct controls over consumer and mortgage credit, terms can be changed quickly. And such changes will affect expenditures more rapidly than general monetary policy. Credit terms can also be changed with some frequency, although not as frequently as general monetary measures.

The economic effects of decisions to increase government expenditures are felt generally as soon as orders are placed and before actual expenditures are made. A decision to curtail or slow down expenditures would similarly affect advance orders before the expenditures themselves. The impact on the economy of decisions to increase expenditures will take different lengths of time, depending on the type of government expenditure in question and the amount of advance planning which has been done. With advance planning of the type recommended in Chapter Five, an increase in government *expenditures* can be achieved within less than a year from the time a decision is made to undertake them. The impact from the *placement* of orders will be felt much sooner.

Although it is generally advantageous to have policy measures that can be quickly activated and reversed, there may be occasions when it is desirable to stimulate expenditures for a period longer than a year without becoming committed to changes in the basic tax structure or to new permanent government expenditures. To achieve this purpose, various measures are required. Some could take effect quickly, and others could start more slowly but have more sustained effects. These measures might consist of temporary tax changes and changes in monetary policy or government expenditures.

VOLUME EFFECTS

The magnitudes of the effects of expenditure changes induced by changes in policy measures are also important. Because over $30 billion of the revenue from the federal personal income tax comes from the application of the first bracket rate, a large change of expenditure can be induced or curtailed by changes in this rate. The desire not to overuse so powerful a measure led the Commission to impose a limit on the tax change it recommends. There is the danger that the proceeds of a large tax reduction would be only partly spent in a recession, and the addition to consumer liquidity from the unspent portion of the proceeds would create the possibility of a durable goods boom after recovery was well under way. Allowing for the limit recommended, consumer expenditures could be raised or curtailed by as much as an annual rate of $5 billion within a few months.

Changes in monetary policy have resulted in large changes in expenditures on residential construction. The increase in the annual rate of expenditure induced by changes in monetary policy from tight to easy money ranged from $4 to $5 billion in 1953-54 and in 1957-58. However, the size of the effect has been partly due to the large backlog of housing demand in the postwar period. So great an impact on housing from changes in monetary policy cannot be expected if the demand for housing should be weak.

Monetary policy has had unmeasured but undoubtedly substantial effects on other types of investment. However, the stimulating effect of an easy monetary policy on non-housing investment during a slump is generally believed to be much smaller than the restrictive effect of a tight money policy during a boom. In part this is because some of the investment projects most easily restrained by the effects of tight money are the ones which are also canceled by a decline in demand.

At present the increase or decrease in the volume of public expenditures which can usefully be achieved with the same speed as those induced by changes in monetary policy and without interference with the efficiency of longer-run programs is probably quite small—perhaps in the order of $1 billion. But with long range planning of the type recommended in Chapter Five the figure might be doubled.*

COMPOSITION OF DEMAND EFFECTS

The various policy measures also have different effects on the composition of aggregate demand. General monetary measures have their major direct impact on capital formation with smaller effects on the demand for consumer durables. Among the major components of capital formation, residential construction has been affected most, with lesser

---

* STANLEY H. RUTTENBERG—I do not agree that the increase or decrease in the volume of public expenditures which can be achieved with adequate forward planning of the type recommended in Chapter Five can be no more than $2 billion. The possible doubling of $1 billion is, it seems to me, grossly underestimated. Adequate long-range planning in an economy with public expenditures of about $100 billion should make possible a much larger sum that is susceptible to speedy flexibility.

Mr. NATHAN wishes to be associated with Mr. RUTTENBERG'S comment.

effects observed in state and local government construction, commercial construction, and private plant and equipment expenditures.

If fiscal measures are used, the effects on the composition of final demand depend upon whether and how expenditures are changed, or transfer payments are altered, or tax rates are changed. If tax rate changes are employed, the effects will depend on changes in the distribution of the tax burden between individuals and corporations.

Changes in government expenditures have their greatest direct impact on the capital goods industries, and because part of the expenditure change consists of wage payments, there is also an immediate indirect effect on consumers goods. Changes in transfer payments will affect the demand for consumption goods primarily.

If tax rates on individuals are changed, this will affect the demand for both consumer and capital goods. The distribution of the effect between consumer and capital goods will depend on whether the tax change bears more heavily on lower or higher income groups. An alteration in corporate tax rates will have its major impact on the demand for capital goods.

BALANCE OF PAYMENTS CONSTRAINTS

During most of the postwar period the United States was able to adopt domestic stabilization measures with little concern about their repercussions on the balance of payments. The achievement of external currency convertibility by the major European countries at the end of 1958 was a major step in the restoration of an international money market. Since then short-term capital flows have displayed markedly increased sensitivity to interest rate differentials among countries. Because interest rate differentials result in short-term capital movements and because the United States is a large debtor on short-term account, the choice of stabilization measures to combat domestic recessions must now take into account their balance of payments effects.

If monetary policy is used to counter recessions, the Federal Reserve should pursue those measures which provide monetary ease with minimal depressing effects on short-term interest rates if the balance of payments situation requires such action. This would attack simultaneously both the recession and short-term capital outflows. For example, increasing the reserves of commercial banks by open market purchases of other than short-term securities will result in a lesser direct impact on short-term interest rates than by purchasing short-term securities.

By placing more emphasis on fiscal policy (either increasing expenditures or decreasing taxes or some of both) as an anti-recession measure, the amount of monetary ease needed to secure business recovery can be reduced. Such a combination of measures entails a somewhat larger deficit, and the increased needs of government finance would result in upward pressure on interest rates. If this deficit is financed with short-term issues, short-term international capital flows would be discouraged, and because there would be no direct upward pressure on long-term interest rates, there would be minimum interference with domestic recovery.

Long-Run Policy Mix

There is no unique, ideal combination of policy measures which is best suited to the achievement of our major economic objectives at all times. Our economy is dynamic; it is in a constant state of flux as consumer tastes change, as new products are developed, as production processes change with new technology, as the size, geographic distribution, and skill distribution of the labor force changes, and as variations occur in many other factors which affect the level and composition of output. Most of these changes require adjustments to restore new balances between demands and outputs of particular products, and these adjustments are induced by changes in prices and responses thereto. The market mechanism is most effective in adapting to such changes if aggregate demand and its broad composition are adequate to keep production at or near high-employment levels.

The long-run rate of economic growth of a high-employment economy, depends to an important degree on the level of private capital formation. While private capital formation depends significantly on the level and rate of growth of consumption expenditures, it also varies independently of consumption. When the incentives to private capital formation are strong, a high-level investment demand requires greater levels of saving to free the resources from consumer goods output for the production of capital goods. Unless the flow of saving responds voluntarily to the increased investment demand, strong inflationary pressures will develop if other measures are not taken either to reduce consumption or to reduce government expenditures or to hold in check the increased investment spending. Contrariwise if the incentives to private capital formation are weak, the level of investment spending will be less than the flow of saving at high-level employment, and total output and employment will tend to decline. Unless current saving falls and consumption expenditures expand voluntarily to offset the decreased investment, unemployment will grow, if other measures are not taken to stimulate spending.

Monetary, credit, and fiscal policies can influence significantly the composition of demand among broad classes of expenditures as well as the aggregate level of demand. The problem of the mix of policy measures is so to influence the level and composition of demand that the aggregate levels of public plus private demands will result in sustained high-level output and employment and that the share of capital formation in total output will generate an adequate rate of growth.

At any given time there exists a basic tax structure, a pattern of government expenditure programs, a set of government credit programs, a level of money supply, a structure of interest rates, and other monetary and credit conditions. All of these inevitably affect the level and composition of demand in the economy. Both the opportunity and the necessity of adapting our programs and policy measures to the underlying trends in the economy must be continually faced. The opportunity exists because the continued growth of the economy provides more resources to use for all purposes. Also because the tax structure is progressive, tax revenues will grow more rapidly than total output in the economy. The existing monetary, credit, and fiscal structure will inevitably influence the pattern of use of the added resources. Thus the opportunity and the necessity exist to affect the way the additional resources will be used because the policy measures must be adapted to the growing size and ever-changing trends in the private sector of the economy.

As aggregate output grows the three broad classes of expenditures will also grow. Personal consumption expenditures will grow steadily with the personal incomes generated from production. Private capital formation will also grow with the level of total output. And permanent government expenditure programs will grow just because of population growth and the upward trend in pay rates. The key questions, however, are whether under the influence of existing policy measures the *total* of the three broad classes of expenditures will generate and sustain a high-employment level of output at reasonably stable prices and whether the *proportions* of the three classes of output will generate an adequate and sustainable rate of growth.

Several basic decisions by the government are involved. One is an evaluation of proposals for government expenditure programs against the alternative of an equivalent amount of private consumption expenditures and private investment. These are political decisions and should be made through the democratic process. They do have an economic impact. The Commission urges that the decisions on the introduction, continuance, or elimination of government expenditure and direct lending programs should be made in terms of a high-employment budget and on the basis of judgments as to the value of these programs relative to the value of the private consumption or investment which must be sacrificed if the government expenditure is to take place without generating excess demand and inflationary pressure.

It should be noted again as in Chapter Five that some types of government expenditures contribute directly to the pace of economic growth and should be evaluated in these terms. Some forms of public capital formation result directly in increased goods and services, other forms complement private capital and are necessary for increased private investment, and still others lead to new advances in technology which in turn stimulate private investment. If the government wants to stimulate the growth rate, expenditures such as these should have high priority.

A second set of decisions relates to the basic tax structure. As indicated in Chapter Five, the Commission believes that there should be a clear separation between the basic tax structure and temporary tax adjustments for stabilization reasons. However, because taxes affect the level and composition of personal consumption and saving, of private investment expenditures, of business saving, and work and investment incentives, the basic tax structure should be related to the strength and stability of the underlying trends in the economy. It should be designed to influence the levels of private investment and consumption and take into account the desired stimulus to private investment so that these, together with government expenditures, will generate high-level employment.

A third decision relates to changes in the money supply. In Chapter Three the Commission urged that the money supply be increased over the long run at a rate commensurate with the high-employment potential of the economy. The public chooses to hold portions of its current saving in the form of money and highly liquid earning assets, such as savings and time deposits, savings and loan shares, savings bonds, short-term government securities, and other readily marketable short-term debt instruments. The demand for money as a liquid asset is not a constant proportion of total output in the economy. The preferences of the public for liquid assets shift between money and other liquid assets with changes in their relative yields and their relative availabilities. The monetary authority must allow for these changing preferences in providing the proper amount of money to match the proportion of saving that the public wishes to hold in this particular form.

The supply of another important type of liquid asset is under the control of the Treasury. By its debt management activities the Treasury can vary the proportion of its debt which is in the form of short-term bills and savings bonds. As the economy grows there will be an increased demand for liquid assets such as these, and the Treasury needs to take this demand into account in its long-range debt management policies. The Treasury and the monetary authority should work in harmony in the provision of money and short-term securities because to a degree at least one form is substitutable for the other.

A fourth set of decisions relates to the choice among general monetary measures, broad fiscal policy measures, particular kinds of taxes, and selective controls in regard to their influence on private investment.

There has been considerable discussion in recent years of what the level of interest rates should be to maintain a healthy growing economy. The Commission believes that Federal Reserve actions can and do affect the level of interest rates, but that there is no uniquely right interest rate level independent of the state of private investment demand and saving habits, and if the level of aggregate demand is satisfactory, if the policy for controlling the money supply outlined above is followed, and if there is no change in the private investment and saving situation, then a recommendation that interest rates should be higher or lower than they actually are requires a simultaneous recommendation for a change in fiscal policy. Under these same conditions a reduction in interest rates can only be achieved by reducing the share of government expenditures in total output or by tax measures which reduce the share of consumption, or by tax measures which reduce business investment, or by direct controls on credit which affect selected expenditures. The opposite moves would be required if an increase in interest rates were desired.*

With given economic conditions, there is more than one set of taxes, expenditure patterns, debt management policies, monetary conditions, and selective controls which is consistent with a given level of total demand, of private investment, and rates of growth. The choice among the alternative combinations should be made on the basis of their impact on such things as the level and composition of investment, private consumption expenditures, the level and types of saving, international capital flows, the distribution of income, and the degree of reliance on the price system for allocation decisions.

Monetary policy and fiscal policy are to a degree substitutes for each other in their effect on private investment. Changes in mortgage credit terms and variations in business taxes (corporate tax rates, depreciation formulas, or investment allowances) are also partial substitutes for changes in interest rates. However, these measures differ in their direct effects on the composition of investment, for example, as between housing and industrial investment, and in their side effects.

For example, if it is desired to encourage business investment as well as residential construction, lower interest rates will help. If it is desired to encourage business capital formation but not residential construction, an appropriate procedure would be to get more favorable tax treatment for business investment, either through accelerated depreciation or an investment credit. If it is desired to encourage residential construction but not business investment, easing of mortgage credit

---

* CHARLES B. SHUMAN—This paragraph places too much emphasis on efforts to influence interest rates. While Federal Reserve policies inevitably affect interest rates, the criteria for policy decisions should be the economy's needs for money and credit rather than the interest rates that will result. The purposeful use of governmental powers to determine interest rates is a form of price control and, therefore, an undesirable interference with the operation of a market economy.

terms may be appropriate. Thus different combinations of policies affect the over-all level and mix of capital formation differently.*

Many more alternative combinations of measures could be set forth for a variety of circumstances. The choice of a combination at a particular time involves a balancing of effects on many diverse economic and noneconomic elements in the economy; this is necessarily a broad political choice and no firm guides are available. It is important to emphasize strongly, however, that the various measures are coordinate and to some extent substitutes for each other. The decisions on the use of one type of control measure need to be made with knowledge of its ramifications and harmonized with decisions on the use of other measures. This calls for effective coordination among all government agencies involved in monetary, credit, and fiscal policies.

Stabilization Policy Mix

The general objectives of stabilization policy are to maintain levels of demand which will lead to low levels of unemployment without inflation. Not only is it necessary to have a demand target, but allowance must be made for the margin of error between the actual and the predicted course of events. How large an allowance for uncertainty must be made in the choice of policy measures depends on the flexibility of available policy measures and the speed with which they can be modified or reversed to correct errors once a mistake is recognized. It will also depend on the cost of making an error, i.e., how much of a price increase will result if demand exceeds the desired level for a given length of time or how much unemployment will result if demand is inadequate.

The stabilization problems are discussed in two parts. First, recessions are examined. This is followed by a discussion of periods of recovery, prosperity, and inflationary booms. In each case emphasis is placed on the necessity of conducting policy in such a way that efforts to solve the immediate problems do not create a new set at a later point.

RECESSION

Recessions and depressions do not have uniform patterns. Each is in a sense unique. As a result, policy guides for dealing with them are expressed only in general terms.

---

* CHARLES B. SHUMAN—The investment credit approach is an undesirable effort to influence decisions that should be determined by the interaction of economic forces in the market place. In my opinion, it would be far better to reduce tax rates, or give taxpayers more leeway in the determination of depreciation rates, than to authorize a selective form of tax relief on the basis of the way in which earnings are utilized.

The objectives of anti-recession policy may be outlined as follows: when income is growing at an inadequate rate and unemployment is high and rising, measures are needed to insure that a recession does not develop; when income actually declines, action is necessary to insure that the initial decline in income does not lead to a cumulative downward spiral. In both cases action is desired to stimulate a recovery to a high level of employment.

When income fails to increase in line with our growth potential for any length of time, actions aimed at increasing demand are normally required. When unemployment and excess capacity are still modest but rising, only those policy measures should be used which can be reversed quickly and which can be applied in small increments. Monetary policy can be gradually eased and the debt structure can be shortened to provide downward pressure on interest rates; credit terms for federally insured and guaranteed mortgage loans can be eased. Placing of government orders can be expedited and government expenditures on existing programs can be increased to expand demand.

If action is confined to these policy measures, which can be moved gradually and quickly reversed, the chance that a recession will develop is reduced, while the risk of creating excessive demand is minimized.

If demand resumes its upward course, we can—according to the rapidity of its growth—refrain from further expansive action or reverse the action already taken. If demand fails to increase sufficiently, stronger policy measures to encourage demand can be undertaken gradually.

Ordinarily, temporary tax reductions should not be used before an actual decline in income has occurred. But when income grows slowly for any considerable length of time, and when unemployment and excess capacity have risen to unsatisfactory high levels, the balance between tax revenues and government expenditures should be reassessed to ascertain whether our basic fiscal policy is unduly restrictive.

When income turns down for whatever reason, there is danger that the decline will lead to a cumulative downward spiral. The first object of policy, therefore, should be to ensure that such a spiral does not develop. The automatic stabilizers have already greatly reduced our vulnerability to downward cumulative processes. All the measures appropriate in a situation where income fails to grow can be used here. It should be emphasized that those measures which have the longest lag in taking effect should be introduced at an early stage.

Temporary reductions in the first-bracket rate of the personal income tax are appropriate as soon as it is certain that income is declining. This can prevent the occurrence of any substantial reduction in disposable income and consumption expenditures. The size of the tax reduction should be based on both the rate of decline in output and the level of unemployment; it should be larger when output is declining rapidly and when unemployment is high.

STIMULATING RECOVERY

If a serious decline in consumption is avoided, a reversal of the decline is often likely within six to nine months after the onset of a recession because inventories often decline rapidly in the early stages of a recession and then level off. When inventories are declining, production is below final-product sales. When they level off, production and employment rise. The resulting increase in income should add to the strength of consumer demand and contribute to recovery.

The reversal of the movement of inventories and the stimulus to consumption provided by the tax cut and the easing of monetary and credit terms all help to stimulate private investment. Finally, those government expenditures can be undertaken which will be completed within perhaps a year from the time a decision is made to initiate them.

The policy measures just discussed are by their nature reversible so that they may be used with somewhat less caution than others. But the extent of their use and the reliance on one instrument rather than another must be varied with circumstances. If unemployment is already high or if for any reason there are strong indications that private fixed investment is declining significantly, all the policy measures under discussion should be used fully as soon as possible.

When the investment situation is less clear, and when initial unemployment is not high, it is desirable to proceed with more caution. The total effect on income of the actions taken should substantially offset the decline in private fixed investment. This should set the stage for a full recovery. The amount of action to take depends on the amount of decline in private investment to be expected and on the expected responsiveness of investment to changes in monetary and credit policy and to increasing consumer demand.

POLICY DURING THE RECOVERY

Once a recovery is under way, different policy problems arise. In the early stages of a recovery it is impossible to tell whether the measures previously taken and the underlying factors influencing private demand will increase income to a satisfactory level, generate inflationary pressures, or produce only a weak recovery.

On the one hand if restrictive action is taken too early and too strongly in a recovery, there is the risk of preventing a full recovery to a satisfactory level of unemployment. On the other hand, it is necessary to recognize that restrictive measures take effect only after a lag and that action should be taken to prevent an excessive increase in demand *before* an inflationary boom situation has actually developed. If restrictive measures are based on price movements as the principal guide to action, they will usually start too late and continue too long. Also the rate of growth of income cannot be used as the sole guide, because clearly the rate of growth of income during a recovery must be higher than the long-term growth rate if high-level employment is to be restored. These and many other indicators must be used in judging the likelihood that demand will become excessive.

In the early stages of a recovery few changes in policy measures are necessary. If, as time passes, output grows slowly and does not reach a high employment level, the measures required are those appropriate for recession policy when income fails to increase.

When an upswing is definitely under way, the temporary tax cut should be terminated and the Federal Reserve should take action to reduce bank liquidity. This latter policy should not be carried so far as to restrict bank lending; it should be designed to reduce the time required for a more restrictive policy to take effect should it later be deemed necessary. The Treasury's debt management operations can also be used to reinforce general monetary policy in reducing the liquidity of the economy and in affecting the structure of interest rates.*

Because monetary measures can be moved gradually in either direction, it is not necessary to make an all-out decision to take strongly restrictive action. If the economic indicators show progressively greater likelihood that excess demand will develop, Federal Reserve policy should move gradually and continually in the restrictive direction. If the first signals prove to have been false, the movement toward restriction can be reversed with little harm done.

A restrictive monetary policy will slow down the rate of increase of demand to some extent even though its direct impact may not be on the sectors in which the greatest expansion has taken place. It will take some time, however, before the expenditure effects of a restrictive monetary policy will be felt. It is important that the Federal Reserve System should take action as soon as it has a reasonable basis for judgment of the future to compensate for the lag between decision and effect. But there will be times when the need for restrictive action cannot be foreseen in time for restrictive action to become effective when needed.

If the speed of effectiveness of monetary policy cannot be substantially increased, it may be necessary to use other measures which have a more assured and rapid influence on private expenditures. These include the regulation of credit terms on government guaranteed mortgages, and

---

* STANLEY H. RUTTENBERG—Note my comments in Chapter Four, page 105.

direct control of consumer credit terms.* The Commission has recommended that the ceiling on interest rates on government insured and
guaranteed mortgages be dropped and that direct controls on the terms
of such mortgages be used to influence expenditures on residential construction.**

Finally, government expenditures should be slowed down if this action
does not interfere with vital governmental functions. If federal expenditures cannot be reduced, they should be held constant or their rate of
increase held to a minimum to slow the growth of income. The same
general rules apply to government credit extensions.

Despite these restrictive measures, a vigorous recovery may develop
into an overinvestment boom, inventory speculation, and strong inflationary pressures. General overinvestment booms involving many sectors
of the economy are most likely to arise when income is rising at a particularly rapid rate. In a period of general optimism, the real danger is
that some capital formation will be carried to the point where it yields
little or no return, and that some of the more speculative ventures will
be carried out on a thin equity base so that a decline in profits will result in a wave of failures.

A stock market boom is also a danger. A rise in stock prices as earnings increase to new highs is of little concern. But when stock prices rise
rapidly and for a considerable period, some people will buy stocks without reference to their earnings prospects but simply because prices have
been rising. This kind of pyramid club can go on for some time, but
history shows that it always ends. Because of losses suffered and because
of the adverse effect on general expectations, a collapse of stock prices
will also cause a decline in consumption and investment expenditures.

The general overinvestment boom, the growth of speculative investment, and the stock market boom reinforce each other in the boom
phase, and when the downturn comes, they reinforce one another in
the downward direction.

In such a situation, the objectives of policy should be to reduce the
rate of growth of aggregate demand and, where possible, to curb investment in the particular sectors most susceptible to an overinvestment
boom. The first objective can be achieved by policy measures which re-

---

* FRED LAZARUS, JR.—As explained previously, I am opposed to additional selective credit controls.

** STANLEY H. RUTTENBERG—My comment in Chapter Six, on eliminating interest rate ceilings on government insured and guaranteed mortgages, is applicable at this
point as well. Interest rate ceilings on FHA and VA mortgages have tended to act
in a counter-cyclical fashion. They should be retained for their counter-cyclical effects
as well as for their social policy effect. Standby credit controls in the field of consumer
and mortgage lending are essential, but they should be a supplement to, not a substitute
for, interest rate ceilings.

strain expenditures. These would include continuous tightening of monetary policy aided by further lengthening of the public debt. As soon as it is certain that a vigorous recovery is developing into a boom, a temporary increase in the first-bracket tax rate should be activated.*

The use of whatever selective controls are available may contribute to meeting the second objective. Increasing the margins on security loans may restrain stock market speculation. Other selective controls can be made more restrictive, although as was pointed out earlier, there may be other objections to their use.**

A restrictive monetary and debt management policy will impinge with special force on speculative investments which are largely financed with borrowed funds. It is likely to restrain such investments because higher interest rates reduce their profitability. Also when money is tight, institutional lenders generally impose tighter restraints on regular borrowers and are reluctant to take on new customers. †

A large part of business cycle history is a chronicle of speculative boom and bust. In some ways, the U.S. economy is better protected from such developments than it used to be. But it would be folly to forget the dangers of speculative booms. They are great enough to justify restrictive measures in any period in which income is rising rapidly and demand is threatening to press against capacity.

A variety of stabilization instruments are available, and in many in-

---

* See Mr. RUTTENBERG'S comment on page 105.
** See Mr. LAZARUS' comment on page 256.
ROBERT R. NATHAN—See my comment on Chapter Three, page 76.
STANLEY H. RUTTENBERG—Selective credit controls are necessary as important policy tools to be used in an inflationary or over investment boom situation. However, it is not sufficient just to have selective controls over consumer credit and mortgage lending. These tools should be supplemented by selective controls over loans for inventories as well as plant and equipment expenditures. Certainly, if one examines the business cycle changes of the post World War II period, the most volatile sectors in the economy have been inventories and plant and equipment. There is no justification in my mind to try to control inventory and plant and equipment expenditures indirectly through restricting consumer and housing credit controls. The attack should be more directly on the specific volatile sector of the economy, namely inventory and plant and equipment expenditures.
Mr. LUBIN wishes to be associated with Mr. RUTTENBERG'S comment.
† STANLEY H. RUTTENBERG—I am not satisfied with the concept that monetary restraint and higher interest rates will act as a leverage on investment by imposing tighter restraints "on borrowers who are not regular customers." The rationing that takes place with higher interest rates is done by the lenders and bankers when they tighten up their requirements for loans. This could very well be discriminatory against legitimate borrowers. Selective controls in the field of inventory and plant and equipment expenditures could be exceedingly useful as a supplement to monetary and fiscal policy in a period of over investment booms.
Messrs. LUBIN and NATHAN wish to be associated with Mr. RUTTENBERG'S comment.

stances a choice can be made among them. The considerations involved in the choice and combination of individual instruments are the speed with which they can be activated, take effect, and be reversed; the potency of the effect; and the sector of the economy they will influence.

The degree of freedom available in the choice of measures is limited also by other considerations. The Commission has already indicated the desirability of having the basic decisions of government expenditure, lending programs and the tax structure made in terms of a budget related to a high-employment economy. Departures therefrom for stabilization purposes would be limited to those for which temporary variations would not jeopardize the purpose of these programs. The Commission also prefers not to use direct control measures if they can be avoided. Balance of payments considerations also affect the choice of stabilization measures. All these considerations suggest that reliance cannot be placed on any single measure but that aggressive, imaginative, and integrated use of our general instruments of stabilization policy is necessary within a framework appropriate to a healthy growing economy.*

---

* GAYLORD A. FREEMAN, JR.—In general, I endorse the whole body of the recommendations of the Commission. I am concerned, however, that if adopted their net effect might be to increase governmental intervention in the economy. But if we accept (as I do)

   (i) the goals set forth herein,

   (ii) the fact that recurrent economic cycles interfere with the realization of such goals, and

   (iii) the conviction that such cycles can be moderated by proper use of monetary, fiscal and debt management tools,

then we are faced in each case with a decision as to whether the benefits in terms of economic stabilization more than compensate for the additional exercise of governmental influence upon the economy.

Increased governmental intervention is not desirable since

   (a) it might interfere with the performance of free markets,

   (b) it tends to concentrate greater economic power in the hands of the Executive, and

   (c) as an elected official, he is likely to err on the side of the more popular expansionary policies rather than the always unpopular restrictive policies.

Such additional power heightens the risk of a continuous bias toward inflationary pressures. On the other hand, a widely fluctuating economy not only interferes with our total productivity and distorts purchasing power, but subjects millions of our citizens to the indignity of recurrent unemployment. These conditions must be avoided and modern government has the responsibility to follow soundly conceived policies that will minimize them.

Thus with some reluctance but with no uncertainty, I accept the underlying theses of the Commission's Report. But I urge that its recommendations be enacted and administered with a scrupulous regard for the interference with long-range economic advancement that unsound or politically motivated policies might create."

Mr. SHUMAN wishes to be associated with Mr. FREEMAN'S comment.

CHAPTER TEN

ORGANIZATION AND COORDINATION FOR NATIONAL ECONOMIC GOALS

Material shifts in public policy call in question the adequacy of governmental institutions for accomplishing newly defined objectives, since organizational forms tend to mirror avowed purposes and interests. The Commission's policy recommendations in the preceding chapters touch the jurisdictions of a wide array of departments and agencies, state as well as national—establishments created at different times and devoted to differing objectives, marked in their evolution by contrasting traditions, and characterized by the variety of their relationships to each other, to private groups and to the national executive and Congress. This chapter considers what changes in their organization and articulation may be needed.

The Commission recognizes but does not dwell here on the political difficulties of carrying out recommendations that affect the respective responsibilities of state and national regulatory authorities. The traditions of federalism and the "dual system" are firmly implanted in our political, electoral and governmental system. It is no part of the Commission's purpose to do away with them, even if that were feasible. For federalism as a principle is a scheme of organization aimed at enlisting and holding the allegiance of a people to a larger national whole by tolerating and encouraging local diversity in enterprise and policy within constitutional limits. But as a principle, federalism does not furnish the criteria for the distribution of power or the division of labor within the system. Except as the Constitution is explicit, or is interpreted by the courts in particular cases, these are matters for political settlement.

It is the genius and the paradox of federalism at once to unite and to divide. In the name of a national right, a national authority may override a local majority or their authorized agents. In the name of states' rights, a local majority may stand against a national interest. In the wider spaces of the nineteenth century the division of constitutional powers tended to govern the division of governmental labors, though precedents of cooperation and of conflict can alike be traced to the earliest days. In the closer-knit society of the middle decades of the twentieth century, federal–state cooperation has resulted in much more interpenetration, as well as in the expansion, of authority and activities at both levels. Yet rivalries between them remain and will continue.

This Commission proposes the abolition of no state authority or agency. It believes that the maintenance of the dual system is not well served by the continued subordination of federal to state standards in matters that affect the safety or competitiveness of financial institutions. It looks to the general benefit to be derived from both state and federal action aimed at broadening the areas and diversifying the channels of competition, and at improving the standards of financial practice under established authority. In the inevitable political contests that the adoption of the Commission's recommendations would entail there is no legitimate room for argument that they would disturb the constitutional division of powers between the nation and the states.

The remaining structural difficulties are mostly traceable to the other great organizing principle of our Constitution, the separation of powers. Here are encountered a cluster of related issues that center on the general problem of *improving coordination* among the many institutions of national government participating in the formulation and administration of economic policy, and of monetary, fiscal, and credit policy in particular.

Coordination is one of the most difficult and delicate of the organizational demands that can be made upon a governmental system as large and as decentralized as ours. It is also one of the most urgent because the goals of policy are multiple, and success depends on their simultaneous fulfillment; and because the instruments of policy are interdependent and to an important degree interchangeable. If unemployment levels, price level stability, and economic growth hang together on the outcome of a combination of a great many moves, how can the actions be knowledgeably and purposefully concerted?

For present purposes, problems of coordination seem especially acute and critical in four areas:

At the top-center of the administration, the President and his Executive Office, including such staff aids as the Budget Bureau and the Council of Economic Advisers.

In the interdepartmental domestic field where monetary, fiscal, and credit policies impinge and where the Treasury, the Federal Reserve, and the major agricultural and housing credit agencies operate.

In the also interdepartmental foreign field where the balance of payments is an object of concern and State, Treasury, Defense, Agriculture, and the foreign lending agencies pursue their several objectives.

In the interactions between the executive and the Congress.

The remainder of this chapter deals with these topics.

Coordination in the Executive Branch

The first prerequisite of effective coordination, and the hardest to get, is unity of purpose—not of all purposes, to be sure, but of those that influence official action. In the years since World War II a consensus has arisen in this country on the proposition that the government of the United States has a proper and positive responsibility for the health and growth of the nation's economy and for minimum standards of well-being for its citizens. This does not mean abandoning our basic reliance on private enterprise; on the contrary, the continuing enterprise of our people is a main source of our national health and strength. But it does mean a determination to try to prevent the severe business cycles that have plagued the past and that might in the future imperil national survival or welfare. And it means a recognition that public authority has a legitimate and important role in attending to national economic goals. So much was embodied in the Employment Act of 1946.

The consensus breaks down, however, in specific contemporary applications. The experiences of the deep depression and of World War II have not recurred, and no current national consensus prescribes the medicines and dosages, and their timing, for the succession of moderated booms and recessions of the postwar years, for the lagging growth rate, for the creeping inflation, or for the balance of payments deficits.

So particular policies are disputable and disputed. Economic programs for agriculture, education, health, housing, foreign aid, social security, transportation, and the like have been adopted and adapted from time to time to meet specific and insistent problems and demands. The variety of governmental agencies and of the programs they administer testifies to the divergent, uneven, and piecemeal development of a national economic policy.

The practical consequence is that the bits and pieces which, added together, make up national policy, tend to be made individually by the separate departments and agencies, each of them in a unique position and with a distinct outlook. Each has its statutory goals and responsibilities, the special tasks it is skilled and accustomed to perform, and a clientele it has come to serve and to reckon with. In such a complex, each agency tends to be in business for itself and to enjoy a considerable measure of autonomy in policy from its nominal superiors.

This increases the reliance that agencies are prone to place, directly and in conjunction with the congressional committees they answer to, on the support of pressure groups. In turn, it weakens the influence of central policy controls.

One effect, usually counted a boon, is easy access to the centers of decision for interested and affected parties. With so many centers to choose from, ordinarily there is hardly a cause that cannot find some agency, some committee, as a forum for a sympathetic hearing, as a fulcrum for leverage and influence, or at least as a listening post for intelligence.

The dramatic difficulties are the recurring cases of conflict when government agencies deliberately pursue divergent policies. No major department or agency concerned with economic policy has wholly avoided such conflicts in recent years. Acknowledging that harmony is not the only goal, that each party to a controversy may have some part of the right on its side, that competition in policy may broaden the perspectives of ultimate decision, it is nevertheless clear that bystanders have been hit and progress hurt on some of these occasions. Less striking but probably more important is the government's chronic difficulty in taking firm and concerted action on a broad front when economic indicators point adversely. On both counts—the reduction of conflict and the timely concert of action—better coordination of government programs for the economy is needed.

Yet coordination is not an end in itself. It is not neutral, because organizations and procedures are not simply "mechanisms," but are manned by people animated by purposes. Inevitably, depending on who controls it, coordination tends to promote some interests, some perspectives, at the expense of others.

The call for coordination therefore need not and should not imply a demand for the elimination of "special interests," or of the official channels of information and persuasion now open to them. It is not a call to override congressional decisions that determine which special groups and interests should receive what particular benefits or burdens at the hands of the government. Nor is it a way of prejudging decisions when economic objectives themselves appear to be in conflict, or when they may need to be subordinated to some more important goal, such as national defense. It is not, in short, to be confused with a call for the elimination of politics from political decisions.

The justification for steps to improve coordination is the aim of creating conditions in which organization becomes the servant of purpose, so that accidents or complexities of structure are not obstacles to the formulation and execution of a concerted and energetic policy. Proper coordination should bring a better appreciation of national goals.

Coordination is not to be had for the asking; it is an elusive phenomenon in organized endeavor. The search for improved coordination within the government of the United States must be guided by an understanding of the working of our institutions and of the real obstacles to be overcome.

UNIFYING THE MANDATE

A formula of words, even enacted into law, will not by itself guarantee unity of purpose among those who are charged to give it effect. But its absence is an invitation to misunderstanding and disagreement, for the publicly avowed purposes of government agencies are expressed in their separate organic statutes. A useful initial step toward coordination is therefore to unify legislative statements of purpose.

A main concern of the original Federal Reserve Act was to provide a "flexible currency," to expand and contract in response to business needs. The Banking Act of 1935, which reorganized the Board, carried over old language and added new, but rejected an attempt to write a fresh charter of general credit policy. The Employment Act, coming at a time of widespread fears lest renewed massive unemployment attend the postwar readjustments, focused on "maximum employment, production, and purchasing power" as the government's economic goals. The act did not speak expressly to the Federal Reserve Board, though Board spokesmen have several times testified that its objectives are taken into account by the Board. Nevertheless, the accumulation of policy guides for the System over the years now consists of a collection so varied as to be no longer coherent. The time is ripe to address to the Board specifically a statutory guide which embodies unambiguously such consensus as can be reached on the nation's economic goals, makes them explicit goals for the System also, and enlists the System's powers for their attainment.

The same language should be introduced into the Employment Act to emphasize the unity of purpose. Efforts in recent years to amend that act by adding price-level stability to its stated objectives have been debated and lost in controversy. The Commission's proposal seeks to limit controversy by voicing a newly defined consensus on three mutually linked objectives and applying it simultaneously to all federal agencies participating in economic policy.

The Commission recommends that the Congress modernize and make consistent the legislative mandates which set out national economic goals in the two statutes that bear most directly on the field of the Commission's concern, namely, the Federal Reserve Act and the Employment Act of 1946. Identical language should be incorporated simultaneously in each to formulate the goals of a low level of unemploy-

ment, an adequate rate of economic growth and reasonable price stability as applicable to all federal agencies administering economic programs.

AN ORGANIZATIONAL FOCUS

A second prerequisite of coordination is an organizational focus. Where is central responsibility to be lodged? To this question there can be only one realistic answer for our national government: in the presidency, or nowhere. A brief discussion of the possibilities is enough to show why this is so.

The Congress has ultimate legislative power across the whole field of economic policy, and all strands in the policy web lead sooner or later through some parts of Congress. It would be idle, therefore, to seek solutions that aim to bypass Congress. But it would be equally futile to seek to center responsibility for coordination of policy in Congress. For a leading characteristic of congressional organization and operation is the dispersion of power, between the two chambers and among the committees and members. Individual members, in their dealings with executive agencies, ordinarily expect, when necessary, to summon the backing of their committees. The committees expect, in case of need, the backing of the full House or Senate. So by a sort of delegation that commonly goes unchallenged because it rests largely on anticipated ratification, each member wields, in a degree, the power of Congress when he confronts outside agencies.

In this general framework, experienced members of Congress with some accumulated seniority, and knowledgeable in a subject matter specialty, can exert great influence and become skilled in negotiating settlements of cases and problems that cut across agency jurisdictions. So it may well be that the interagency coordination that produces a particular action owes as much to an interested member of Congress as to any command structure in the executive branch.

Yet what can be done piecemeal in this way, Congress cannot do either for the executive branch as a whole, or for the broad span of agencies and policies encompassed in an economic program. For here, many committees in each house (taxing, appropriations, and government operations, not to mention such subject matter committees as banking and currency, labor, and so forth) as well as the Joint Economic Committee, have a rightful claim to take part. And the history of past efforts to coordinate these coordinators—to concentrate power in either house sufficient to control the committees—warns against expecting satisfactory solutions to the general problem of coordination by devices that in operation would strengthen the seniority rule.

For the most part, Congress acts by reacting. It serves well in responding to, restraining, and even goading leadership. It is not so organized as to be ordinarily capable, on its own initiative, of developing and enacting comprehensive programs in a controversial field—as the history of tariff legislation teaches. The search for coordination of economic policy must, as a practical matter, begin in the executive branch, with Congress continuing as stimulator, critic, and ultimate judge of what will be and will not be given the sanction of legislation.

Within the executive branch, coordination commonly starts with the establishment of interdepartmental committees, designed to bring agencies closer together by providing a forum where their accredited representatives can meet regularly, exchange views, negotiate settlements if possible, and refer irreconcilable differences to higher authority. But when a substantial issue is in dispute and stakes are high, concrete determinations that deserve the name "policy" in any specific sense can seldom be reached in an interdepartmental committee unless that committee falls under the domination of one strong member.

For the policy that all committee members can willingly and easily follow is likelier than not to be no policy at all. Conflicts of many sorts, at many levels, are built in by disparate statutory mandates, clientele demands, congressional pressures, bureaucratic loyalties, and personalities. Inevitably, and properly, each committee member interprets the common obligation to coordinate in the light of his own organization's statutory duties and perspectives. The committee collectively cannot for long assume and hold the separate powers and duties of the agencies represented on it. Accordingly, if the committee is more than merely a tail on the kite of its strongest member, coordination by committee tends to produce either a stalemate of inactivity or action only on the lowest common denominator of agreement—commonly a vague formula that plasters over real differences.

The search for an organizational focus must therefore proceed to center on the presidency; if for no other reason, because in no other place is there a jurisdiction so nearly comprehensive as the problem. There are other reasons. The President is elected on a promise to give leadership, and so programs are expected of him. People inside and outside of government take problems to him and look for guidance. What the President does and says is newsworthy; he can use the attention he commands to enlist, to persuade, to mobilize support.

There are difficulties in presidential coordination too. Over military and foreign policy, to be sure, tradition and the Constitution alike give the President overriding powers of direction, but this is not usually so for domestic economic policy. Nor is the appointing power a universal solvent. Ordinarily a President must stay with the choices in appointments he has already made, and reckon with the fact that the statutory powers run mostly to his subordinates—or their subordinates, bureau chiefs—and not to him.

It is no remedy for the difficulties of agency independence to suggest as a general solution that all the relevant powers of departments be given to the President instead, for redelegation as he sees fit, or that he be authorized to command their every move. Such an arrangement might help him in some cases: it was the Budget Bureau's remedy, following the first Hoover Commission report, for the dispersion of statutory powers among bureaus within the executive departments, at the expense of department heads. But the cry of "presidential dictatorship" from the outside, and the overburdening of his office from the inside would be compelling objections to such a sweeping solution in the domestic field; and except in times of grave and evident crisis the Congress would view such a step as abdication of its own responsibilities. Coordination must in the main be achieved by persuasion and consent, perhaps even more than by command and obedience, by stimulating external pressures that will put a higher premium on internal cohesion, and by enabling the President to bring his influence to bear at timely stages before the lines of policy divergence have hardened.

Another difficulty is that the President's time and attention must be divided among many competing claimants, not all of them on errands connected with the state of the economy. Diagnosis and prescription for the economy, moreover, have become highly technical matters, for all their political implications. Effective coordination of national economic policy must accordingly depend heavily on the growing institutionalization of the President's office, by way of staff assistance, without at the same time encroaching on his freedom to exercise his personal talents for leadership. To this end he must feel that his immediate assistants are working for him, rather than for one of the interests or agencies he is expected to coordinate.

The problem in devising coordinating machinery, then, is to transcend at once the limitations of presidential commands and of multilateral negotiations in interdepartmental committees. Past efforts to bring presidential authority more effectively to bear have taken one or the other of two somewhat overlapping but broadly distinguishable routes. One is the "cabinet committee" approach, where an interagency committee of elevated status is attached to the President, usually with the link of a White House assistant. This gives the committee a judge and arbiter, who presumably has the power and means to impose decisions and make them stick. The other is the "presidential staff" approach, where staff takes the place of a committee and attempts coordination by investigation and consultation in the process of preparing documents on which the President must act by a date-certain. An example of the first is the National Security Council; and of the second, the Bureau of the Budget.

Each type has its own limitations and each, pushed very far, may get in the other's way. The NSC machinery, for example, involves the President and other already busy officials in regularly scheduled consultations, whether or not anything has to be decided there by a particular date. In the absence of hostilities or diplomatic crises, which generate such dates, the NSC's agenda has often been filled by discussion of elaborately prepared papers; then when policy has actually to be made in the form of concrete decisions, consultation through the NSC is likely to be short-circuited and previous discussion to be irrelevant. The Budget Bureau mechanism, by contrast, is oriented to inescapable, specific decisions—a message, in print, must go to Congress, over the President's signature, by a set date. It cannot be put into print until a multitude of competing claims and conflicting positions have somehow been coordinated. All parties are under pressure to force a resolution as the date approaches. The budget process thereby escapes the difficulties of unreality and postponement of unpalatable conclusions, but only to raise the painful and familiar problems of staff screening—second-guessing and interference in the relationships between and among the President and the department and agency heads who have political and legal responsibility for action.

Even in the best of circumstances, coordination by means of these devices is imperfect and uncertain. The NSC and Budget Bureau actually exemplify nearly the best of circumstances in our system, for in the one case the President has constitutional powers in virtually every field where NSC members have statutory duties, and in the other the statute runs to him and the actions to be taken by a specified date are his. Though Congress can override him, the law makes every agency acknowledge if not accept his judgment.

By comparison, the field of monetary and credit policy presents a much less hospitable set of circumstances for the working of coordinative mechanisms of either sort. A cabinet committee must reckon with the independence of the Federal Reserve Board and with congressional tendencies to insulate the other domestic credit agencies from central supervision. A presidential staff solution confronts the difficulty that crucial powers are vested in the Treasury, the Board, and elsewhere under laws that leave the timing of decisions up to them.

In summary, neither alternative guarantees the desired results; both offer some limited promise. On the record of the last two or three decades, more progress seems to have been made by the staff route than by the cabinet committee route; and government experience suggests no basically different third possibility to try. The record also sustains the view that it is more efficacious to set in motion, or strengthen, forces working in the desired direction, through whatever machinery is at hand, than to erect structures and mechanisms that are vulnerable to failure

because their operators probably have different motives than their archi-
tects. The history of administrative reorganization is strewn with such
wrecks. The prudent course in these circumstances, accordingly, appears
also to be the most promising: to build from present strength rather than
leap to innovations; to try modest advances along both historically trav-
eled routes; and to concentrate on creating conditions more conducive to
coordination. Starting with a more unified statutory mandate, the most
feasible approach to improving coordination by the presidential staff
method appears to lie in the strengthening of procedures already laid
out in the Employment Act of 1946.

EMPLOYMENT ACT PROCEDURES

The Employment Act as it stands is something of a milestone on the
road to coordination of economic policy. It requires of the President an
annual *Economic Report* to Congress. It furnishes him a staff agency—
the Council of Economic Advisers, located in the Executive Office of the
President—to help prepare his report and to make continuing studies
of the economy. And it establishes in Congress the Joint Committee on
the Economic Report to respond to the President's report with one of its
own and to engage in other studies itself. Taken together, these innovations have contributed to the transformation of the climate and technical sophistication of official and public discussion of economic measures that has occurred over the past decade. They have also given the
President better technical equipment for his coordinating role. What
they have not yet sufficiently done is to increase the pressures on the
operating departments and agencies to modify their policies and behavior correspondingly, or to provide a high-level forum for policy discussion or even tentative policy decisions.

The Joint Economic Committee—seven senators and seven congress-
men, reflecting the partisan divisions of the two houses, and chosen not
from other committee chairmen but from ranking members of related
committees who request the assignment—has been called "the most ex-
citing contemporary invention" in the organization of Congress. The
Joint Committee has always had strong representation from the banking
and currency committee, who are perhaps most aware of the general
framework within which their own work should be considered, and from
the taxing committees. The appropriations committees show little interest in membership.

The Committee has no legislative jurisdiction to introduce bills and
so avoids arousing the jealousy of other committees. It roves at will over
the field of economic policy, studying broadly or intensively any problem
that attracts the interest of the Committee or of the congressional leadership. In Congress it is an anomaly: a planning and theory group in a cul-

ture fiercely devoted to the short run and practical. It is committed to the panoramic view in a system that stresses jurisdictional lines. It signifies recognition that economic problems are related, in a body that deals with them piecemeal.

The Joint Committee has pioneered a method of study that more nearly resembles a graduate seminar or professional conference than the traditional committee hearing. Technical papers prepared by economic experts provide the material for hearings which take on the character of a panel discussion. Direct effects of this educational process can be observed in the members' behavior in their other capacities on other committees and on the floor. Indirect effects on other members of Congress can be traced to the wide dissemination of Committee documents. The result is not always consensus: when one party is in control on the Hill and the other in the White House, majority and minority reports of the Committee will naturally reflect partisan premises. But unquestionably, the Committee's activities and the President's *Economic Report* have served to highlight and focus informed discussion of the behavior of the economy. This in itself is a fact that obliges government agencies to take somewhat more account of each other's policies and activities and of inconsistencies among them. The Committee is a contributing factor, rather than a direct instrument, toward securing coordination.

The role of the Council of Economic Advisers has varied since the Employment Act was passed, depending in part on what the President and the CEA Chairman have wanted to make of it. A good deal of the time a special assistant in the White House has served as economic adviser on immediately pending measures and current developments, leaving the CEA to concentrate on the annual report, national economic analysis, and long-range studies. But in a different conception and with more adequate support the CEA might well become the President's principal staff reliance for economic policy analysis and could be equipped to provide expertise in each of the main fields of economic policy.

The annual *Economic Report,* presented to Congress in conjunction with the state-of-the-union message, is long, detailed, and full of figures on the past; it has sometimes been specific but more often general and cautiously noncommittal on forecasts and recommendations for the future. For the general public, and as a dramatic device, it tends to be overshadowed by the other presidential messages it accompanies. But against these disadvantages—and against consequent suggestions of a later release date for it—must be weighed the existing interest in an up-to-date annual economic review as the congressional session opens.

Major presidential messages to Congress are instruments of coordination in the executive branch, for they tend to make White House business of what would otherwise be departmental responsibilities. Their preparation forces White House action and decision on their contents and phraseology, which in turn requires some prior coordinative staff consultation with the departments and agencies affected by what is to be said or left unsaid. The timetable of preparation compels some resolution of whatever divergence in counsel is uncovered in that process.

The annual *Economic Report* furthers these coordinative tendencies, but in a very mild degree, because of both its timing and its content. The opening of a session of Congress is a ceremonial occasion, suitable for a general expression of the President's aspirations for the labors that are about to commence. Language appropriate for that purpose is as likely to conceal as reveal the hard choices in more specific proposals and commitments. Only by coincidence will the need for short-run action occur in conjunction with a fixed annual date. The annual *Economic Report*, in addition to its reviewing function, may consequently serve as a launching pad for long-range legislative programs; it will not ordinarily be the means of inducing government agencies to respond to shorter-term changes in economic circumstances. The occasion for considering a decisive shift in economic policies may arise infrequently; the time for it is unpredictable. Yet only when such a time comes, and only if it brings forth actions or proposals from the President, will conditions and forces conducive to coordination operate across the board and with a potentially adequate effect. In current practice too little is at stake, politically speaking, in the contents of the annual *Economic Report* to give it the needed leverage on the policies and actions of the operating departments and agencies.

So, whether or not the coordinative machinery and procedures of the Employment Act have met the expectations held for them in 1946, they fall short of present-day needs. Yet no other vehicle of the presidential-action, presidential-staff type is so readily at hand and easily convertible. The effectual changes needed are to highlight the President's responsibility and to hitch the requirement of an evaluative presidential report to an occasion that will give it a higher policy significance.*

---

* STANLEY H. RUTTENBERG—I agree that the annual *Economic Report* of the President cannot adequately deal with the short run problems of the economy. It will only be incidental that the annual report will coincide with the point in time when the President should be recommending policies about short run developments in the economy. However, I do think that the annual *Economic Report* of the President and the Council of Economic Advisers should be used to set forth projections of the goals and objectives of the American economy.

The council should, as the law suggests, describe the "conditions under which there will be afforded useful employment opportunities, including self-employment, for those able, willing, and seeking to work, and to promote maximum employment, production, and purchasing power." These conditions should be reported in enough detail so that a yardstick of achievement will be available.

To do this requires composition and detail. The composition—the whole economic

To this end the Commission offers three related recommendations. The first is aimed at improving the quality and timeliness and enhancing the significance of the statistical series relevant to the appraisal of the performance of the economy. Since 1949 the law has authorized publication by the Joint Economic Committee of a number of economic series which are important for informed discussion of national economic policy. The series appear in a convenient monthly form under the title *Economic Indicators* and are assembled by the Council of Economic Advisers from the statistical services of the various government departments and agencies. *Economic Indicators* carries no interpretive text, but provides some thirty pages of current and comparative series under half a dozen main headings relating to output, employment, prices, credit, and so forth.

The Commission believes that every practicable step should be taken to improve the timeliness, quality, and relevance for policy decisions of such statistics as are published in *Economic Indicators*. The data should be the best that can be obtained to judge the behavior of the economy in relation to major economic objectives. More public funds are urgently needed for this purpose.*

In emphasizing the importance of securing the best available economic statistics, the Commission wishes also to call attention to their intrinsic limitations. Depending on the nature of the raw data from which they are compiled, as well as the methods of treating them, the statistics and the index numbers they yield are, in varying degree, approximations. Their built-in margin of error may be reduced—perhaps in some cases to small proportions—by improved and more elaborate techniques but never altogether eliminated. Consequently, the intelligent use of these series requires an appreciation of their approximate quality and cautions against attributing too much significance to minor variations unless they are persistent over a period of time sufficient to confirm a trend. Exag-

---

pattern—should be set forth so that needed goals in the three major categories that make up the gross national product are clear—the necessary levels of investment, consumption and government spending. These three categories should be related to the projected levels of population growth, labor force growth, and productivity increases, so that the various parts of the economic pattern will fit together.

If this balanced, detailed, composite picture of the economy were developed, it would then be possible to project the needs for the next five years, the next ten years, and the necessary levels in each sector to keep the economy operating at a rate that insures maximum employment, production, and purchasing power.

Mr. NATHAN wishes to be associated with Mr. RUTTENBERG'S comment.

* J. CAMERON THOMSON—Following the word "objectives" I would add the following. "*Economic Indicators* and reports of the Federal Reserve Board should, when appropriate, contain information as to nonsustainable expansion of business inventories, capital expenditures, including business plant and equipment, housing, and consumer durables, also credit extension by bank and nonbank financial institutions and government financial agencies."

gerating either the optimism or the alarm to be drawn from a shift in a fraction may do a widespread disservice.

Beyond this, however more exact the statistics of the nation's economic performance may be made, they require judgments for their interpretation. Statistics measure what is and has been; public policy must prescribe what ought to be. Statistics are guides, and useful as such. The Commission does not expect to see the day when human wisdom in public affairs can be dispensed with in favor of figures alone.

The Commission recommends that *Economic Indicators* **should be issued from the Executive Office of the President.**

Placing the responsibility for publication where the responsibility for preparation already lies, coupled with the necessity of meeting White House deadlines for prompt issuance, should be helpful. It should also tend to encourage them to devise additional series and breakdowns so as to develop more sensitive and reliable indicators for policy purposes.

Second, the Commission believes the prospects of improved coordination in the executive branch will be advanced if, on the foundation of this monthly informational and analytical routine, the President's responsibility is somewhat sharpened. This should be done with care, so as not to bind his judgment of the proper course of policy. Section 3 of the Employment Act presently requires him, in his *Economic Report* to Congress, to transmit, along with much statistical information, "a review of the economic program of the Federal Government and a review of economic conditions . . . ," as well as "a program for carrying out the policy" of the act. It also authorizes "supplementary" reports "from time to time." The annual report, as has been noted, has become too general, and the supplementary reports, after some trial of "mid-year" reports from the CEA, have fallen into disuse, presumably because they offer only an opportunity and impose no duty.

A partial substitute for supplementary reports has emerged in the institution of the presidential press conference. Here, perhaps as often as weekly, and in a relatively informal, highly visible, and easily accessible forum, the President may be asked to comment on economic developments among other topics. The anticipation of reporters' questions and the preparation of answering statements has a tendency, like the more formal message to Congress, to make White House business of what otherwise might be left to the operating departments and agencies directly concerned, with only such lateral clearances as they see fit to arrange. And unlike the annual message, these statements are likely to be addressed to current developments that may call for immediate and specific policy decisions.

The Commission accordingly recommends that the Employment Act be amended to provide that whenever in the President's judgment the

current economic situation, as revealed over a span of time in the indicators issued from his Executive Office or on the basis of other information, shows a tendency significantly counter to the objectives set forth in the Employment Act as amended, and at least quarterly thereafter for so long as the unfavorable tendency prevails, the President shall supplement his annual *Economic Report* with a statement setting forth:

1. His understanding and assessment of the factors in the economy contributing to the unfavorable tendency.*

2. The steps being taken by him and by government agencies, including the Federal Reserve System, to use existing instruments and resources available for better achieving the goals of the Employment Act as amended.

3. Explanations for any seemingly inconsistent use being made of any of these instruments.

4. Recommendations for any congressional action he thinks advisable.**

5. Any other comments he thinks appropriate.

Third, because the Congress has a lively interest and a legitimate concern, not only for the performance of the economy but also for the performance of the executive branch, a regular procedure should be recognized for the expression of that concern, in a manner that will tend to ensure that the sentiments of Congress as a whole, rather than of particular committees, will prevail.

The Commission therefore recommends that the Employment Act be also amended to provide that the Congress may, by concurrent resolution, request the President, if he has not already done so, to furnish such a statement, whenever it finds that the current economic situation reveals a tendency running significantly counter to the objectives set forth in the Employment Act as amended.

All this is within the scope and spirit of the Employment Act as it now stands. It does not preclude the President or the CEA or the Congress from any move now open to them; no relevant subjects are closed

---

* WILLARD L. THORP—The point at which the series of reports shall start is left to the discretion of the President. But there often is a rather confused situation in which some objectives are being well achieved and others less so, and the President might feel that making such a report would create undue uncertainties. Therefore, a regular quarterly report might be preferable.

Mr. RUTTENBERG wishes to be associated with Mr. THORP'S comment.

** J. CAMERON THOMSON—Add, "consistent with the provisions of the Employment Act of 1946 relating to free enterprise and the general welfare as well as our international relations and responsibilities."

Mr. BLACK wishes to be associated with Mr. THOMSON'S comment.

to them by the act as it is presently written. It does aim to increase somewhat the pressure on the President to give attention to the indicators, to deal explicitly with failures in the performance of the economy, and when in his judgment the occasion arises, to take a public position.* The leverage toward that result consists in the expectation that the need for speaking out will be something of a political liability to the President. It should be a liability strong enough to induce him to seek to secure the fullest use of available measures to avoid it, if he can do so without sacrificing other goals he is willing to call more important, yet not so serious as to undercut his ability to act in the future.

The effect of sharpening the President's responsibility should be to strengthen his hand in coordinative moves. The necessity of his taking a formal stand and of explaining and reconciling agency policies will fortify his position against separatist tendencies among government agencies and in Congress and will bring inconsistencies and lags more openly into view. And the preparation of his messages will strengthen the staff mechanism of coordination.

But staff assistance in injecting the President's perspective into the deliberations and actions of the various agencies may well need supplementing to secure the necessary degree and continuity of consultation. This argues for an effort to make use also of the other type of coordinative mechanism, the cabinet-committee approach, provided it will not cancel out whatever gains can be derived from the presidential-staff approach via the Employment Act.

Cabinet-Level Councils

Cabinet-level interagency councils or committees in the field of national economic policy have been frequently advocated, at least since the first Hoover Commission in 1949. In these suggestions two main types can be distinguished. Some of the proposals have limited the scope of the coordination they sought—and, correspondingly, the agencies to be included—to monetary and credit activities. In such plans the Treasury and the Federal Reserve have the leading roles. Other proposals have cast a wider net. Contemplating stronger and more direct and selective measures on a broader front, they have included fiscal policy among the objects of coordination, and so have brought the Budget and Council of Economic Advisers into their councils. The first type shies away from a

---

* CHARLES B. SHUMAN—In my opinion, it would be undesirable to increase "the pressure on the President" as contemplated by these recommendations. The probable result would be to increase political controversy, and reduce the influence of economic factors on the determination of economic policies.

presidential focus and so puts the council chairmanship in an agency head; the second stresses it by giving the chairmanship to the President or to the CEA Chairman.

None of these proposals has been enacted into law, though by Executive Order, or less formally, several cabinet committees have been created for sectors of the general field. The only *statutory* cabinet-level council or committee with a jurisdiction bearing importantly on monetary and credit policies is the National Advisory Council on International Monetary and Financial Problems. The National Security Council, to be sure, is another statutory body with responsibilities for coordination, and its members are not unaware of the domestic economic impacts of the defense and foreign policies NSC considers. But it is scarcely the vehicle for the coordination of national economic policy. To try to make it that, by expanding its composition and jurisdiction, would in effect merge it with almost the whole Cabinet and leave unmet the special and major purposes it now serves.

The NAC was established by the Bretton Woods Agreement Act of 1945. The Secretary of the Treasury is chairman, the Treasury provides staff support, and the other members are the Secretaries of State and Commerce, the Chairman of the Board of Governors of the Federal Reserve, and the Director of the Export–Import Bank. Under Treasury dominance, and despite its apparently broad charter, the NAC for the past decade has kept to a much more limited role, for example, the coordination of instructions given to the U.S. members of the international lending agencies.

Viewing the experiences of cabinet-level councils, some generalizations appear to be tentatively warranted by their operation during the postwar years. Committees not closely tied to the President—in actuality, regardless of formal appearance—tend to take one of two courses.

The committee may wither away after repeated meetings have made it plain that significant issues are not presented for decision or cannot be resolved there. Instead, agency heads or their deputies, under no compulsion to yield their differing positions in that forum, may prefer to take their business directly and separately to the President if higher authority must be consulted. This course is the more likely because any President must open and preserve the privilege of direct and confidential access to him for some of his principal subordinates if he wishes to get candid advice. Agency heads are not apt to air, for the benefit of their cabinet committee colleagues, views that can be more safely or persuasively put to the President privately; and those who do not have that access may save their arguments for the ears of those who do.

The committee may fall under the domination of one strong member. In that case the price of its survival is to restrict its activities to matters on which the strong member can ordinarily make his views prevail. The coordination achieved in such circumstances is likely to appear parochial in the perspectives of government-wide policy.

Committees closely tied to the President have a hard time keeping their ties close. This is only partly because of the many competing claims on the President's time. It reflects also an inherent dilemma. If he insists that he will reach no conclusions on matters within the committee's purview except through the committee's framework, he cuts himself off from the private counsel of individual members. If he listens to them separately he undercuts the committee. Alternatively, if he puts the committee's business in the hands of an assistant on his behalf, he risks widening the distance in another way.

Committees set up by statute and required to report to Congress tend to hem the President in. A report to Congress immediately becomes public property. The timing and contents or omissions of a public report may play into the hands of his adversaries and so make him the object rather than the source of coordination. He cannot repudiate its conclusions without publicly displaying his want of confidence in the committee that endorsed it. If he regards the committee as having been created as a check on him he may decline to use it, and seek to secure coordination by some other means.

Committees established by statute also risk the danger that at some point the dominant member will be an inappropriate one for the business at hand. And with the passage of time their composition may become inappropriate for changing problems.

Finally, coordination by committee tends to give each member a veto. For that reason, committees are sometimes proposed and membership on them sought more for the sake of delaying than for advancing action.

REVIVING AN ADVISORY BOARD

These considerations indicate some of the difficulties to be anticipated if a cabinet-level committee for economic policy is added to the Employment Act, which now embodies the presidential-staff approach. How the two methods could both be employed without friction, and so as to be mutually re-enforcing, is a problem to be worked out. The most promising course appears to lie in the revival or creation of something along the lines of the Advisory Board for Economic Growth and Stability, for which no legislation would be needed.

This advisory board was a consultative instrument attached to the Council of Economic Advisers and headed by its chairman, with representation (nominally at the undersecretary level) from the Federal Reserve Board, the Departments of State, Treasury, Agriculture, Commerce, Labor, and Health, Education, and Welfare, the Housing and Home Finance Administration, and the Bureau of the Budget. It was established by a letter from the President when the Council of Economic Advisers was reconstituted in 1953; it flourished under its first chairman and has been dormant lately. As a working mechanism of coordination it was displaced in 1958 by entirely informal consultations at fairly frequent but irregular intervals between the Secretary of the Treasury, the FRB Chairman and the CEA Chairman, sometimes with the President in attendance. If the changes the Commission has proposed in the Employment Act are enacted, a committee more broadly based than the trio of Treasury, FRB, and CEA is indicated, because of the range of operating programs needing to be canvassed and coordinated. Moreover its composition should be variable, depending on the problems it deals with.

A few steps would suffice to restore vitality to such an advisory board. The President could attend its meetings often enough to assure that heads of agencies would find it wise to represent themselves. He could insist on referring enough significant and pending matters to the Board to keep it from futility. It would be desirable to leave open the question of who is to serve as chairman. One possibility would be to make the CEA Chairman the chairman of the board. In that event the President would be required to make it clear that the CEA would continue to be the source of staff work and that the CEA Chairman would call its meetings, set its agenda and review its results, all on his behalf. This would make the CEA Chairman less than a cabinet member but more than an executive secretary, a deliberate and desirable ambiguity.

A statutory establishment of such a board and its chairman would be positively undesirable. The board's usefulness for coordination purposes would depend almost entirely on the President's willingness to use it and on the personality and capabilities of the chairman. Making both statutory would risk an enforced perpetuation of what could become a paper mill, or presidential time waster, or an artificial prop for an ineffectual chairman.

In sum, assuming the adoption of the changes already recommended in the Employment Act, the President will need to make suitable arrangements, congenial to him, for staff and interagency consultative machinery to assist him in discharging his expanded responsibilities. No statutory council should be created which has the effect of constricting his choice of advisers or formalizing their advice. The Commission recommends that he consider setting up an advisory board along the lines of the Advisory Board on Economic Growth and Stability, under a chairman to be designated by him, and plan its work so that weekly meetings of department and agency deputies, supported by staff assistance from the Council of Economic Advisers, may culminate in periodic meetings of their chiefs in the presence of the President.

THE NATIONAL ADVISORY COUNCIL

The emergence of the balance of payments problem makes a reappraisal of the National Advisory Council timely. It is clear that with the passage of time the composition of the NAC has become anomalous if it were actually to undertake the coordination of all government agencies "to the extent that they make or participate in the making of foreign loans or engage in foreign financial exchange or monetary transactions," as its charter states. The absence of Defense and Agriculture are alike inappropriate for a broadly conceived NAC today, and for such a purpose the terms of reference in the act would need expansion to include grants, trade policy, and other aspects of foreign economic policy as well as loans. Similarly, the Treasury's chairmanship and possession of the secretariat would need reconsideration. The original justifications were Treasury leadership in the Bretton Woods negotiations, the concentration in that department of expert talent in the field, and reassurance to the banking community about the management of the International Bank for Reconstruction and Development and the International Monetary fund. These considerations have long since lost their force. Even apart from the NAC, the importance of factors beyond the financial has made the Treasury's role in foreign economic policy-making disproportionate to its responsibilities. The record may serve as a warning against freezing in a statute the designation of the strongest member of the NAC for the chairmanship and staff work.

When the payments imbalance assumed proportions demanding presidential attention, as it did in 1959, the problem fell squarely within the terms of reference of one, and only one, regularly constituted policy-making group at the time, the Council on Foreign Economic Policy. Despite its formal White House base, this council was passed over; and it has since been abolished. Instead, Treasury and State jointly worked out a coordinated set of actions for the immediate occasion, involving several other agencies. The problem is too important to be left to *ad hoc* improvisations, yet statutory prescriptions of machinery seem out of place. Furthermore, any interagency policy group for this purpose will need to be closely and integrally related to the over-all economic policy council recommended in the previous section, and through that to the President.

The Commission recommends that the President should fix a clear and continuing responsibility, perhaps in a subcommittee of the advisory board recommended above, for the direction and coordination of actions required to deal with the balance of payments problem, and, more generally, for the coordination of grant, loan, and trade policies

as aspects of American foreign policy. To clear the way for this, the Bretton Woods Agreement Act of 1945 should be amended to enable the President to designate the chairman and membership of the National Advisory Council on International and Financial Problems (NAC) and to assign the responsibility for its staff support.

With its statutory base removed, the President would then be free to reconstitute it as an advisory board subcommittee or otherwise relate its work to a more inclusive framework of responsibility.

Coordination of Domestic Lending Agencies

Interagency relationships in the domestic lending field from time to time present significant coordination problems, depending on the magnitude of the impact of an agency's operations on general credit conditions. Serious policy clashes may arise between agencies in particular fields and agencies with broader economic responsibilities, especially the Treasury, the Federal Reserve, and the Budget Bureau. Measures toward coordination within the structural framework of the executive branch frequently meet obstacles in the independent status accorded several of the principal lending agencies, often in the form of government corporations, and the political support in Congress and elsewhere that buttresses that status.

The impact of the operations of the Treasury and the Federal Reserve on the banking and financial system of the country is so great that coordination of their policies is imperative. It may be fostered by the close working relationships and mutual understanding that usually prevail between the two agencies. But when, as in the period prior to the "Accord" of 1951, a sharp conflict of views develops, the stakes are too high to admit of an extended stalemate or of continuing actions which are at cross-purposes. The Commission's recommendations earlier in this chapter and in Chapters Three and Four aim at a greater assurance of coordination between them, particularly as participants in a revitalized advisory board, and in their responses to the expanded responsibilities anticipated for them under the Employment Act.

The same general framework of coordination, with adaptations to suit particular situations, should apply also to the government lending agencies, for example to the Farm Credit and Home Loan Bank systems, the Housing and Home Finance Agency, the Small Business Administration, the Export–Import Bank and others. Given the adoption of the Commission's previous recommendations, no major additional changes in *organization* seem needed for coordination purposes. It is likely, however, that closer working relationships at operating levels will need to be developed to give a fuller effect to the wider monetary, credit, and fiscal policies of the government. The coverage of the President's reports under the Employment Act should include attention to the actions and policies of the credit agencies. Budget controls apply to most of them in varying degrees. And they should be included in the scope of discussions in the advisory board. A further statutory mechanism of coordination, applicable to the agencies established as government corporations, may be found in the terms of the Government Corporation Control Act.

THE GOVERNMENT CORPORATION CONTROL ACT

The Government Corporation Control Act of 1946 undertook to reconcile the rights and claims of government corporations (both wholly owned and mixed) to policy and operating autonomy in their several fields with some central concerns of fiscal and debt management policy. Along with the budget and audit controls it imposed, the act also instituted a Treasury clearance over the public issuance or sale of securities in excess of $100,000 by any government corporation. The statute confirmed and extended a position the Treasury had long contended for, that confusion in the Treasury securities market would result if more than one channel for new issues to that market was open, and that the Treasury's stake in it was of overriding importance. The act accordingly, with one exception, gives the Treasury complete control of the amounts, timing, coupon rates, and other terms of any government corporation offerings. No criteria of review are specified. The exception runs in favor of the farm credit agencies, which must consult but may appeal from the Treasury to the President and Congress.

In practice the Treasury ordinarily routes requests for clearance to the Federal Open Market Committee of the Federal Reserve, which channels the transactions to the Federal Reserve Bank of New York as agent. This partial delegation of the clearance function indicates that the Treasury's concern seems to have been limited chiefly to the technical aspects and timing of offerings to make sure the market does not become congested on any particular day.

There are sound reasons for this special interest in the debt management aspects of these transactions. There are strong reasons also—reinforced by the support the corporations have usually been able to muster in Congress—why the Treasury should hesitate to push its own review beyond those aspects that touch its immediate operating responsibilities. On the other hand, the credit operations of several of the lending agencies, and especially the fluctuations in the scale of their activities, plainly are significant influences on the economy. In the light of its recommendations regarding the Employment Act, the Commission believes the present scope of review of government corporation issuances is too narrowly conceived.

Accordingly, the Commission recommends that the Government Corporation Control Act of 1946 be amended so as to direct the Secretary of the Treasury, in the exercise of his clearance power over the issuance and sale of the securities of government-owned corporations, to take into account explicitly the full range of objectives of the Employment Act as amended, and not merely debt management considerations; and that cases of disagreement be taken to the President.

The purpose of this change is to convert the Treasury's apparently absolute, but actually almost unused and unusable, policy veto into a flagging device for top-level coordination. It should have the effect not only of broadening the criteria of review but also of bringing the decision, in cases involving substantial policy alternatives, into a presidential forum where the over-all economic policy of the government can be dealt with in a coordinated fashion. The Secretary's clearance should reflect that policy, as worked out in consultation with the advisory board recommended above.

Executive Discretion and Statutory Inflexibilities

On the record of the postwar years, the simultaneous achievement of low levels of unemployment, reasonably stable prices, and an adequate rate of growth will require finer adjustments in the use and coordination of the tools of economic policy than our government has so far been able to manage. It is a task for the sixties to do better.

While economics has made vast strides over the past quarter century in improving our understanding of policy, much remains to be done. Chance will intervene, unanticipated side effects will arise, and uncontrollable outside events may frustrate plans and alter problems out of recognition. In the face of such contingencies, pragmatism is better than dogmatism. Experiment, trial, and error still have their place in policy. Some of the conditions of an intelligently experimental approach to the economic challenges ahead have already been suggested in this report. The Commission concludes this chapter with an emphasis on one that raises a perennial issue in our national government, the need for flexibility in the powers delegated to the executive branch. Both the coordination of executive moves within existing law and the prospects of a successful joint legislative–executive approach to new measures depend on it.

There is a normal presumption that when Congress legislates it will phrase its mandates as specifically as circumstances allow, for our traditions run against unrestricted delegations of power. There is an equally normal presumption that a prudent lawgiver will not tie the hands of

the executive where that may defeat the larger ends in view; and states-
men do not seek high office to perform merely ministerial tasks. Historically, Congress has been intentionally specific in imposing duties or
withholding discretion when it distrusted a particular executive or
wanted to reserve to itself the time and manner of deciding later when
a change in circumstances warrants a change in policy. It has been intentionally vague or generous in delegating power when it faced an acknowledged crisis or preferred to avoid the direct responsibility for
controversial or highly technical decisions. Commonly it strikes some
balance between delegation and specification, even within a single
statute.

When specifics are frozen into law, they sometimes prove later on to
be obstacles to the development of a policy that needs to be based on
wider perspectives than were in the minds of the framers of the law. The
Commission has already referred, in this and previous chapters, to instances where it thinks statutory inflexibilities have had this inhibiting
effect and should be relaxed. It has pointed to the first-bracket tax rate
as a case where a limited flexibility should be introduced to convert a
revenue-raiser into a multiple-purpose tool of fiscal policy. It has called
attention to the need for clarifying the authority of the Federal Reserve
Board to free its members' time for the larger issues of monetary policy
by some delegation of its more detailed regulation of the banking structure. More generally, the Commission believes it a good rule to state
objectives broadly, to fix responsibilities sharply, and to make available
in statutory authorizations a variety of means for their discharge. In
fuller observance of that rule lie opportunities for better executive coordination and improved cooperation between Congress and the executive for the furtherance of national goals.

SELECTION COMMITTEE

ROBERT D. CALKINS
CHAIRMAN
President, The Brookings Institution

ARTHUR F. BURNS
President, National Bureau of Economic Research, Inc.

EVERETT NEEDHAM CASE
President, Colgate University

CHARLES W. COLE
President, Amherst College

MORRIS A. COPELAND
Professor of Economics, Cornell University

AUGUST HECKSCHER
Director, The Twentieth Century Fund, Inc.

PENDLETON HERRING
President, Social Science Research Council

J. E. WALLACE STERLING
President, Stanford University

H. CHRISTIAN SONNE
Chairman, National Planning Association

HERMAN B. WELLS
President, Indiana University

ADVISORY BOARD

STAFF

BERTRAND FOX
Research Director
Edsel Bryant Ford Professor of Business Administration
and Director of Research, Graduate School of Business
Administration, Harvard University

ELI SHAPIRO
Deputy Research Director
Professor of Finance, School of Industrial Management,
Massachusetts Institute of Technology

THE FOLLOWING INDIVIDUALS SERVED AS MEMBERS OF THE STAFF OF THE
COMMISSION DURING VARYING PERIODS OF ITS EXISTENCE

ROBERT Z. ALIBER	WILLIAM F. HELLMUTH
GEORGE K. BRINEGAR	VIVIAN C. HOWARD
JOSEPH W. CONARD	DAVID KETTLER
JOHN C. DAWSON	HARVEY C. MANSFIELD
JAMES S. DUESENBERRY	LAWRENCE S. RITTER
WILLIAM B. FAIRLEY	IRA O. SCOTT, JR.
BURTON C. HALLOWELL	WILLIAM L. WHITE
MARY C. WING	

ROBERT F. LENHART
Executive Secretary

PORTER McKEEVER
Director of Information

KARL SCHRIFTGIESSER
Assistant Director of Information

HARRY E. RABEY
Comptroller